LIGHTING YOUR HOME

Inside and Out

Design ■ Select ■ Install

by Jane Cornell

CREATIVE HOMEOWNER PRESS®

Author: Jane Cornell
Editorial Director: David Schiff
Editor: Margaret Gallos
Assistant Editor: Patrick Quinn
Copy Editor: Beth Kalet

Art Director: Annie Jeon
Graphic Designer: Fernando Colon Jr.
Illustrators: Jim Randolph, Norman Nuding
Photo Researchers: Jane Cornell, Alexander Samuelson
Cover Design: Fernando Colon Jr.
Cover Photograph: Courtesy of Intermatic Inc.
Spring Grove, IL

We give special thanks for their technical review of this book to Mr. Richard H. Dowhan, Manager, Corporate Communications, Osram Sylvania, Inc., Danvers, MA; and to Ms. Judy Collins of Judy Collins Interior Designs, Mendham, NJ.

The following companies also helped in developing this book:
Design With Lighting, San Francisco, CA
General Electric Lighting, Cleveland, OH
Intermatic Inc., Spring Grove, IL
Lutron Electronics Co., Coopersburg, PA
Michael De Luca & Associates, Santee, CA
Real Goods Catalog, Ukiahi, CA
Thomas Industries, Inc., Louisville, KY

Manufactured in the United States of America
Electronic Prepress: TBC Color Imaging, Inc.
Printed at: Webcrafters, Inc.

Current Printing (last digit)
10 9 8 7 6 5 4 3 2 1

Lighting Your Home Inside and Out
Library of Congress Catalog Card Number: 95-70917
ISBN: 1-88002-67-7

Though all the designs and methods in this book have been tested for safety, it is not possible to overstate the importance of using the safest construction methods possible. What follows are reminders; some do's and don'ts of basic carpentry. They are not substitutes for your own common sense.

- *Always* use caution, care, and good judgment when following the procedures described in this book.

- *Always* be sure that the electrical setup is safe; be sure that no circuit is overloaded, and that all power tools and electrical outlets are properly grounded. Do not use power tools in wet locations.

- *Always* read container labels on paints, solvents, and other products; provide ventilation, and observe all other warnings.

- *Always* read the tool manufacturer's instructions for using a tool, especially the warnings.

- *Always* use holders or pushers to work pieces shorter than 3 inches on a table saw or jointer. Avoid working short pieces if you can.

- *Always* remove the key from any drill chuck (portable or press) before starting the drill.

- *Always* pay deliberate attention to how a tool works so that you can avoid being injured.

- *Always* know the limitations of your tools. Do not try to force them to do what they were not designed to do.

- *Always* make sure that any adjustment is locked before proceeding. For example, always check the rip fence on a table saw or the bevel adjustment on a portable saw before starting to work.

- *Always* clamp small pieces firmly to a bench or other work surfaces when sawing or drilling.

- *Always* wear the appropriate rubber or work gloves when handling chemicals, heavy construction or when sanding.

- *Always* wear a disposable mask when working with odors, dusts or mists. Use a special respirator when working with toxic substances.

- *Always* wear eye protection, especially when using power tools or striking metal on metal or concrete; a chip can fly off, for example, when chiseling concrete.

- *Always* be aware that there is never time for your body's reflexes to save you from injury from a power tool in a dangerous situation; everything happens too fast. Be *alert!*

- *Always* keep your hands away from the business ends of blades, cutters and bits.

- *Always* hold a portable circular saw with both hands so that you will know where your hands are.

- *Always* use a drill with an auxiliary handle to control the torque when large size bits are used.

- *Always* check your local building codes when planning new construction. The codes are intended to protect public safety and should be observed to the letter.

- *Never* work with power tools when you are tired or under the influence of alcohol or drugs.

- *Never* cut very small pieces of wood or pipe. Whenever possible, cut small pieces off larger pieces.

- *Never* change a blade or a bit unless the power cord is unplugged. Do not depend on the switch being off; you might accidentally hit it.

- *Never* work in insufficient lighting.

- *Never* work while wearing loose clothing, hanging hair, open cuffs, or jewelry.

- *Never* work with dull tools. Have them sharpened, or learn how to sharpen them yourself.

- *Never* use a power tool on a workpiece that is not firmly supported or clamped.

- *Never* saw a workpiece that spans a large distance between horses without close support on either side of the kerf; the piece can bend, closing the kerf and jamming the blade, causing saw kickback.

- *Never* support a workpiece with your leg or other part of your body when sawing.

- *Never* carry sharp or pointed tools, such as utility knives, awls, or chisels in your pocket. If you want to carry tools, use a special-purpose tool belt with leather pockets and holders.

Contents

1
The Many Facets of Light

"Let there be light," "You light up my life," "The light dawned" — the importance of lighting is embedded into our consciousness. Lighting has been both a symbol of comfort and a practical tool stretching back to the caveman's first welcoming fire.

Today, at the flick of a switch, a home can be illuminated inside and out. Entire lighting scenes can be programmed and stored. On command, a homeowner can, for example, create bright lighting for work, then change the mood to casual, comfortable, and cozy, and then change it once more to complement an activity such as television watching — and all this using the same set of controls! Lights can be timed, remotely triggered for security and safety, or adjusted to create a sense of warmth in an otherwise sterile environment. Lighting can be an interior designer's dream or curse; it is the element most of them agree makes the biggest difference in the overall effect of a room.

For complicated situations, a professional lighting expert may be the best resource. However, the average homeowner can do many lighting projects without professional help. This book teaches you the steps of planning, designing, and installing effective home lighting, and it presents suggestions for specific lighting situations.

Before you start, though, you need to know what lighting is and how it affects people, places, and things. Then, you need to learn about individual components of lighting equipment, such as the many types of bulbs available. Finally, there are fixtures to be considered. Each of these elements—the light itself, the bulbs, and the fixtures—has its own effect on your lighting scheme, and you will want to consider them all from the beginning in making your plans.

Understanding lighting terminology will help you talk to lighting experts and sales staff most effectively. For instance, you may consider a "lamp" something with a shade, cord, and a plug, but lighting professionals often refer to bulbs as "lamps".

In addition to lighting terms, you need an understanding of light itself—its qualities, how it is measured, and its effect on color. To make effective choices from among the wide variety of lighting types available, you need to compare them on a level playing field, and that's what lighting measurements can help you do.

Armed with the knowledge of choices available, you can begin sketching lighting plans, which are devised to cover areas within one room and to create a flow from one space to another. This book will show you how good plans make the difference between quality home lighting and haphazard, downright dangerous situations. This book also will

Practical lighting that makes the staircase easy to see and dramatic accent lighting work together in a well-designed plan.

teach you about wiring lamps and fixtures and how controls work so that, with the help of the do-it-yourself installation instructions on most lighting products, you will be able to plan and/or install almost any lighting you wish.

But whether you plan to do the work yourself or get help from an electrician or lighting specialist, understanding wiring is essential to making sure the job is done safely, economically, and effectively. This book includes step-by-step instructions and diagrams that will help you ensure that your wiring is properly installed.

Outdoor lighting can make even a modest home seem like a palace. It follows many of the same principles as indoor lighting, but with a whole different range of products and special effects to choose from. Outdoor lighting can be line or low-voltage, can be timed, triggered by motion, or can have photocells that turn on fixtures of enormous strength and brightness as darkness approaches. Any garden takes on aspects of Eden when properly lit.

So, lighten up! Attack these projects on the light side. Brighten your outlook and your family's, and add that sparkle and brilliance that only you can bring to your home by making its lighting perfect.

How Lighting is Used

Effective lighting makes rooms and outdoor spaces look good; it makes us feel good and it keeps us safe.

Aesthetically, use lighting like an artist uses a brush, to hide or enhance elements of any room. Lighting focussed on an object draws the eye to that object in contrast to its background. For instance, lighting a room's corners makes it seem larger, as eyes take in its entire volume. In contrast, creating a cozy pool of light around a sofa focuses your eyes on the furniture. The rest of the room vanishes into shadow so it seems smaller.

Lighting Functions

The functions of lighting fall into three basic categories: to provide task lighting, general or ambient lighting, and accent lighting.

- Task lighting makes it easier to see what you are doing. Individual fixtures concentrate light in specific areas for chores such as preparing food, applying makeup, reading, or doing crafts.
- General lighting provides overall brightness for an area. Furnishing background illumination, it can vary with day and night, winter and summer, or for different moods and activities.
- Accent lighting highlights an area or object, emphasizing that aspect of a room's character. These mood-makers of lighting, to be effective, must contrast with their background of ambient lighting, the way a star performer relies on the rest of the cast to deliver a stunning performance.

Lighting for Safety

Poorly lit spaces are accidents waiting to happen. It is no surprise that many home accidents occur in the bedroom, when sleepy people are disoriented, vulnerable, and often in the dark. When it comes to safety, the kind of lighting, its placement, and how it is controlled are all important.

Lighting's Effects on Well-Being

Not everyone reacts to light the same way. Some are more photosensitive than others, preferring a lower field of general lighting. In contrast, the toned-down lighting suitable to photosensitive people is downright depressing and dour to others. Consider the personal preferences for all family members when you design your lighting.

Plan to light common spaces, such as family rooms, living rooms, and kitchens for everyone in the family, but err on the side of brightness. On the other hand, gear lighting to individual needs in private areas such as a study, bedrooms, or a workshop.

And so, individual preferences do count, but there are some effects of lighting that should figure in all lighting plans.

Seasonal Affective Disorder

Scientists have recently proven what they long suspected—that changes in light accompanying the seasons affect peoples' moods. It is estimated that during the winter, as much as 6 percent of the population in northern climates becomes severely depressed and sluggish because they are suffering from lack of sunlight. Exposure to sunlight suppresses production of melatonin in the blood. People with Seasonal Affective Disorder (SAD) Syndrome have measurable elevated levels of melatonin in their blood that is in direct proportion to their depression. Doctors treat SAD syndrome patients with highly specific light exposures that can run 10 times higher than what is frequently used in office buildings. If you suspect you suffer from SAD syndrome, see a doctor. But even if you don't, be aware that everyone's spirits can be lifted by a well-lit environment. If you live

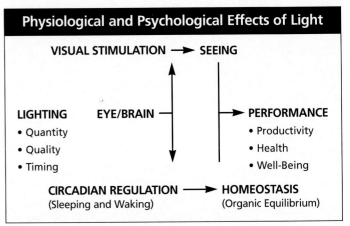

Lighting and health. Lighting affects well-being as well as seeing well.

in a northern climate, increase indoor light in wintertime to compensate for nature's dimming effect.

Avoiding Eyestrain

You can avoid eyestrain by having plenty of ambient light, thereby reducing the contrast to task lighting. Start by determining the level of light needed for the activity or task, then relate it to the surroundings. Task lighting, lighting immediately nearby, and then the lowest lighting in the area (as in a room's corners) should range no more than a ratio of four to one, preferably three to one near task lighting. You can compare watts and footcandles cast by various light sources to determine the ratios or approximate them with your naked eye.

Professional lighting designers develop precise illumination plans based upon exacting formulas that vary by area and type of lighting fixture. If areas are four times dimmer than task lighting, eyes constantly have to adjust to the difference, causing eyestrain. For instance, with the bright intensity of a television screen it is necessary to have some ambient light in the room. This keeps eyes from having to process both dark and light at the same time and allows eyes to focus away from the screen without a major adjustment to a new light level.

Recommended Ranges of Light Levels for Seeing Activities in the Home

	Easy-Short Duration	Critical or Prolonged
Billiard or pool table	low to moderate	moderate
Card table games	low to moderate	moderate to high
Craftwork*	moderate	high
Dining	low	low
Entertaining	low to high	low to high
Grooming	moderate	high
Hand sewing*	low to moderate	high
Ironing	low to moderate	high
Kitchen, laundry chores	low to moderate	high
Machine sewing*	moderate	high
Music scores	low to moderate	high
Reading	low to moderate	high
Study	moderate	high
TV viewing	low to moderate	low to moderate
Typing, computer	moderate	high
Writing	low to moderate	high
Workbench*	moderate	high

*Benefits from supplementary directional light.

Activity lighting demand. Intensity of activity determines the light level you need.

While it may seem wise to conserve energy by reducing the light level, do not compromise to the point that eyestrain is a risk. Balance of lighting is important, as is the comfort level of the direct task light for the specific activity.

Eyestrain may have no lasting health effects, but it can cause headaches and fatigue. When you are straining to see, you cannot produce your best work or enjoy an activity to its fullest.

Anyone who has repainted a room or added a carpet in a vastly different color knows how profoundly a room's lighting can be affected. What seemed ideal lighting in a pale room seems barely adequate in a darker room whose walls absorb the light. The colors, amount of direct daylight, darkness or lightness of hues used, amount of reflectance of surfaces, and the textures all influence the usefulness of a light source. It may take some trial and error to determine the amount of light you need to be most comfortable.

Design lighting to match the specific tasks you call upon your eyes to do. For instance, provide more lighting for sewing a same-color seam or cross-stitch needlepoint than for reading a book, where black lettering stands out in sharp contrast to a white background. Consider the time to be spent at the task as well. Eyes that feel little strain during 20 minutes at a computer need more light when subjected to regular three-hour computer sessions in a home office.

Consider also age and health in planning your lighting. Older eyes need as much as 50 percent stronger lighting, especially in stairways or other places where there is a change of level. Older eyes also take longer to adjust from glaring outdoor sunshine to the soft lighting of an interior. They may benefit from supplementary lighting in a foyer to make a smooth and safe transition from outside. Make task lighting for food preparation, reading, and other activities brighter for older eyes as well.

Cutting Glare

Everyone has at one time or another been blinded by the glare of a track light or exposed bulb. Victims of indirect glare may not know the source of the problem, but all the same may experience headaches, eyestrain, and general discomfort. Any good lighting plan eliminates direct and indirect glare.

Direct Glare. Bare-bulb glare is obvious. Eliminate it by changing a shade, adjusting the angle of a fixture, or replacing the bulb with one of a lower wattage or thicker frosting.

Lighting professionals caution against "glare bombs," fixtures that produce unavoidable, uncomfortable light. A common offender is a bathroom globe or strip light over the vanity. First, since strip lights usually take between three and ten bulbs per fixture, use 10-, 15- or 25-watt (rather than 40- or 60-watt) bulbs in each socket so that no single bulb is uncomfortably bright. Also, try switching from clear to frosted or from thinly frosted to thickly frosted bulbs. If necessary, add another light source on a ceiling or wall. Or change the fixture. In recessed lighting, baffles can either absorb unwanted light or shield the light source from direct view. These and other design advances can minimize or remove glare almost entirely.

With any new furniture layout, reassess for glare. For instance, reorienting a family-room sofa to face a game table might cause those seated on the sofa to look directly up into the exposed bulbs of a suspended pendant fixture. A spotlight installed for a new hallway piece may blind anyone coming in the front door. In this case, shift the fixture, select a different bulb, or replace the fixture for one with a diffuser.

Indirect Glare. Any flat reflective surface can be the source of indirect glare. Shiny desktops, countertops, and tables are prime offenders, as are mirrors, computer screens, glass over pictures, and television screens. Even enameled or metallic surfaces can cause glare, as can window glass.

While not as obvious as direct glare, reflected, or indirect glare also can cause eyestrain.

To determine reflected glare, estimate the angle from the source or empirically test it with a mirror. In the first instance, you know the reflectance angle from the surface affected is the same as the angle from the light source. By measuring the first, you can estimate the angle where glare will be strongest from the reflecting surface.

A second method is simply to place a mirror in front of or on top of the surface that you suspect is causing reflecting glare. This method is especially helpful when the surface, such as a computer monitor, is patterned and backlit so that its glare-reflecting qualities are hard to separate from the monitor's projected light. The mirror will isolate reflected light glare. You can place a light temporarily where you want a permanent source to be, then check for glare before making your final installation.

To solve reflected glare problems, shift light sources or furnishings. The more flexibility you build into a layered lighting system, the easier it will be to manage glare.

Eliminate glare. Use a mirror to determine the lighting reflections off a TV or computer screen.

Contrast

Sharp contrast with deep shadows can be dramatic or annoying, depending upon the situation. For everyday living, it is important that ambient, accent, and task lighting are compatible.

All environments benefit from contrast in lighting. It brings out natural textural elements, it pleases the eye by providing a realistic sense of three dimensions, and it makes moving from one area to another safer. A good design integrates contrasting light levels plus the pleasant arrangement of changes in colors and textures.

While shadows from contrasting light levels and light offer a sense of shape and depth, deep shadows call for eyes to make difficult adjustments and can be hazardous, especially outside at night.

Reflectance of Surfaces

When light strikes a white surface, it is reflected and magnified, maintaining its brightness. Like a sponge, black surfaces will absorb the light. Tones along the spectrum of grays from white to black will proportionately augment or detract from the light. The same principle applies to colors in a range from light to dark. For instance, colors such as white reflect back 70 to 80 percent; light blue, 40 to 50 percent; dark blue, 10 to 15 percent; navy blue, 5 to 10 percent; and black, 5 percent.

The surface texture also makes a difference. Smooth, mirror-like surfaces can reflect as much as 90 percent back in light tones. Consider the reflectance differences between a high-gloss enamel paint or resilient flooring and a highly textured carpet, or between deep nubby or velvet upholstery and patterned cotton chintz. You will need less lighting in a room where light, reflective surfaces predominate.

Understanding Light

A hands-on understanding of lighting begins when we replace that first light bulb, but the best lighting plans come from an appreciation in more sophisticated terms of what light really is.

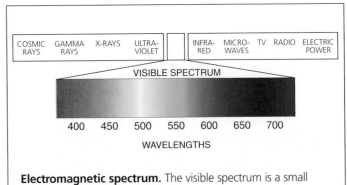

| COSMIC RAYS | GAMMA RAYS | X-RAYS | ULTRA-VIOLET | | INFRA-RED | MICRO-WAVES | TV | RADIO | ELECTRIC POWER |

VISIBLE SPECTRUM

400   450   500   550   600   650   700

WAVELENGTHS

Electromagnetic spectrum. The visible spectrum is a small segment of the total electromagnetic spectrum. We only are aware of light waves and audio waves.

Light is the visible spectrum of electromagnetic radiation that falls along the continuum of long and short waves. The human eye and brain interpret these waves as light. We interpret their *intensity* as brightness (hence the SAD syndrome on darker winter days). We interpret *wavelength* as color. A beam of sunlight passing through crystals or a prism is refracted or broken up into different wavelengths, at different angles, producing a continuous spectrum of colors in a rainbow.

Colors in light, graded from shortest waves to longest waves, are red, orange, yellow, green, blue, indigo, and violet. All light breaks down into these colors, but in varying degrees. The visible light portion of the electromagnetic spectrum extends from 770 nanometers (infrared end) down to 380 nanometers (ultraviolet end). Light measured from different bulbs can be expressed in graph form to identify its quality. For instance, a bulb whose light is extremely warm and simulates candlelight would have an entirely different spectrum profile than one with a bright, blue-white light.

Psychologically, people respond positively to indoor light that simulates firelight or candlelight and sunlight. Bulbs vary in the degree that they match these psychologically pleasing light balances. A fixture and the reflected light it creates can alter the perception of the light from its bulb, making it appear warmer or colder, brighter or dimmer.

The entire electromagnetic spectrum, from its longest to its shortest waves, encompasses energy commonly discussed today, but the spectrum was relatively unknown 75 years ago. Consider radio waves, infrared waves, light waves, ultraviolet waves, X-rays, gamma rays, and cosmic rays.

The Language of Lighting

What follows are definitions common to the lighting industry, which help you understand the many facets of lighting available today and make attractive, functional, and energy-efficient selections for your home.

Amperes

Measurement of current flow is amperes or "amps." The amp rating is marked on many electrical products and special-purpose lights to ensure that adequate wiring will be used for the application.

Bulbs and Tubes. Experts often refer to these light sources as lamps, encompassing the bulb, its base and the filament or arc, the internal part that produces light.

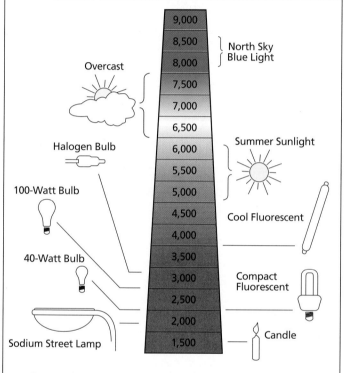

Color temperatures. These vary from extremely cool to candlelight warm. All are "natural" colors.

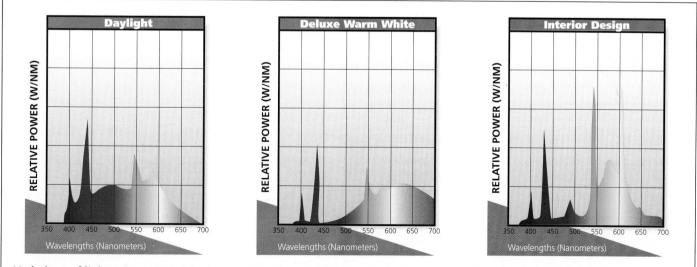

Variations of light color. Light bulbs of different types have different profiles of the amount of colors that make up their light.

Lighting Levels and Intensity

Quantity	Unit
Intensity of light (candlepower)	Candela
Amount of nondirectional light	Lumen
Illumination level per square foot	Footcandle
Brightness of surface	Footlambert

Candela. A measurement for luminous intensity roughly equivalent to 12.57 lumens.

Candlepower. The luminous intensity of a beam of light, total luminous flux, in a particular direction from an international candle measurement standard, the candela. Similar to horsepower, the higher the intensity of light the more candelas it represents and the higher the candlepower.

Efficacy. The efficiency of a lamp (bulb or tube) measured in ratio of lumens per watt (LPW). The more lumens per watt, the more efficient the lamp. Under the National Energy Policy Act (EPACT), bulbs must meet certain minimum LPW standards. A higher LPW means the bulb converts power into light in a more efficient manner, saving more energy. Wattage and lumen ratings are on packaging for bulbs.

Efficiency. Efficiency relates to the light output from a luminaire (fixture) as a percentage of light output from the bulb or bulbs it uses. For instance, a fixture with a fluorescent bulb that emits 1,000 lumens may have a shade or cover that decreases the direct light emitted to only 900 lumens. That fixture would be considered 90 percent efficient.

Footcandle. A unit of illuminance equal to one lumen per square foot of surface. One footcandle equals 10.76 lux. Lux is the standard international unit of illuminance equal to one lumen per square meter. Designers determine light needs by using suggested footcandle levels for different activities and areas. Footcandles are used primarily for directional lights.

Footlambert. The brightness of a surface which emits or reflects 1 lumen per square foot of its surface. The metric equivalent is candela per square meter.

Illuminance. The density of light on a surface when it is uniformly illuminated, measured in footcandles and lux. Lighting professionals recommend certain illuminance levels for various lighting applications, such as when someone's visual performance, like accuracy, is important. The recommendations are based on type of activity, the ability of the observer to see, and the age of the observer.

Lamps. Lighting professionals often refer to "lamps" when they mean the light sources commonly called "bulbs" or "tubes." This is because the "bulb" is actually only one part of the unit that makes up the "lamp." In this book, we will generally follow the industry norm and use the term "lamps," although we do use "bulbs" or "tubes" if the context makes that less confusing. The term lamp also is used to refer to free-standing, plug-in luminaires, as in desk, floor, or table lamps.

Lux. One lux is equal to the illuminance provided by an ordinary wax candle on a spherical surface with an area equal to one square meter, from one meter away. One lux equals 0.0929 footcandles.

Lumen. The amount of light cast upon 1 square foot of the inner surface of a hollow sphere of 1-foot radius with an international candle in its center. It is used to measure quantity or intensity of omni-directional light. The light output of a bulb or tube is measured in lumens. One lumen is approximately equal to one footcandle. Lamps differ in the total amount of light emitted and also differ in the rate at which the light output decreases over time, a phenomenon called lamp-lumen deprecation. The light output rating on a bulb package, expressed in lumens, is the light rating before any decrease takes place. Lumens are used to describe general lighting, while candlepower is used in task lighting.

Lumens Per Watt (LPW). The ratio of the amount of light provided to the energy (watts) used to produce the light—the measurement of the bulb's efficacy. This measurement is increasingly important in both bulb design and usage because it enables the consumer to compare the light output of bulbs relative to the electricity it takes to produce that light.

Luminaires. The lighting industry uses this term to encompass "lighting fixtures" or "fittings." Luminaires are grouped by mounting type and locations: ceiling-mounted, suspended, recessed, architectural, wall-mounted, furniture or cabinet-integrated, plug-in, and exterior luminaires.

Voltage. The electric potential difference that drives the current through a circuit or the force of electrical pressure. A generator creates the pressure that keeps the electric current flowing through the conductors or wires. Bulbs and luminaries are marked with their voltage capacity, such as 120 volts, 110-115 volts, or low-voltage, such as 12 volts. Products designed to operate at the voltage specified may burn out if installed on a higher voltage circuit.

Watt, Wattage. A unit of active electric power; the rate at which electric energy is used. Wattage is the electrical power consumed by a device. It equals volts multiplied by amps. The wattage rating of a circuit is the amount of power the circuit can deliver safely, which is determined by the current-carrying capacity of the wires or cables. Wattage also indicates the amount of power a fixture or appliance needs to work properly.

Wavelength. In lighting, the distance between two similar points of a given wave, as measured in nanometers (1 nm equals 1 billionth of a meter). Wavelengths are important in ensuring that various parts of a lighting system—ballasts, bulbs, and incoming current—are compatible. Also, wavelength differences in bulbs determine quality of the light itself. Manufacturers have taken into account these issues when they recommend use of compatible types of bulbs, ballasts, and transformers.

2
Selecting Light Bulbs and Tubes

From the trusty fluorescent tube over the workbench to the flickering candle-flame bulbs in the foyer fixture, lamps, as lighting professionals call them, are available in a variety of sizes, shapes, and strengths to suit every conceivable need. You can make a major change in your fixtures simply by replacing lamps. However, once you discover how many lamps are available, it will be almost impossible not to rethink your overall lighting schemes.

Lamps function as a light source, and it is this quality that differentiates them from each other. To understand the differences, you need to know the quality of light we use as benchmarks as well as the measurements by which lamps are judged. Then you will be able to make the best selections for the specific lighting qualities you want.

Standard Measurements for Color

Scales used universally in lighting assess the color temperature the lamp or bulb gives off and how the light from that lamp affects the objects it is lighting.

Correlated Color Temperature Range

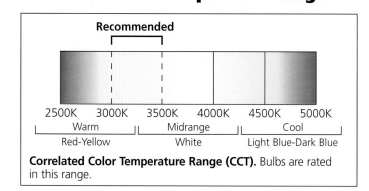

Correlated Color Temperature Range (CCT). Bulbs are rated in this range.

The term Correlated Color Temperature (CCT) is used in comparing the warmth or coolness of the light as it is produced, or the source as it appears to the viewer. This describes the color appearance of light in terms of warmth or coolness. To define this in measurable amounts, in the lab a reference source of metal is heated, producing different colors as it heats. These range from red to orange to yellow to blue to blue-white and are designated according to the Kelvin (K) temperature scale. When lamps or bulbs are rated

according to their Kelvin (K) color temperature, you can select those whose light is closely matched. Or you can vary the coolness or warmth of lighting for specific situations.

The blue of the sky is near the top of the Kelvin scale at 10,000K. The measurements then range down to neutral color, which is neither extra warm nor extra cold, from about 3,200 to 3,600K, then to below 1,000K, which is the ruddy warmth of candlelight. Generally, light sources below 3,000K are considered warm sources, while those above 4,100K are considered cool sources.

Be particularly careful in selecting the color of light produced around artworks. In this case, the ceiling almost has a sunset glow without distorting the painting.

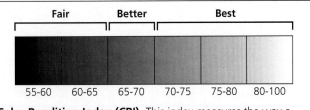

Color Rendition Index (CRI). This index measures the way a light source renders color. The higher the index number, the closer colors are to how an object appears in sunlight. An index of at least 75 percent is recommended.

Color Rendition Index (CRI)

Color rendition describes how a light source affects the sense of the colors of objects it illuminates, such as room decor and flesh tones. Color rendering capabilities of lamps are rated from 1 to 100, with 100 being closest to how an object looks in sunlight or how close it is to the colors people expect to see. "True" color is at 100, while lower numbers in proportion relate to the amount of color distortion from the lamp in question. In decorative usage, a range from 75 to 100 is most often chosen.

Two lamps with similar Correlated Color Temperature (CCT) but with different Color Rendition Indexes (CRIs) will light the same object differently. Conversely, two lamps may be similar on the Color Rendition Index (CRI) but may differ in Correlated Color Temperature (CCT), and they may also light an object differently.

Match and compare Correlated Color Temperature (CCT) first, then color rendition (CRI), to achieve the same effects from two different lamps.

While light may have the same Kelvin numbers (CCT) and rendition (CRI), the balance of individual wavelengths which comprise the light of each kind of lamp or bulb are as unique as fingerprints. Some will have a broader band of green, some a broader band of red or blue.

If you want true color matching, use lamps with similar color spectral power distribution (SPD). The spectral distribution often is illustrated in bulb/lamp catalogues.

Color Schemes and Light

Did you ever buy a table or floor lamp, get it home and find its light changes the color of everything in the room? Consider first the color schemes you are most likely to be using when selecting bulbs/lamps. You can start by learning what parts of the spectrum a light enhances, and what parts it depresses or neutralizes.

Cold, blue light intensifies blue and green tones and diminishes warm tones such as oranges and reds. Warm light makes blues and greens less intense and more muddied while intensifying the reds and oranges.

Lighting can intensify colors in these polarized color schemes. However, since most homes include a combination

of warm and cold tones (even blue rooms usually include the red-brown-orange tones of woods), selecting bulbs that provide balanced lighting, comfortably close to what appears normal to the eye, is usually the most attractive choice. It is equally important to make sure flesh tones are attractive.

When trying to achieve a look similar to lighting you have, experiment with various alternatives. Consider, also, changing the look of your interior by changing the bulb's color rendition and quality of light. For instance, if you have matching fixtures flanking either side of a sofa, you probably want to match colors identically. Conversely, you may want a specific light to be totally different than other lights around it. For instance, a cooler, whiter light such as a halogen bulb often is more effective as an accent light. It will stand out more sharply than a bulb with matching warmer color temperature and a lower color rendition index than that of other bulbs in the room.

When changing to a different kind of ambient bulb, such as from incandescent to energy-saving compact fluorescent, consider how the difference in color will affect the entire room's look. Generally, fluorescents are cooler, but new developments in fluorescent lamps now make it possible to find a product that produces almost the same visual effects as incandescent bulbs.

By replacing bulbs/lamps alone and experimenting with different looks, you can transform a room without changing a single fixture. So it's a good idea to read this chapter about bulbs and tubes before you consider the fixtures that use them. The following is a list of lamps/bulbs and their characteristics.

General Incandescent Bulbs

It is hard to imagine a home without the most commonly used and least expensive of all bulbs, the incandescents. Their soft, warm glow is reminiscent of candlelight. However, they are the least efficient lighting sources. Approximately 90 percent of their electricity goes into heat generation rather than light production. But even incandescents are becoming more efficient. A variety of styles is offered, many with capabilities unheard of as recently as the 1980s. For example, you can now purchase a bulb that turns itself off after 30 minutes.

The path to current developments in lighting technology spans the last 200 years. The arc light was developed by Englishman Sir Humphrey Davy in 1809. Then in 1841 Englishman Frederick DeMoleyns patented an electric lamp made of platinum and charcoal, which went out when the platinum melted. In 1874, Russian Aleksandr N. Lodygin developed a graphite lamp, but it proved too expensive to produce. In 1879, American Thomas A. Edison used a bamboo fiber which, after charring, lasted for hours and produced a reasonably good light. These first practical incandescent bulbs were installed in New York City in 1882. The incandescent has been used ever since.

Incandescent lamps have heated filaments that can be used decoratively with clear bulb exteriors, as in this fixture.

Bulb filament. Incandescent bulb coils are double-coiled.

How It Works

Today's most common incandescent bulbs/lamps are composed of vastly superior substances and are inexpensive to make. The bulbs convert electric power into light by passing electric current through a filament of tungsten wire. The wire consists of minicoils, which are coiled into larger coils. The current heats the tungsten filament until it glows. Tungsten's high melting temperature slows the filament's evaporation,

and to further retard it, the lamps usually are filled with an inert gas mixture primarily of argon with nitrogen. Attached to the filament are lead-in wires that hold the filament in place and carry the electrical current from the base.

The bulb itself is usually made of glass, which defines its overall shape. The bulb can be clear, diffuse, tinted, or colored, and can have a reflective coating inside. It can be designed to be directional or nondirectional.

An exhaust tube below the filament is used during manufacture to remove air and introduce inert gases inside the bulb. The base typically is made of aluminum or brass with one lead wire soldered to the center contact at the bottom and the other lead wire soldered to its upper rim.

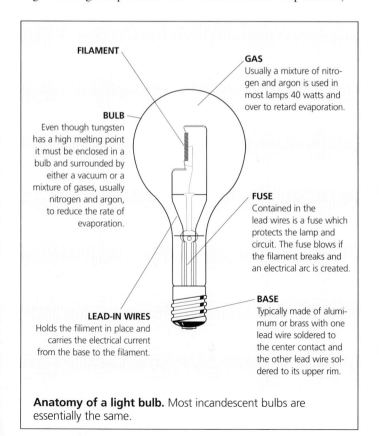

FILAMENT

GAS
Usually a mixture of nitrogen and argon is used in most lamps 40 watts and over to retard evaporation.

BULB
Even though tungsten has a high melting point it must be enclosed in a bulb and surrounded by either a vacuum or a mixture of gases, usually nitrogen and argon, to reduce the rate of evaporation.

FUSE
Contained in the lead wires is a fuse which protects the lamp and circuit. The fuse blows if the filament breaks and an electrical arc is created.

LEAD-IN WIRES
Holds the filament in place and carries the electrical current from the base to the filament.

BASE
Typically made of aluminum or brass with one lead wire soldered to the center contact and the other lead wire soldered to its upper rim.

Anatomy of a light bulb. Most incandescent bulbs are essentially the same.

Advantages and Disadvantages of Incandescent Lamps

Advantage	Disadvantage
Low initial cost	High operating cost
Creates inviting environment	Fragile
Enhances skin tones	Short life
Immediate starting	Low lumen per watt
Easily dimmed	High heat output
Variety of shapes, sizes, and applications	
Easy to use/install	

The most common bulb/lamp bases are screw-in or bayonet shape, although other base shapes and sizes are used. Most screw-in type bulbs/lamps have medium bases, also known as standard or Edison bases. But there are also intermediate screw-in bases, such as for a refrigerator or other appliance bulbs, candelabra screw-in bases, used in chandeliers or other multiple-socket fixtures, and finally, mogul bases, the large bases for three-way incandescent bulbs used in some floor lamps.

Bayonet bases have two round contacts at their base. Insert them into the socket, turning until the contacts lock corresponding slots. They are often used in high-intensity lamps.

Lamp Life and Efficiency

The average rated life of a bulb or lamp, which is usually printed on the package, indicates the number of hours at which 50 percent of bulbs burned out. Using the proper bulb for the fixture or luminaire will lengthen bulb life. Incandescent bulbs can be easily dimmed, which lengthens their life.

Shapes and Sizes

Most luminaires are designed to take a specific shape and size bulb.

Shapes. Letter designations are used to refer to incandescent bulb shapes.

- "A" bulbs are the commonly used, pear-shaped bulbs. They come with candelabra, intermediate, medium, or mogul screw-in bases.

- "G" bulbs are globes and are often used when the bulb is exposed to view. They range in size from about 1 to 5 inches in diameter and can be frosted or white. Smaller sizes have candelabra bases and larger sizes have medium screw-in bases.

- "T" tubular or "showcase" bulbs are used in cabinets, and desk and freestanding lamps such as pharmacy lamps. They can be screw-in medium bases or bayonet bases and can be clear or frosted.

- Decorative candle bulbs are used in chandeliers, sconces, fan light kits, vanity lights, and old-fashioned fixtures. They come in a variety of sizes and shapes such as flames, teardrops, and others. They may be clear or frosted, and can have either medium or candelabra size screw-in bases.

BULB	NAME	WATTAGE RANGE	TYPICAL APPLICATION
C-7	Cone	4-7W	Night lights
S S-11	Straight	3-40W	Sign, Decorative, High-Intensity, Appliance
B-10	Decor	12-60W	Chandelier and Decorative Light Fixtures
F	Flame	15-60W	Decorative Light Fixtures
T	Tubular	6-60W	Aquariums, Appliances, Showcases
GT	Globe Tubular "Chimney"	60W	Outdoor Post Lamps
G	Globe	10-150W	Kitchen, Bath, Decorative Lighting
PS	Pear Straightneck	50-1500W	Most Commonly Used as Utility or Three-Way
A	Standard	15-250W	General-Purpose Lighting
R	Reflector	30-1000W	Indoor Directional or Downlighting

Bulb selection. Determine the best bulb for your application for aesthetic appeal and efficiency.

BULB	NAME	WATTAGE RANGE	TYPICAL APPLICATION
ER	Ellipsoidal Reflector	50-120W	Indoor Directional or Downlighting
PAR	Parabolic Aluminized Reflector	35-500W	Indoor/Outdoor Directional Lighting
MB	Mid-Break Halogen A-Line	42-100W	General-Purpose Lighting
MR-16	Mirrored Reflector	20-75W	Display, Audiovisual Lighting
An 48	Aluminized Reflector	20-100W	Display Audiovisual Lighting
T	Single-End Quartz	75-1500W	General-Purpose Lighting
Bi-Pin	Bi-Pin	10-75W	Display Lamps
T	Double-End Quartz	100-1500W	Indoor/Outdoor General Lighting

Sizes. These are designated in ⅛ inch, measured at the bulb's widest point. A bulb 1 inch wide at its widest would be an A-8. An A-17 bulb has a maximum diameter of 1⅞ inch, or 2⅛ inches (17 divided by 8).

Specialty Bulbs

Bulbs are getting smarter all the time. New bulbs with capabilities such as built-in dimming and timers are available, and new smart designs undoubtedly will be introduced as new needs are identified. Bulbs that encourage plant growth, and those with extra-strong filament protection

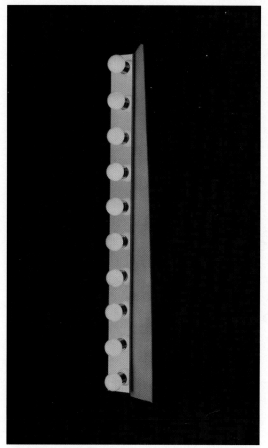

Use white globe bulbs for fixtures that are in plain view so they will look as nice when off as when on.

for areas of high vibration (such as in ceiling fan fixtures), or bulbs with shatter-proof exteriors are some examples of specialty bulbs.

Reduced-Wattage and Long-Life Bulbs

Often bulbs are both reduced-wattage and long-life combined, although not always. You'll save money and energy by reducing wattage. Be sure, however, the amount of lumens is sufficient for the effect—that is, be sure you'll get enough light—before replacing an "A" bulb with another of reduced wattage.

Long-life bulbs are most suitable wherever replacing bulbs is difficult or inconvenient, such as in a chandelier, a fixture attached to a high ceiling, or in a post lantern that is hard to take apart. The cost-per-wattage ratios may not be as great as for ordinary bulbs, by the time the additional cost is factored in.

Three-Way Bulbs

These bulbs have two filaments, and when used with a corresponding three-way socket, either or both filaments can be lit to provide three light levels.

Incandescent Reflector and PAR Bulbs

The lamp efficiency or lumens per watt (LPW) of some models of reflector and PARs do not meet the energy-efficiency standards mandated by the National Energy Policy Act of 1992 (EPACT). But more efficient replacements for restricted bulbs are available, often halogen or compact fluorescent variations. Both offer savings in wattage use and protection of the environment over the life of the bulb.

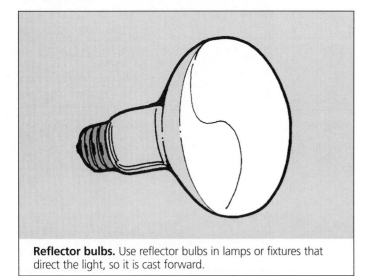

Reflector bulbs. Use reflector bulbs in lamps or fixtures that direct the light, so it is cast forward.

How It Works

Reflector bulbs are designed to project light forward. Shape and silver coatings give these lamps beam spreads from the diffuse, wide spread of a floodlight to the more narrow, focused beam of a spotlight. The more concentrated the light beam, the narrower the distribution and the greater the intensity of light at the center.

The next factor is the beam angle or field angle. Beam angle is the center of the beam, which is the area of the lamp that delivers 50 percent of its candlepower. Often this is the only measurement given in catalogues since it is the critical information for task lighting. In addition, there is an area of spill light which has only 10 percent of the candlepower. The beam angle and spill light together make up the field angle.

Many manufacturers tell you the number of footcandles and the diameter covered by the beam angle at various distances from the source or illustrate the strength and distribution of light in a distribution cone. For instance, a flood with a maximum intensity of 2,600 candelas will have a footcandle distribution 24 inches below it of 2,650 over an area of approximately 18 inches. At 48 inches below it, this drops to 163 footcandles covering approximately 36 inches; at 72 inches below, 72 footcandles, covering 52 inches. To apply the knowledge, start with what you need to light and then study charts provided by manufacturers to see which bulb/lamp will suit you best. For instance, if you have a

table 60 inches in diameter that is 72 inches from the light source, you can see that the flood described above will almost cover the table surface with a generous 72 footcandles.

Light that falls outside the concentrated beam is called spill light. The sharpness of definition between the beam and spill varies and can also be altered by the fixture in which the bulb is used.

Incandescent Reflector Bulbs. These "R" bulbs direct light out in front by bouncing it off their cone-shaped, silver-coated inside walls, unlike incandescent "A" bulbs, whose light spills out in all directions from front and sides. The reflector's concentrated beam requires fewer watts to brightly light a specific area.

The most common "R" lamps are used in track and recessed lighting. But both the popular 75-watt R30 and 150-watt R40 bulbs are no longer manufactured due to EPACT. Some lamps, though, are exempt from EPACT, including lamps with diameters of less than 2¾ inches, such as the R20. Halogen and compact fluorescent bulbs are available to replace the less energy-efficient models.

Incandescent ER Ellipsoidal Reflector Bulbs. The ER bulb focuses its beam of light approximately 2 inches in front of it, making it an efficient choice for deep, well-shielded recessed fixtures. Since they are recessed, these bulbs project more light forward without producing glare. Conversely, though, since they are longer than regular "R" bulbs, they will cause glare unless they are recessed in fixtures that keep them at least 2 inches from the aperture or opening.

Incandescent PAR (Parabolic Aluminized Reflector) Bulbs. Vaporized aluminum on the glass backing of the lamp forms a reflective coating that forces light forward. The back and front lenses are made of hard, heat-resistant glass, and stippling of the front lens determines the angle of the beam. These produce about four times the light of "A" bulbs. While PAR-38 styles have become widely used, EPACT dictated no further manufacturing after 1995. Those below 2¾ inches in diameter such as PAR-16 and PAR-20 are exempt.

Halogen Bulbs

Although basically an incandescent, the tungsten-halogen lamp has several characteristics that make it superior to conventional incandescent lamps. Not only are halogen lamps the replacements of choice for energy-wasting incandescent lamps no longer produced because of EPACT, but also they actually are energy-efficient upgrades. (See "Compact Fluorescent Bulbs," page 23 for another option.) Although halogen lamps may cost more than common incandescent bulbs, they usually pay for themselves over the life of the bulb.

Advantages and Disadvantages of Halogen Lamps

Advantage	Disadvantage
Greater efficiency	Higher initial cost
Longer life	Heat generation
Compact size	
Easily dimmed	
Excellent lumen maintenance (brightness)	
Bright, white light	

How It Works

Halogen incandescent lamps have a slightly different shape and thicker, heavier glass bulb than general service "A" lamps. Halogens also produce light when electricity heats a tungsten filament, but in the ordinary incandescent, the filament evaporates over time and the bulb wall blackens

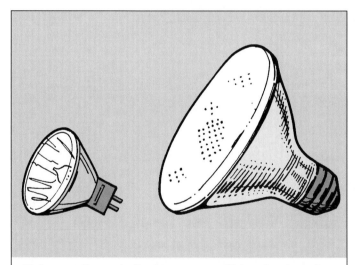

Halogen reflector bulbs. More energy-efficient than incandescent reflectors, halogen reflector bulbs are available for use with 12-volt current (left) or 120-volt current (right).

Halogen bulbs. Use halogen bulbs in lamps to replace incandescent bulbs for longer life and efficiency.

slowly as tungsten is deposited on it. In the halogen lamp, this process is altered through a regenerative process known as the tungsten-halogen cycle. The halogen gas in the bulb causes the particles of tungsten to be redeposited onto the tungsten filament. That means the lamp lasts longer and is whiter and brighter throughout its life.

To maximize the effects of the tungsten-halogen cycle, the filament and halogen gas are contained under pressure in a quartz capsule. To contain a possible rupture, many tungsten-halogens are further enclosed, a "lamp within a lamp." Others do not have the extra shielding, though, because the floor lamp or fixture they are used in provides it.

Halogens usually can be dimmed, but this decreases the effects of the tungsten-halogen cycle and the glass of the bulb begins to darken. The tungsten returns to the filament most effectively when the lamp is at its hottest interior bulb temperature. And so, if your halogen begins to darken, briefly turn it up to its brightest setting to clear the glass and restore light output.

Shapes and Sizes

Halogen lamps can replace "A" and general incandescent PAR bulbs. Their designs are constantly being upgraded to provide alternatives to popular general-service incandescent bulbs, including those made obsolete by EPACT.

Halogen PAR-20 and PAR-30 lamps with long necks are easy retrofits for obsolete "R" lamps. PAR-16 lamps are excellent for dramatic accent lighting effects.

IR PAR Halogen Lamps. An infrared-reflective coating redirects infrared energy onto the filament of these bulbs, giving them even greater efficacy and a true color rendition. They cost more initially but provide longer lamp life and lumens per watt.

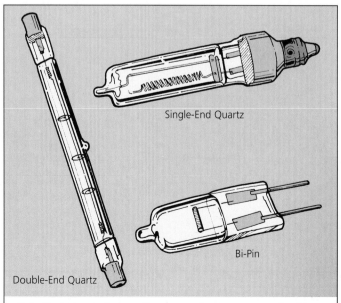

Single-End Quartz

Double-End Quartz

Bi-Pin

Tubular halogen lamps. Some capsules are not contained in a protective bulb, and must be encased by a fixture to provide sufficient shielding.

Tubular-Shaped Halogen Lamps. These specialty bulbs are designed for specific luminaires such as chandeliers, sconces, desk lamps, and recessed lighting. They usually can't be used in anything but the unit for which they are initially intended. Often the luminaire will come with the bulb.

For safety reasons, Underwriters Laboratories requires that all halogens it tests or that are manufactured in compliance with its standards, be shielded. The lamps must be protected by a glass sleeve or jacket to prevent potential damage from lamp rupture and filtering of ultraviolet radiation.

Use a soft cloth or glove to handle an unencapsulated halogen tubular lamp. This prevents oils from your hands from touching the bulb. Its quartz glass walls can withstand high operating temperatures, but may crack if etched with hand oils. Be sure also that combustible materials, such as drapery, do not come into contact with the lamp.

Unshielded lamps include single-end quartz, bi-pin (low-voltage) quartz, and double-end quartz.

Low-Voltage Halogen Lamps

Compact but effective, low-voltage halogen lamps require less than 30 volts (usually 12 volts) rather than line voltage electricity, such as 120-volt. While halogen PAR lamps are up to 40 percent more efficient than regular incandescent bulbs, low-voltage halogen lamps provide up to 50 percent more light than conventional line voltage halogen systems using the same amount of energy.

Unobtrusive and small, these lamps are the hummingbirds of the lighting world, providing highly focussed light. They can be placed close to the surface to be illuminated without get-

ting in the way. As such, low-voltage halogen lamps often are used for accent or display lighting, suspended downlights or track lighting. Some of them employ a dichroic reflector that projects the light forward while deflecting the heat backward toward the socket so that the light beam itself is cool. These must be used in open fixtures or fixtures designed specifically for them that allow the heat to be safely dissipated. Some recessed fixtures are specifically designed for use with halogen bulbs to accommodate the heat buildup.

How It Works

Luminaires that use low-voltage lamps require a transformer to convert line voltage to low voltage.

Some transformers are an integral part of the luminaire, as in low-voltage, halogen desk lamps. Transformers often are integrated into the fixture for track and recessed lighting systems. However, other transformers can be a separate component (as is the case in low-voltage outdoor systems). Remember to factor in cost of transformers and whatever electrical draw they add when choosing your lighting system.

Since some transformers, especially magnetic, emit interference with other electrical appliances, lighting designers often locate them where problems like noise and heat emissions will not intrude on living areas. They can tuck them away in closets or other little-used areas. Often, a lighting system will be composed of both the fixtures and lamps specified to work with one another.

A thick, short filament combined with a highly efficient reflector system allows for the compact design of these bulbs. Dimming is easy with them but remember to operate them periodically at full strength to clear the blackening on the glass and preserve efficiency of the tungsten-halogen cycle. Then they maintain their brightness.

Shapes and Sizes

The smaller size of low-voltage, halogen lamps makes it possible to use them in tight quarters. For instance, a standard PAR bulb may require a recessed light fixture depth of more than 8 inches, but low-voltage halogen can be installed in fixtures of half the depth. For ceilings or soffits without much clearance above them, this kind of recessed lighting application has obvious advantages.

PAR Lamps. These often are used in track, recessed, and other lighting applications.

MR (Multifaceted Reflector) Lamps. This term describes two popular low-voltage halogens, the MR16, which is ⅝ inch or 2 inches wide, and the MR11, which is ⅛ inch or 1⅜ inches wide. Baffles, beam spread (degree of spot or flood dispersion), concentrations of light, filters, and other adjusting capabilities are

Low-voltage halogen bulbs are so much smaller that designers have created new ways of using them, as in this track system where wires in Icarus wings conduct electric current to the bulbs.

Advantages and Disadvantages of Low-Voltage Halogen Lamps	
Advantage	**Disadvantage**
Saves energy	Can require separate transformer
Lasts longer	Cannot be used in conventional fixtures
Compact size	Costs more than incandescents
Excellent lumen maintenance	
Wide range of effects	

increasingly used to make these systems highly adjustable. The key in purchasing the systems and lamps is to be sure the lamp will provide the light needed. With good planning, a system also can be updated with different lamps and adjustable fixtures. Should you change the furniture arrangement or need to redirect light for some other reason, this system provides unusual flexibility for virtually any anticipated need.

Fluorescent Lamps

From kitchen to classroom to office, fluorescent lamps have had a recognized place in lighting since their successful introduction in 1938. Experimental until then, they became practical when the standard fixture began to include both tube and ballast. More light is produced worldwide by fluorescent lamps than any other light source.

Classic lineal fluorescent tubes are becoming more energy-efficient.

Old-fashioned fluorescent lamps used to buzz when started and sometimes throughout the time the lamp was on. They also discolored objects and gave skin color a strange appearance. Aesthetically, fluorescents were second-class. They were often used in undiffused, glaring fixtures and tended to be unpopular with interior designers. Despite all that, they came to be widely used because they were more efficient than incandescent lamps.

The good news is that today's fluorescent lamps are totally different. They are easier to use and more efficient, and they are constantly being upgraded.

Much has changed about the way fluorescent lights can be used today. They adapt to many lighting situations and can represent a substantial savings over incandescent or halogen lamps.

EPACT has sparked even further upgrading of fluorescent lamps by banning production of the least energy-efficient models. Fortunately, manufacturers have more energy-efficient replacements for popular fluorescent models that will no longer be produced.

Until something else revolutionary comes along, the major changes in lighting continue to be in the field of fluorescent lamps, including compact fluorescents covered separately in this section.

How It Works

Fluorescent lamps are based upon a system entirely different from the filament technology of incandescents. Fluorescents are glass tubes coated on the interior with phosphor, a chemical compound that emits light when activated by ultraviolet energy. Air in the tubes is replaced with argon gas and a small amount of mercury is added.

Conventional circular fluorescent tubes now may come with decorative fixtures that are easy to install.

When a fluorescent lamp is turned on, the electricity heats cathodes at each end causing them to emit electrons, which in turn create an electric arc between the cathodes. The electrons in this arc collide with mercury vapor and argon or other gas atoms to produce invisible ultraviolet rays. These rays excite the fluorescent phosphor coating, producing visible light. Fluorescents are highly efficient because 80 percent of their light comes from the phosphor coating.

Ballasts. Unlike incandescent lamps, fluorescents cannot control their current consumption. Unless the current is regulated, the lamp burns itself out immediately. To avoid this, ballasts that provide the necessary high starting voltage and limit current to the proper operating value are part of fluorescent fixtures. Only ballasts labeled "high-power factor" can accommodate some of the new energy-saving fluorescent lamps. In upgrading, consider the whole unit. Fluorescent tubes may not be interchangeable with existing fixtures, such as those that are merely labeled "normal power factor" or that are not the right length. Also, the bulb contact may not be properly spaced for the fixture's receptacles.

The two types of ballasts commonly used for residential lighting are magnetic and electronic. The majority sold today are energy-efficient magnetic ballasts, but electronic ballasts are gaining in popularity because they are even more energy-efficient than magnetic ballasts, are lighter weight, operate more quietly, and do not cause the lamp to flicker as much as their magnetic counterparts. They are becoming more price-competitive with magnetic ballasts as innovations are introduced.

Basic Components of a Fluorescent Lamp

Bulb. Usually a straight glass tube. The tube can be circular, U-shaped, or curved and bent to fit into a compact fluorescent screw-in base.

Phosphor. Coating inside the bulb that transforms ultraviolet radiation into visible light. The color of the light produced depends upon the composition of the phosphor.

Base. Several different types, single-pin, bi-pin, and four-pin, are used to connect the lamp to the circuit and support it in the fixture. Single-pins have one contact at each end of the tube. Bi-pins, the most common, have two pairs of electrical contacts, one pair at each end of the lamp. A miniature bi-pin is used for T-5 (⅝ inch) bulbs and a medium bi-pin for T-8 and T-12 bulbs. In circular lamps, the cathodes are connected to a four-pin base located between the junction of the two ends of the lamp.

Cathode. Located at each end of the lamp. Cathodes are coated with a material that emits electrons and usually are made of coiled-coil or single-coil tungsten wire.

Gas. Argon or a mixture of inert gas at low pressure. Krypton sometimes is used.

Mercury. A minute quantity of liquid mercury is placed in the bulb to furnish mercury vapor.

Shapes and Sizes

Straight tube fluorescent lamps are used so frequently that almost everyone has seen them. However, it is necessary to coordinate ballasts, bulbs, and fixtures to plan effective use of these energy misers. (Since screw-in compact fluorescent lamps often are used to replace common incandescent bulbs, they will be covered separately.)

Common fluorescent tubes are designated by the code letter "T" followed by the diameter of the tube expressed in eighths of an inch. Fluorescent tubes vary in diameter from T-5 (⅝ inch) to T-17 (2⅛ inches). In nominal overall length, fluorescent lamps range from 6 to 96 inches, which is measured from the back of the lampholder to the back of the lampholder instead of bulb end to bulb end. Higher wattages go with longer tubes so that, for example, a 20-watt T-12 tube is shorter than a 40-watt T-12 tube.

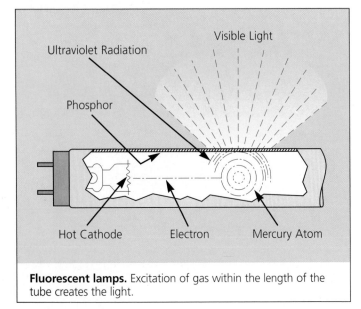

Fluorescent lamps. Excitation of gas within the length of the tube creates the light.

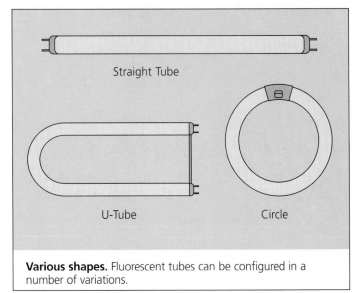

Various shapes. Fluorescent tubes can be configured in a number of variations.

Various manufacturers may name the specific configuration of their fluorescent lamps in their own codes or proprietary names. However, such terms as "U-shaped" or "U bulbs" and "circlines" are universal. Newer twists in sizing allow use of fluorescent lamps in areas where they previously would have appeared bulky and oversized. For instance, extra-slim models can now fit in small cabinet spaces that would have been a tight fit for their predecessors.

Color Rendition

Fluorescent color rendition varies from manufacturer to manufacturer and from bulb type to bulb type. Some tubes emit light that is close to the cool side of the spectrum and others, a close approximation of sunlight, and still others, even warmer tones.

The most common lamps have a single coating of phosphors called halophosphors. Phosphor in varying proportions used in the tube coating determines its color rendition, Correlated Color Temperatures (CCT), and Color Rendition Index (CRI).

Color temperatures from 4,100K (cool), 3,500K (midrange), to 3,000K (warm) are recommended for home use.

Rare Earth Phosphors (Triphosphors). These either are used in addition to the single coating or alone and can make lamps have a color rendition that more closely approximates daylight. Rare earth lamps are more energy-efficient, have better color properties, and are more expensive than single-coated lamps that are basically sold as "cool white" or "warm white." Rare earth lamps are identified as being either within the 70s CRI range or the 80s CRI range, which is excellent color rendition for fluorescent. As with other lamps, the CRI should only be compared with lamps of similar color temperature (CCT).

Because fluorescent lamps are nondirectional (except those used with reflectors), they tend to be used for ambient, background lighting. In this application, the color rendition is more critical than in that of a spotlight.

Lamp Life and Efficiency

When it comes to energy efficiency and length of life, fluorescents have it all over incandescents. They are truly impressive.

Typically, these lamps are four to five times more efficient. For example, a 40-watt incandescent lamp produces 445 lumens, while a 40-watt fluorescent lamp produces 3,050 lumens, about six times the amount of light. The average rated life of the 40-watt incandescent is 1,500, while the 40-watt fluorescent has an average rated life of 20,000 hours. A new, more efficient generation of fluorescent bulbs promises to outdo even that.

Efficacy. The efficacy of commonly used incandescent bulbs is 10 to 23 lumens per watt, while there is a substantially

Advantages and Disadvantages of Fluorescent Lamps	
Advantage	**Disadvantage**
Long life	Not easily dimmed
Low operating cost	Temperature-sensitive
Variety of colors	May require separate ballast
Start fast	
High lumen output	
Low surface brightness or glare	

better range of 60 to 95 lumens per watt for fluorescent lamps (including bulb and ballast).

Quality of Light. The quality of light (lumen maintenance) of fluorescent lamps over their lifetimes is far superior to that of incandescent bulbs. After stabilizing for 100 hours, fluorescent lamps maintain their lumen output over many hours.

Life Expectancy. The life expectancy of fluorescent bulbs is based on an industry standard of three hours use time per start. Bulb life is greatly extended by increasing the burning cycle per start and greatly shortened when the lamps are used for periods of less than three hours. Keep this in mind in determining where to put fluorescent fixtures. For example, a fluorescent might not make sense in a storage area where light is only needed for a few minutes at a time here and there. On the other hand, installing a fluorescent fixture as your overhead kitchen light makes sense because it's likely to be on for hours at a time.

Dimming Fluorescents. Most fluorescent lamps cannot be dimmed and should never be used with dimmer switches. Incandescent dimmers do not regulate voltage for fluorescent lamps properly and will blow out the bulbs, posing a fire hazard. There are, however, special systems of ballasts and dimmers that, combined with specific fluorescent fixtures, provide this capability. You will need to purchase an entire system designed for dimming, usually with all components specified from the same manufacturer.

Starters. In recent years the rapid-start feature incorporated into the ballast for conventional tubular fluorescent lamp fixtures has made these devices unnecessary. However, there may still be starters available for old fixtures.

Compact Fluorescent Bulbs

If you are not saving yourself at least $50 in bulbs and electricity over the life of the bulb by using compact fluorescent bulbs, consider it now! More sure than a stock market investment, compact fluorescents return not only money savings to individuals, in the long run they cost less in environmental impact on our natural resources.

Screw-in compact fluorescent bulbs are heavier and broader at the neck than incandescent bulbs, but the fluorescents are much more efficient.

Additionally, some utility companies have provided special rebate programs for purchase of compact fluorescents that make the money-saving ratio even higher.

There is a compact fluorescent bulb substitution for most popular incandescent bulbs. With medium screw-in bases, they are a fluorescent tube and ballast combined as one. Modular units come in two pieces, so that the ballast can be reused and disposed of separately from the bulb. Ballasts can last up to three times longer than the bulbs. Two types are available: magnetic and electronic ballasts. Compact fluorescent bulbs with magnetic ballasts are less expensive, but may start slowly and flicker for a moment when first turned on. These ballasts operate at 60 cycles per second, which creates a subliminal "strobe" effect some people find annoying. Electronic ballasts start instantly and have no strobe effect. They also weigh less. Electronic ballasts are most often used, although magnetic ballasts also are available in some units. The compatibility of tube and ballast are ensured when they are in one unit. These one-piece units usually are smaller and may fit into a luminaire more easily than a modular unit.

Advances in design are making all screw-in compact fluorescents both lighter weight and less unwieldy. Check with your home center, lighting showroom, hardware store, or utility company from time to time for the latest innovations.

How It Works

Compact fluorescent lamps function like other fluorescents, except they screw into medium or Edison bases just like incandescent bulbs. In compacts, manufacturers have bent narrow fluorescent tubes to make units shorter and able to fit where incandescent bulbs are used. Usually, more than one tube is used to produce additional light. Four joined tubes are called quads.

These bulbs do not function well at extreme temperatures. Don't use them where excessive heat might build up. Don't use them outdoors in cold weather unless they are specified

for use within your climate range. As with other fluorescents, use compacts only with dimming systems specifically meant for fluorescents. Keep this in mind if you are putting compact fluorescents where you have previously used incandescents, such as in a set of recessed lights hooked up to an incandescent dimmer.

Estimating Lighting Needs. Generally speaking, replace incandescent bulbs with compact fluorescent lamps that are one-third to one-fourth the wattage. Most compacts have the comparison information on the package.

Color

Most compact fluorescent lamps are designed to simulate incandescent bulbs. Quality phosphors that produce a warmer Correlated Color Temperature within a warm visual range are used in these bulbs where aesthetics are important. Color Rendition Indexes (CRI) are considered "fair" from 55-65, "better" from 65-70, and "best" from 75 on up. Many of these lamps have a CRI of around 80. While the color is not the same as incandescent, you may find the trade-off in efficiency makes up for it.

For uniform color and overall visual effect, use the same bulb types within a room. Don't mix bulbs of various manufacturers. It is particularly important to use matching bulbs in matching fixtures, such as where two table lamps flank a sofa or in arms of a wall sconce.

You can use a fixture's surroundings to adjust the color of its lighting. For instance, to warm up cooler lighting, use a warmer lamp shade color and warm colors where the light will reflect, such as on the shade's interior. You can change the lamp base to a warmer hue or change the interior of a track or recessed light fixture to a warm hue like gold.

Shapes and Sizes

While lighter-weight, more compact fluorescent bulbs are becoming available, most are still heavier than incandescent bulbs. Some compact fluorescents can make lightweight,

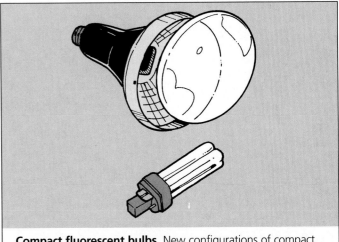

Compact fluorescent bulbs. New configurations of compact fluorescent bulbs make them adaptable to screw-in applications. This version has a twist-on lens and a replaceable inner lamp.

standing fixtures top-heavy. In some table or floor lamps, try adding counterbalancing weight made of materials like plaster of Paris or metal. However, floor and table lamps with wide and weighted bases are the best candidates for compact fluorescents. Shop around to find compact fluorescents with a shape and heft best for you.

It is relatively easy to solve the problem of compact fluorescent bulbs that are too wide to fit into some lamps. Various types of accessories that fit beneath the socket and hold the harp (the metal frame that holds the shade) are designed to accommodate the wider bulb ballast. They are inexpensive and are available through home centers, lighting showrooms, and utility companies.

Make sure also that the bulb height suits the fixture, since some compact fluorescents are taller than incandescents. Since lamp shades are scaled to suit the table and floor lamps they match, be sure your alterations are still attractively in scale.

Shapes. A variety of shapes is available. The most common has a circular or square ballast base with a "U" tube extending from it. Alternatives include units with multiple "U" tubes, two or three in the same base. Ultra compact lamps may have three shorter tubes replacing one longer "U" tube and are closer in shape to conventional bulbs.

In some models the tubes are covered with a circular or cylindrical plastic or glass outer casement designed to avoid glaring, concentrated spots of lights called hot spots. Because they resemble traditional incandescents, these models are a good selection when the bulb will be exposed.

Make sure circular screw-base fluorescent bulbs fit into the fixture.

In reflective compact fluorescents, a reflective cone surrounding a "U" tube concentrates the light forward. These are good adaptations for using compact fluorescent

bulbs in track or recessed light or where reflector lamps are specified. Lensed reflectors serve to concentrate the light even more than plain reflectors. As with all reflectors, positioning within the luminaire is critical so that the lamp is neither too far forward nor too recessed. These can replace R, PAR and ER incandescent and some halogen lamps. Some reflector designs are handsome enough inside and on the exterior to be used as their own fixtures in some installations.

Energy-Saving Advantages

Using compact fluorescents saves energy and money in various ways. Here's how:

Bulb Replacement Cost. One 23-watt lamp lasts as long as 13 incandescent bulbs, thereby saving the cost of replacing those bulbs. Most compact fluorescent bulbs last 10,000 hours, whereas common incandescent bulbs last 750 hours.

Power Consumption. Compact fluorescent lamps generally use one-quarter of the electricity of incandescent bulbs they replace, as illustrated in the comparison based on information in the chart below.

Cooling Savings. Since these bulbs operate efficiently they do not produce wasted heat, which you then need to eliminate through increased air conditioning. The significance of the savings varies depending upon conditions such as how many incandescents you are replacing, your house, and your area's climate.

Ecological Savings. Reducing electricity consumption at home is only part of the beneficial story of compact fluorescent bulbs. Because they are so much more efficient,

Some compact fluorescent bulbs have a casing so that they look like globes or elongated globes, and are attractive exposed in a lamp or fixture.

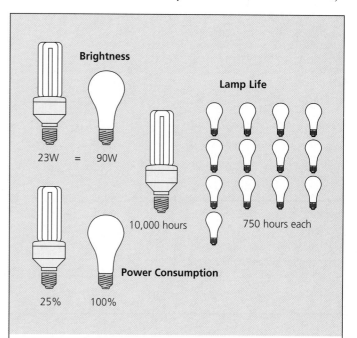

Efficacy comparison. Compact fluorescent bulbs are more efficient than incandescent bulbs in brightness, power consumption, and lamp life.

Advantages of Replacement with Compact Fluorescent Lamps

Incandescent Wattage	Fluorescent Replacement (1)	Rated Fluorescent Life	Yearly Savings (2)
2-60W	1-20W Straight Tube	9,000 Hours	$60.30
1-100W	2-20W Straight Tubes	9,000 Hours	$42.30
2-75W	1-40W Straight Tube	20,000 Hours	$196.00
2-60W	1-32W Circle Tube	12,000 Hours	$93.60
3-60W	1-32W+1-40W Circle Tubes	12,000 Hours	$126.00
2-100W	2-40W U-Tubes	12,000 Hours	$124.60
1-60W	1-13W Compact Twin	10,000 Hours	$43.00
1-100W	2-13W Compact Twins	10,000 Hours	$66.00
1-75W	1-18W Compact Quad	10,000 Hours	$53.00
1-60W	1-15W Compact Screw-In	9,000 Hours	$40.50

(1) Includes allowance for ballast wattage.
(2) Calculated @ .10 per KWH based on deluxe warm white color.

Estimating Savings

Use this formula to estimate your savings per bulb:

Add cost of incandescent bulbs (13 X price)   _____

Add estimated energy savings (see chart above) _____

Total: _____

Less cost of compact fluorescent bulb   _____

Total: _____

Less utility company rebate, if any   _____

Total: _____

they don't deplete natural resources as much when the electricity is generated. They also reduce atmospheric pollution caused by power plant production of electricity.

If you replace a 90-watt incandescent with a 23-watt compact fluorescent, it saves 630 pounds of coal, or 51 gallons of oil, or 6,700 cubic feet of natural gas from being consumed. The same compact fluorescent saves 1,072 pounds of carbon dioxide (agent of the Greenhouse Effect), 7.8 pounds of sulfur dioxide (a contributor to acid rain), and 4.1 pounds of nitrogen oxide (smog) from being released into the atmosphere. Imagine the benefits if you use more than one bulb!

Other Options

With technology advancing at the rapid rate of recent years, new, more efficient lamps will probably supplant the options available now. Some may come from the types of lamps being used primarily in public spaces. Others may come from variations on existing exterior lighting technologies. Among these are high-intensity discharge (HID) lamps, including metal halide lamps and sodium lamps.

Fiber-optic systems, with one extremely bright lamp transporting light to one, 40, or 100 destinations through fiber optic conduits, is even now used dramatically for accent lighting to highlight art objects. Since fiber optics does not generate ultraviolet rays or heat at the end of the fiber, it is an ideal choice for illuminating some artwork and the like where heat buildup or degradation from light are to be avoided.

For now, the lamps and bulbs currently available are enough to revolutionize most home lighting systems. And the bulbs are just the beginning.

Fiber-optic fixtures rely on a transformer that then serves as the source for many fiber-optic fixtures. The fixtures can be colored as shown here.

3

Lamps to Light Our Way

Before built-in fixtures, there were lamps. Prehistoric man used wood with high pitch content to make torches. Later, in Babylon, thick flax wicks were used in bowls capable of holding 50 pounds of animal fat. Ancient Romans developed the candle, the wax torch (flambeau), and the horn lantern.

Lamps can reflect designs from almost every age of man, such as this lamp with classic elegance.

Shetland Islanders for centuries captured and dried the stormy petrel, a bird with a high percentage of grease in its body, to fashion a lamp.

Early American settlers contented themselves with tallow and bayberry candles until the 1600s, when whale oil became a basic fuel for lighting. When oil was discovered in Titusville, Pennsylvania, around 1860, the shift to kerosene lamps was underway, and later, kerosene faced competition from gas lights. When the electric bulb was introduced in the late 1800s, it was a quantum leap that changed the future of all lamp design.

Today's lamps often are styled to reflect the designs of the past. From candle lamps to rustic terra cotta jars that could have held oil wicks, traditional lamps add style as well as light to a room. Of course, lamps are also available in contemporary styles. Often, modern lamps showcase new lighting technology with wit and high-tech humor.

Whatever your fancy, be sure the lamps you select fit into your decorating scheme and provide the best possible, most useful light.

Most lighting plans are built around or inspired by decorative plug-in lamps. Since plug-ins often are the style-makers and are sometimes necessary for task lighting, consider them first in developing your overall scheme. Keep in mind that you may be able to eliminate some plug-in lighting with fixtures if you so choose. However, consider first the advantages and purposes of most plug-in lamps by category as discussed here: floor lamps, table lamps, desk lamps, task lamps, spotlights, picture lamps, cabinet, curio and kitchen cabinet lights, night lights, and add-on dimmers and timers.

Portable plug-in lamps solve both lighting and decorating problems. When designing your room, ask yourself these questions:

▪ Will this lamp provide the lighting I need?

▪ Which lamp type suits my activities best?

▪ Can I make an energy-efficient selection with this lamp type?

▪ How will the lamp style fit into my overall decorating scheme?

▪ Is the lamp well balanced and properly weighted?

▪ Does the lamp have flexibility features such as dimming, three-way lighting, adjustable light angle, or can I alter the lamp to provide these qualities?

- Can I provide electricity for the lamp without extending cords across normal pathways?
- Will bulbs and tubes for this lamp be hard to replace, and do they have a long lifetime?
- How will the lamp fit into the overall lighting scheme, including built-in lighting and fixtures I may want to add?

Floor Lamps

Up, down, all around — floor lamps can propel light in all these directions. They are a design solution for areas unsuited for a table lamp that need task and ambient light. For instance, you can position a traditional floor lamp for reading near a comfortable chair. The lamp and the pool of light it throws around that chair are an integral part of the inviting warmth of a cozy nook you have created. Without the floor lamp, the entire area would be flat, lifeless, and uninviting.

Styles

Floor lamps run the gamut from far-out modern to those reminiscent of Early American candle tables. In fact, some traditional lamps have tables incorporated into the bases.

Working Lamps. These are used for reading or close work and should be flexible. Adjustable lamps include those whose angle of light can be altered and styles where the lamp itself can be repositioned on a movable hinge. Popular accent lamps such as pharmacy or banana lamps and traditional wrought-iron country lamps often are adjustable in height as well as articulated for lamp position.

A torchiere casts light both out and up.

Most task or accent floor lamps are less than 5 feet high. For reading, the bottom of the shade should be just at eye height when seated, which is 38 to 42 inches from the floor. If the lamp also emits light upward, make sure you will not see a glaring bulb when you pass the lamp. Lamps that can be dimmed or set on low maintain decorative light while conserving energy when task light is not needed.

Torchieres. These are designed to direct most light upwards. While they may provide an attractive glow at the source, most of their light is thrown against the ceiling and reflected back. They work best in rooms with relatively high ceilings that are painted a light color so that light is diffused over a wide area. Avoid putting torchieres where their glare will be visible from a stairway or balcony. Be careful, too, to place them well away from flammable materials such as curtains. Most torchieres are about 6 feet tall, so that bulbs don't create glare for people of average height.

Torchieres can produce a strobe-like effect if placed directly under a rotating ceiling fan and also can create unpleasant light patterns if placed too close to a wall. They are best used just like the torches from which their name is derived: close to seating but standing relatively alone.

Floor lamps. For reading, position floor lamps behind and to the side.

A flattened globe atop a sleek base defines this floor lamp.

Sleek light tubes cast light from floor to their tops, another variation on the floor lamp.

Bulbs. There are floor lamps designed to take everything from incandescent "A" bulbs through halogens and even compact fluorescent or circline bulbs. A torchiere with the equivalent of 250 incandescent watts of uplight provides soft, even, shadow-free overall illumination for rooms up to 400 square feet.

Torchieres are the perfect application for halogen bulbs, and many designs come with 300- to 500-watt halogen bulbs. Foot dimmers or knobs on the lamp column control the light, which is thrown out and up, filling the room. Yet the heat from the bulb rises up high, away from the people nearby.

Table Lamps

Everyone's lamp. It's hard to imagine a home without table lamps. Like floor lamps, they are decorative as well as practical lighting sources for both ambient and task lighting.

Styles

Most table lamps are designed to coordinate with home furnishings. Many come in more than one color so that you can coordinate very closely. Many are made of neutral colors such as white, ivory, or beige, and materials that go with everything such as crystal or metals like brass, pewter, or wrought iron.

The designers of lamps coordinate shades and bases in size and color. Classic traditional lamp designs include candlestick designs, ginger jar designs, vase shapes, and oil lamp reproductions. Contemporary designs are made with ceramic, glass materials, metals, and high-quality plastics. Some are more for show than for practical illumination, but so interesting that they are wonderful decorative accents. Shades are an integral part of the overall design, and replacing a shade with one that does not fit the lamp alters its look dramatically.

Sizes

Since all tables are not the same, take measurements before you go to a store to purchase a table lamp. The top of the lamp base plus the table height should be about 38 to 42 inches above the floor. That will place the bottom of the shade just at eye height for someone seated nearby.

Shorter tables call for taller lamps and vice versa to have the shade bottom positioned best.

For conventional table lamps, if the shade bottom is at least 16 inches wide, it will provide an ample pool of light. In lampshades to be viewed from above, the bulb should be recessed well below the top edge. If you need to change the shade to accomplish this, try one whose frame (where it attaches to the lamp) is recessed. However, be sure the shade is proportioned so that it reaches to just below the socket. Lampshade harps come in many sizes, and risers are available that screw on to the top of the harp, adding height just below the decorative finial. Diffusers are incorporated in some lamp designs so that there is no bulb glare from above.

A reeded pole table lamp is the kind of transitional style that will fit right into many furniture styles.

A ceramic lamp in the pottery tradition can look classical with artful embellishments.

Table lamps. Depending upon table height, select a lamp that has the shade lower edge just below eye level.

Efficiency and Bulbs

Lamps with semitransparent shades can provide both accent or task light and ambient light. They make the most of the bulb. Do not use bulbs of higher wattage than the manufacturer recommends. A bulb too hot and too close to a shade can cause uneven light diffusion, glare, or even "hot spots" that burn the shade brown and create a fire hazard.

The most energy-efficient shades are semitransparent, providing ambient light as well as allowing light to spill from top and bottom. Always check the quality of light a shade imparts before buying the lamp. What may seem like a solid white shade may have an undertone of creamy yellow, a cool bluish cast, or a linen texture that substantially darkens the shade while providing textural interest. Coordinating lampshade and lamp with light on and off is a necessary part of overall lamp design. You can alter shades by changing the harp to raise them or lower them, even replace them for an entirely different style, but check first that the end result will be as pleasing as what the original designer intended. Calculate the amount of light that comes through the sides as well as from top and bottom in judging a lamp's contribution to the overall room scheme.

A less efficient but highly dramatic lamp style employs opaque shades. Examples are candlestick lamps and lamps with pierced shades, both of which are traditionally designed with opaque shades. These dark lamps work best in rooms with dark walls, such as paneling, where they visually blend in. However, since they do not provide light through a semitransparent shade, more lamps or other light sources may be needed with opaque shades to illuminate the darker walls.

Many opaque shades have reflective white interiors to boost the bulb's efficiency for uplighting and downlighting. A rich effect is produced with gilded lampshade interiors, which cast a light that is usually flattering to both wood and flesh tones. Designers have also been known to use palest peach

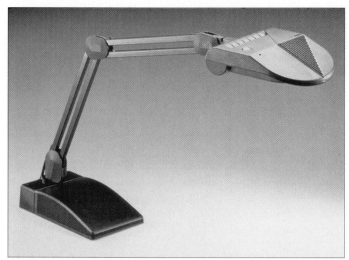

An ergonomic desk lamp is designed with baffles that direct light to the right, beyond the head, so the head cannot block your view.

Lighting for tabletop tasks. Position a lamp to the side and toward the table/desk front edge so hands do not produce shadows.

or pink tones on opaque lamp interiors to provide an intimate and flattering light, kind to faces.

Table lamps are now designed to accommodate halogen, compact fluorescent bulbs, and three-way bulbs. If you replace an A-type incandescent with another bulb, be sure that the lamp will not be top-heavy. If you are rewiring a lamp yourself, figure out what kind of bulb you want to install and make the necessary changes in the planning stage. Use dimmers and three-way switches to turn lights down when bright light is not needed, making sure first that the rewiring is appropriate for the type of bulb.

This desk lamp diffuses light in all directions.

Desk and Task Lamps

Forget those old-fashioned desk lamps that were positioned directly across from the person seated at the desk. They created the worst possible surface glare, throwing light directly into eyes. Recent emphasis on ergonomic office design can be carried over into the home in lighting designs for desks, craft areas, and sewing centers. The principles for many tabletop projects are similar.

Styles

Miniaturization, in bulbs like halogens and compact fluorescents and in the designs of desk lamps themselves, has broadened the possibilities. Modern renderings often include long-legged designs and articulated necks that allow you to position light exactly where you want it.

When it comes to task lighting, efficiency takes precedence over design. Eyestrain can result from poorly adjusted lighting that is not customized for tasks. Be sure your desk lamp suits your needs. Check out the lamp in the store, sitting as you would sit to use it. Lamps for left-handed people should be placed on the right, and those for right-handed people belong on the left so that hands and arms do not shadow the work or writing field.

Avoid lamps that provide bright light to a small viewing area only by creating glare when you are seated in your

For a formal, old-fashioned desk, select a lamp that echoes the candleholders of old, such as this double candlestick base.

Bulbs

Bulbs include everything from high-intensity halogen lamps (sometimes designed with a low-voltage transformer in the base) and linear or compact fluorescent lamps to incandescent bulbs. Be sure the lamp is properly balanced if you use one of the heavier bulbs. Consider, too, how the bulb will make your work look. A cool crystal-white halogen bulb or cool compact fluorescent may give you the best definition, if color is not important to you. However, if you are using a task light for sewing or craftwork with textiles or wood, the warmth of a traditional incandescent may be better. In this case, make sure you are comfortable with the way the work's colors are rendered, or your enjoyment of the task itself will be diminished.

Consider, too, the amount of heat a desk lamp will generate, since you will be close to it. If excessive heat will bother you or affect your project materials, check out lamps that take compact fluorescent bulbs since they are the coolest choices. Also, even small halogen bi-pins can have casings around them very hot to the touch, so always be sure to adjust the desk lamp by using the special adjustment arm or pin incorporated in many halogen desk lamp designs. Some styles are designed to vent or direct heat back from the beam, but not necessarily far enough away from the person using the desk. Test the lamp in the store.

Portable Cans/Spotlights

The light source is unobtrusive, but the lighting effect is one of high drama. Portable spotlights in can-shaped, plug-in fixtures point the way to highlight special features of a room. Often they show off indoor plants, with the can positioned on the floor to display not only leaves, but to create an interesting shadow play on a nearby ceiling and wall. These lamps can highlight a hanging quilt, bottom-light a sculpture or decorative vase, or pick up the elegant colors of a flower arrangement.

Whether clip-ons, mounted on the wall, attached to bases, or simple cans, these spotlights can be positioned closer or further away from the featured object to create the best possible highlighting effect.

With incandescent or halogen bulbs, these lights may run hot. Be sure to use the bulb rated for the unit and remember that spotlights generating a lot of heat should be kept at a safe distance from fabrics and plants.

Portable spotlights are inherently contemporary in design, so keep them out of sight in traditional and country surroundings by placing them behind sofas, chairs, or with another decorative object such as a churn placed in front. For other interior styles, the lamp itself may be a decorative asset.

Adjustability is critical when you use spotlights because you want to be able to disguise the light source and prevent glare. Some spots have adjustable louvers that allow you to restrict the pool of light to precisely where you need it.

normal relationship to the lamp. The entire lamp design, including distance the bulb extends towards you beyond the base, amount of shielding of the bulb, range of light thrown, and opacity of the shade are all factors that make a desk lamp convenient or inconvenient for your specific needs. A lamp whose shade rim is below your eye level (usually 15 inches above the desk surface), that can be positioned 15 inches beside your working area and about 12 inches centered from the edge of your desk, is an efficient choice for most desk work.

If your tasks vary, you will need an easily adjustable lamp. For example, you may need to position the lamp down closer to the surface for fine detailed work at one time and have the same lamp amply light the entire desktop for a different project. Task/desk lamps are available that will readily adjust to different needs, while some others are best set in one position and kept stationary.

Unless there is a fair amount of ambient light on the working surface and surroundings, select a desk lamp that projects a broad cone of light. Check the lamp label to be sure that the lamp will accept a bulb bright enough for your requirements.

If your desk lamp will be used adjacent to your computer, be sure it will fit and properly light the materials you need to read while doing computer work, without creating glare on the computer screen.

Spotlights. Keep the lamp unobtrusive, and use it to cast creative shadows or spotlight a selected object.

Select a picture light that is wide enough to provide light across the entire picture.

Use a picture light to keep a painting from going into dark shadows between flanking table lamps.

Others may be pivoted or adjusted up or down. Remember, too, that you can change the way the light falls by moving the spotlight in or out in relation to the featured object.

Bulbs

PAR, ER, and reflector bulbs most often are used for these fixtures. There are screw-in fixtures that are one unit with a socket which fit directly into an outlet and have an adjustable reflector bulb articulated at the base. Reflective compact fluorescent bulbs also may be suitable for these units.

Picture Lights

Nothing brings a picture to life more than proper lighting. A subdued background and a properly lit picture show off the artist's intentions to best effect. Consider two factors when choosing a picture light: protecting the artwork and the best way to light it.

Museums commonly restrict lighting for famous works to protect them from the ravages of light. While the human eye discerns from 1 to 10,000 footcandles, many museum pieces are lit in the range of 5 to 10 footcandles to avoid degradation of the art. Art lamps often are low wattage for the same reason.

Strip lights are effectively used vertically, lighting books in shelves evenly.

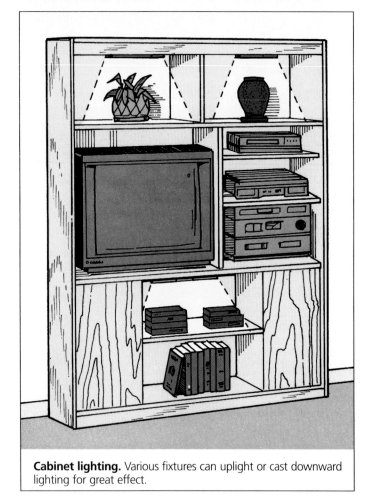

Cabinet lighting. Various fixtures can uplight or cast downward lighting for great effect.

Such extreme precautions may be overkill for artwork that can be replaced. By lighting your artwork, you increase its impact and importance as a decorative focus in a room.

Styles and Sizes

Clip-on and bracket art lights can be attached easily to many frames. Free-standing miniature lights placed on a shelf or table also can be used to light artwork. The latter may be best for illuminating miniatures or small sculptures.

In any case, art lights should be adjustable so that they won't glare on framing glass. Often, the lamps are from 7 to 14 inches long, with one or two low-wattage tubular incandescent bulbs. Linear fluorescent picture lights with attractive casings ranging up to 2 feet long are available with filters to screen ultraviolet radiation from the art.

Clip-on or bracket picture lights usually fit on the frame either below or above, rather than to the side, of the artwork. Most have adjustable louvered covers to close down onto the artwork without illuminating the wall as well. Traditionally, picture lights have been made of brass or a bronzed metal to blend in with the frames of the past, or in neutral colors that will not conflict with the artwork.

Consider also modern methods of illuminating artwork. Install custom lighting strips of thin fluorescent and/or the "starlight" type inside a recessed cove frame for a piece of artwork. Fiber-optic fixtures are used in museum lighting because they are cool and do not transmit ultraviolet rays. They require a remote light source. In the future, these fixtures may become more common in home use.

Bulbs and Efficiency

Picture lights use compact fluorescent, incandescent, fluorescent, or halogen bulbs and provide varying degrees of color accuracy and brightness.

Cabinet and Curio Lights

Customizing a china or kitchen cabinet or a curio cabinet with light can transform a humdrum unit into a showpiece and make humble accessories take on the look of true beauty. Some cabinets come with lighting already in place, some don't. In most cases, augmenting the lighting will multiply its effectiveness.

Since the principles are pretty much the same for all kinds of shelf, cabinet, and curio units, see how many areas in your home would benefit from auxiliary lighting. The soft, warm glow of cabinet lights also provides attractive low-level ambient lighting.

The first step is to consider the cabinet design and what's going to be in it. Carefully arrange permanent collections such as glassware, pottery, figurines, and trophies and light them to best effect. Bright lighting usually works best. Soften the light when you want to blend disparate objects, such as books, fancy bookends, china, or other eclectic elements.

Many units, including curios with glass shelves, come with ineffective lighting. The worst offender is a cabinet with a single bulb centered at the top that is supposed to illuminate a series of glass shelves. That unprotected bulb can glare directly into your eyes when you are seated nearby, and often it lights only the objects on the top shelf, casting everything below into shadow. This classic situation calls for change. Adjusting the lighting using one of the many choices below will upgrade the unit and make it much more effective.

tube. They take thin fluorescent tubes such as the T-5, that are a mere ⅝ inch wide, and they come in various lengths. Use these for such matte-finish treasures as books or wooden objects since the strips often are hard to baffle for glare. Light strips of incandescent bulbs or units with incandescent tubes are also choices. Of these, the incandescent produce the most heat and are least efficient.

If you have many objects to display on a wall or in cabinets, investigate fiber-optic units. A single light source can produce many pin-dot light spots. Fashion shielding strips from the same material as the cabinets. Conversely, the light strip shields themselves also can be a decorative contrast. What's key is that the strips keep the lamps hidden. Before you attach the light strip, experiment with putting it on the shelf's front edge, slightly further back, midway back, or at the rear for best effect.

Apply the same technique to uplighting with fluorescent tubes. This lighting usually is positioned along the front edge.

Backlighting is effective from both top and bottom. Use it to show off the wood grain of the furniture back and to backlight and outline decorative objects placed on the shelf. Balance highly dramatic backlighting with some frontlighting or sidelighting on objects such as pottery, colored glassware, or figurines so they are not totally in shadow.

Strip lights placed at the top inside recessed alcoves are effective as long as objects themselves do not block the flow of light.

Styles

Some lighting units are designed for use within furniture and come with the unit. You also can design your own lighting, adapting existing lamps for cabinets. But do not select lamps that will unduly heat up the cabinet interior, especially those enclosed by glass doors.

Miniature lamps of many shapes can be clipped or set upon shelves to spotlight specific items. Miniature track lighting, strips of low-voltage mini-lights, and all-in-one fluorescent units also can do the job.

Depending on what you want to light and how you want to light it, you can install light at the top, bottom, back or sides, or combine light positions.

Toplighting brings out the sparkle of crystal and china. Consider using miniature MR low-voltage lamps, which direct heat away from the lamp front, to spotlight such objects from above. Be sure the unit has shields or is otherwise designed to prevent glare. Check for glare when you are both sitting and standing nearby. Check out lighting units that have baffles or eyeball shields.

Light nonreflective surfaces from the top by installing thin fluorescent undercabinet units that combine a ballast and

Many professionals favor sidelighting to balance the light at the front and sides of objects as well as the background through overall illumination. Install shielding strips along either side of a unit in matching or inconspicuous material. Notch shelves for vertical fluorescent tubes that run the height of the unit on either side. Create contrast between the objects and background through color not light, since the entire interior will be aglow.

Do not overlook the cabinet or curio top as a lighting opportunity. Collectibles or plates arranged up there can be highlighted or backlit with many of the same techniques as those used inside the cabinets. Often, cabinet tops have ready-made railings or molding that will disguise the lighting source.

Incorporate lighting controls for displays so that they either light separately or all turn on at once. Make sure to provide additional ventilation, especially in glass-fronted cabinets or curios, to counter heat from lighting you added. Use common sense and don't place combustible objects near the light source.

Bulbs

As noted, MR low-voltage halogen bulbs, incandescent bulbs (especially tubular), linear and compact fluorescent bulbs, and fiber optics all are possibilities. You'll find them in cabinets already outfitted with lighting or you can install them yourself.

Portable Control Devices

Lights that automatically turn on at dusk and off at dawn, timers both for random times and at set daily intervals, and dimmers that allow you to readily conserve energy and control a room's mood are all adjuncts to portable lighting. These features can be integrated into a lamp or can be separate, controlling more than one luminaire. You also can connect controls directly and permanently to your house wiring. Electricians call this hard wiring. Start a lighting remodeling plan by thinking about installing controls even for portable plug-in fixtures.

The simplest method of controlling portable lighting, aside from using the switches that come with it, is to attach inexpensive portable timers and dimmers. With these accessories, existing fixtures and lamps take on custom qualities without the need to hard wire.

You may find exactly what you want built right into the bulb. New bulb models have microchips in the base of the bulb that control light functions. One type automatically shuts off after 30 minutes, another adjusts to four different light levels with the flip of the switch, and a third has a "safety" filament built in that provides a backup light when the main filament fails. (This also can be used out of doors.)

Compare the cost and efficiency of these built-in "smart" bulbs with older models of portable controls. Over the long run, it might be best to use conventional bulbs with separate timers or dimmers. However, the newer bulbs may be ideal for some uses, such as where space or other considerations make using separate dimmers impractical.

Portable plug-in controls are easy to set for timing intervals, and can give the appearance that someone's home when they're not.

Consider also button-like devices inserted into the socket that act as dimmers.

Dimmers

Dimmers for portable fixtures operate in much the same way as hard wired dimmers. See "Choosing Dimmer Switches," page 149.

Dimmers must be matched to the fixture and bulb to be used. A dimmer could overheat and become damaged or cause a fire if used incorrectly. Dimmers can cause bulbs to burn out if the maximum dimmer load does not tally with the bulb specifications of the lamp. *Never* install an incandescent dimmer for a fluorescent lamp, or plug an appliance into a dimmer. Some fluorescent lamps can be dimmed with special ballasts and dimmers designed specifically for them. Low-voltage halogen lamps also need specific dimmers. Check, also that the dimmers will not cause interference with computers, radio, television, and other equipment. Dimmers can be outfitted with electromagnetic interference and radio frequency interference (EMI and RMI) filters or should be placed sufficiently distant from electronic equipment to avoid interference.

Two styles of dimmers are popular: those that are installed in line and those that are socket and cord dimmers. In-line dimmers are attached directly to the cord of the portable plug-in fixture. Many are based on the use of a circular control, a button that you rotate. Attach the dimmer along the cord so that it will be within easy reach when the lamp is in use, usually directly behind a table lamp.

Socket and cord dimmers are made of a plug and adaptor unit that is wired to a dimmer switch. The adaptor plugs into the wall, the luminaire plugs into the adaptor, and the dimmer unit controls the lamp. These are particularly useful with floor lamps or torchieres, since the hand or foot control can be placed away from the lamp but within easy reach.

Dimmers save energy and extend lamp/bulb life. If you dim an incandescent lamp by 50 percent about 50 percent of the time, you use three-quarters of the energy and almost double the bulb life. Often, you don't need the brightest light level. For example, dim a task light down for low-level ambient light when you are not using it for work.

Even a reduction of 10 percent light about half the time will save a corresponding 10 percent in power and increase the lamp life by about one-third.

Make sure the dimmer is totally turned off when not in use. Conversely, keep in mind that halogen lamps need to be used at full strength occasionally to maintain their brightness.

Timers

Plug-in and screw-in timers are used for safety, convenience, energy conservation, and extension of bulb life. By turning lights on, timers give the impression someone is home. Timers also can automatically provide safe illumination as soon as you walk into a room. They ensure lamps are not

Use an automatic security light control that plugs into a lamp. Some are motion detectors, others are activated by light levels to turn on at dusk.

left on longer than needed and so conserve energy.

Socket-located timers have a small, button-shaped insert that screws into a medium socket. They delay turn-off by a fixed duration, such as 10 to 30 minutes. They are ideal in detached garages, attics, crawl spaces, and pantries, where you might need light to see but have no easy way of turning the light off.

Plug-located interval timers operate as miniature clocks, which can set to go on or off at any time of day. Security systems even have random patterns, slightly varied from day to day to better simulate normal light use. The device can be either spring-wound or electronic and should be easy to read. It should also have an easy-to-use manual override. Check that the timer and lamp are compatible. Most timers are designed to take the wattage lamps demand. Important exceptions are low-voltage and fluorescent lamps, which may not be compatible with timers.

Locate the timer where it will be easy to reach once the light is off, or make sure that another lamp can be used to light your way into an automatically darkened area.

Automatic Night lights

Automatic night lights contain a photocell that automatically switches the light on at dusk and off at dawn. They are used for safety and to reassure children at bedtime. All-in-one units are plugged directly into any polarized wall outlet, and most come with a replaceable bulb. Fanciful designs are geared to the most often used locations, such as bathrooms, children's rooms, kitchens, and bedrooms. Hallways and stairways are other areas where this tiny lamp can actually save lives by helping people avoid accidents. They use only four to

Use night lights wherever visibility might be needed, such as in the bathroom or hallway. The lower wattage required makes them economical choices.

This plug-in light comes on when the power goes off. You won't need to rummage for flashlights and batteries during a power outage.

seven watts of electricity, which is adequate for most night-adjusted eyes.

Photo-Control Devices

These units operate with photocell sensors as do night lights, but regulate conventional lamps and bulbs. Models include screw-in types for both "A" and PAR bulbs and plug-in controls that can be positioned to eliminate radio static. Some can be used with some screw-in fluorescent PAR bulbs. While these devices are often used out of doors, they also are effective inside.

Emergency Power Failure Lights

Especially handy in rural areas but useful in almost any home, emergency power failure lights are designed so that a light automatically comes on when the power goes out. Use them as a handy rechargeable flashlight that plugs directly into a wall outlet. Position these at stairways or within easy view.

Miscellaneous Controls

A number of controls have reached the mainstream in recent years and suit specific needs. Motion sensor units, either hard wired or separate, are controls that have become more popular. These devices automatically turn off lights after no motion is detected for a period of time. In many cases, the time interval can be programmed. These devices also serve as security lights and promote energy efficiency.

Touch controls or controls that react to noise make portable lamps much more accessible for anyone who may have trouble turning on switches, such as people whose dexterity is limited by arthritis. As such needs become more prevalent, new products that are easier to use will become available.

With variations in the controls and the built-in flexibility of portable lighting, these products will adapt to today's lighting schemes and lead the way to the schemes of the future.

4
Fixtures and Their Effects

Fixtures are the stage setters of lighting. With them we are able to direct and manipulate light today in ways unknown as late as the 1970s. In large part, the variety of lighting fixtures available today is a testament to the international as well as national way of rethinking lighting. New lighting techniques and improvements in bulbs and fixtures started in the theater, stimulated by such demands as light-driven stage designs. Residential designers were quick to adapt the same techniques, such as using banks or rows of lights in their own designs.

In another vein, interest in classical design motifs prompted designers and architects of the post-modern school to incorporate lighting into architectural detailing. Moldings, pillars, cove ceilings, and the like all were used as lighting foils.

Use fixtures to set or complete your design in addition to providing lighting. Signature fixtures are essential in this landing that dominates a foyer.

Styles range from the highly traditional to the most contemporary of modes. Energy concerns have sparked some of the most innovative designs. As manufacturers have created more energy-efficient designs, fixture designers have capitalized on these intriguing advances with designs impossible before. Smaller energy-efficient, low-voltage halogen bulbs are used in equally exciting small fixtures. More accurately calibrated bulbs throw light farther and are brighter for the same wattage, so designers have greater flexibility in positioning fixtures for the best effects.

Tried and true favorites are also part of the bountiful selection of fixtures, from chandeliers that echo those used in lavish Versailles to humble wall sconces that resemble candle lamps. With so much to choose from, you can make a lighting plan that is perfect for every room in your home.

Fixtures can be divided into two groups. First, there are those meant to be seen and to be part of the overall design of the space, such as ceiling pendants, chandeliers, wall sconces, surface-mounted ceiling fixtures, and track lighting. Second, there are unobtrusive fixtures, such as cove and recessed lights, which provide light without calling undue attention to themselves.

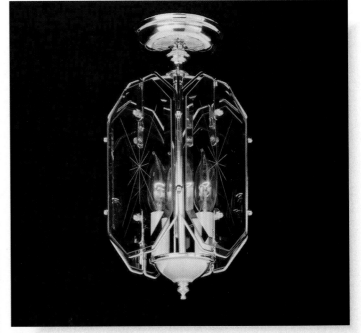

Chandeliers often are designed with faceted glass panels that reflect the light without interfering with it.

Regardless of the type of lighting fixture you choose, follow these general guidelines when installing them:

- Locate switches where they are easily accessible. Usually they are most convenient near a doorway. Consider three-way switches for the same fixtures in rooms with more than one doorway.

- Use dimmer controls to allow most fixtures to provide lighting for mood as well as tasks. Don't wire more than one fixture with the same dimmer. One dimmer to one fixture will provide the greatest control over lighting levels.

- Always see how a fixture looks when lit before purchasing it. Also, before you buy, make sure you have adequate electrical circuits located where you want to place all the fixtures. See "Mapping Electrical Circuits," page 119.

- Coordinate fixtures that will be seen together, including those within sight from one room to another.

Relate fixtures within a room to portable lighting as well. Transitional styles that blend elements from various decorating periods like a brass and glass pendant and restrained styles such as a sleek circular opaque wall sconce need not exactly match other furnishing styles but usually will work well with them.

- Expect to pay more for some surface-mounted fixtures, which must be decoratively finished all around, than you might pay for recessed fixtures only decoratively finished at the front.

- Consider choosing a fixture that combines lighting effects such as downlighting, uplighting, spotlighting, and intimate mood lighting. Some fixture styles offer more options than others. For instance, chandeliers will light a whole room, but some also have separately controlled downlights in the center that throw light directly onto a table below.

- Where possible, use fluorescent lamps as the most economical long-term light source. Some fluorescent lighting systems as well as individual units have ballasts that allow dimming with a dimming switch for even more energy saving. Initial costs may be higher, but the payback usually overrides the expense.

- Consider convenience in bulb or tube replacement for hard-to-reach fixtures, such as foyer pendants.

- Make sure that specialty bulbs used in any units will be easy to replace.

- Make sure the placement of the fixture is attractive as well as efficient.

- Avoid both reflected and direct glare.

- If you plan to move, opt for surface-mounted lighting that you can take with you. If you plan to alter your rooms or furniture arrangement, select movable or adjustable fixtures such as track lighting that can be easily repositioned, in preference to recessed lighting that stays put.

There are many kinds of lighting to chose from, and here are the general benefits of the most popular choices:

Chandeliers

These are the jewels of most lighting plans, the showiest manifestations of lighting. Based on the branched, highly ornamental hanging candlesticks that predated electricity, traditional chandeliers often have prisms and crystals that play with the light they produce. Chandeliers were introduced to England by French emigrants in the late 1600s and were emulated in the American Colonies as well.

Styles

For best effect, coordinate your chandelier's style with your furnishings and your home's style. Simplified styles are made of materials such as copper, brass, pewter, pottery, porcelain, chrome, or wood. The most elegant styles have graceful lines and crystals, used in either modern or highly traditional designs. Install dimmers to control the chandelier's light level. As a rule, at least 150 total watts will produce the best effect. Many chandelier manufacturers make coordinated wall brackets that enable you to carry the look throughout the room.

Size

It is critical to make sure your chandelier is both in scale with its location and adjusted to the proper height. Most chandeliers are adjustable up and down so that they can be positioned properly. Chandeliers come with long lengths of chain and wire so that there will be a sufficient length for

Chandeliers such as this are scaled to be long enough to look pleasing in a high-ceiling area such as an open staircase foyer.

Chandelier placement. Allow enough room to avoid bumping heads, and keep the light high enough so it isn't directly at eye level.

Chandelier Proportions Centered in a Room	
Room (in feet)	Diameter of Chandelier or Pendant (in inches)
10 X 10	14-20
12 X 12	20-26
14 X 14	24-30

Bulbs

Use decorative candle or clear globe bulbs to enhance the sparkle of crystals. Otherwise, translucent globe bulbs are popular choices. You may be able to use halogens or compact fluorescents in chandeliers that have diffusers or glass globes to cover the bulbs.

Pendants

Chandeliers are a part of the pendant family, which encompasses many styles including Victorian, classic, country, and contemporary. Pendants give uplight, downlight, or a combination of both.

Bulbs and Efficiency

Combination uplight and downlight fixtures make the most of the bulbs used. Use pendants under light-colored ceilings for most efficiency in reflecting ambient uplighting. But make sure the ceiling is attractive, even if it is dark-hued, since it will be lit. Virtually every kind of bulb is used in pendants, with halogen and compact fluorescent being most energy efficient. Always use the bulb specified for the fixture, especially if the bulb is enclosed in a globe that traps

various ceiling heights. When installing the chandelier, carefully measure the height you need, then cut the cord and, with chain pliers, remove the number of chain links to obtain the appropriate length. Be sure of your measurements before you cut the cord because if a chandelier cord is too short, you must rewire it with longer cord. A chandelier designed with cable or unusual types of lamp cord may need to be rewired before you take it home. Many manufacturers will honor special requests for cord and chain length, and most lighting showrooms will rewire chandeliers to your specifications.

A chandelier positioned over a table should be at least 6 inches from each edge of the table. Hang the chandelier 30 to 36 inches above a table, unless the ceiling is higher than 8 feet—then the chandelier may look best raised even higher than 36 inches.

Allow for door clearances when choosing a foyer chandelier. Hang the fixture comfortably above tall people's heads (generally, at least 7 feet high) unless it will be over a table.

To proportion the light from the fixture in the room, follow the guidelines in the chart "Chandelier Proportions Centered in a Room."

Pendants come in a variety of shapes, sizes, and styles to suit your furnishings, such as this turn-of-the-century style.

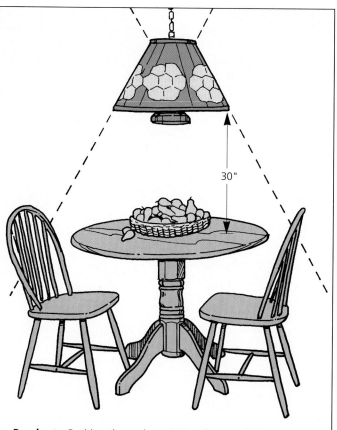

Pendants. Position these about 30 in. above a dining table. For demanding tasks, pendants should be about 15 in. above the work surface.

ing the fixture to accommodate new furniture arrangements in the future, or if the electrical box is not quite where you need to hang the pendant.

Home centers and lighting showrooms sell swag kits. You can also ask the lighting showroom or manufacturer when you order about converting a direct wire fixture to a swag, or whether there is any provision for slight changes once the pendant is installed.

Downlighting Pendants. These usually are equipped with shades or globes to eliminate glare and are practical over dinette tables, game tables, kitchen counters, or other work areas. A pendant is a good solution above end tables or other surfaces because they free up space otherwise occupied by table lamps.

Locate pendants' lower edges just below eye level to provide light for demanding tasks. That's about 15 inches above a work surface. For dining, pendants can be about 30 inches above the table. When installing such a pendant, be sure to check for glare while you are seated and standing. Turn on the fixture in the store, check it for reflected glare and be sure it isn't too bright.

heat. Check with the fixture manufacturer or with the lighting showroom staff to be sure you can retrofit a fixture with a more efficient lamp.

Styles. You have a choice from a wide range of pendant styles and even a choice of how they are installed. Most are designed to be wired directly into the ceiling. In permanent installations, chains, metal stems, thin cables, and retractable cords support the fixtures. Some pendants come with counterweights so they can be lowered and adjusted at will.

Many pendants can be converted to plug-in swags. In these, the fixture does not hang straight down from the canopy; it hangs from a hook in the ceiling. From the hook, the cord and chain are either looped over to be wired through the canopy and directly into the electrical box, or they loop down to plug into a wall outlet No canopy is needed in this arrangement.

A classic globe pendant provides diffused light in almost all directions except straight up.

Install a swag-chain arrangement if you anticipate mov-

A contemporary pendant can direct light downward as well as sideways through glass.

Uplighting Pendants. Softly glowing hemispheres of alabaster, almost translucent material entwined with classic antiqued metals as supports: this is just one example of a beautiful contemporary pendant. There's something almost mystical about many uplighting fixtures. Most cast some light downward, defining themselves as a decorative element. Like torchieres, uplighting pendants light the room by throwing light up to be reflected downward from the ceiling. They use the entire ceiling and upper wall as a giant reflector. Consequently, those surfaces must be attractive to spotlight. The entire room will be bathed in the color of the ceiling, so most designers use crisp white on ceilings that are uplit. The best uplight pendants are designed so that light is diffused over a wide area and without hot spots directly above the light source.

In many cases, the fixtures are designed to be positioned at least 18 inches below the ceiling for the best light spread, making them most suitable for rooms with high ceilings. If you are putting an uplight pendant above clear floorspace, as in a foyer, make sure there is sufficient headroom below it.

Combination Uplights and Downlights. The classic globe fixture and wonderful Nogucci Japanese rice-paper lantern pendants are examples of uplighting and downlighting pendants. Other examples include glass models that not only light upward, but cast light through glass along the sides as well as provide spotlighting below.

Some, such as collections of miniature halogen lamps with exotic Italian Murano shades and delightful shapes, are like miniature planets in a room's decorating universe. Some fixtures are combined with a crossbar, like the traditional pool table pendants, with green cased glass shades or gaslight-style fixtures used in stores and large rooms.

Functional pendants such as those used over game tables or dinettes may incorporate separate switches for ambient and task lighting. Some pendants, such as those with shades made of Tiffany-style or channeled-glass panels, include a center downlight in the trunk of the fixture. The downlight usually takes a reflector bulb, which can be operated separately from the fixture's main switch, giving you the choice of the downlight alone, the ambient lighting from the main fixture, or both at the same time.

In most cases, light is more efficient in one direction than the other, so decide which you need most before you buy. For instance, if you use a Tiffany-style lamp over a kitchen table mostly for mood lighting when eating, it's not so important that downlighting is bright. If you use the same space for homework or projects, good downlighting may be the highest priority. The design itself will determine how functional a pendant is.

Ceiling Fan Lights

Ceiling fans with built-in luminaires can project light upward above the fan or downward below it. Fans also can accommodate light kits, either a globe or a set of branched decorative lights radiating below the fan itself.

Fan light kits with projecting downlights can produce direct glare from exposed bulbs, but this can be minimized with a dimmer switch, frosted bulbs and glass, or a combination of all three. Generally, globe fixtures can be less glaring, but they may not take the wattage that "branched-style" light kits can provide.

When you buy a fan, read the installation directions carefully. See "Replacing a Light Fixture with a Ceiling Fan," page 134. Manufacturers will describe proper clearances from the ceiling and the space below. The first consideration is to be sure that sufficient clearance is possible in mounting the fan with the lighting fixture, generally 7 feet.

Light kits attach to fans in slightly different ways, depending upon which manufacturer makes them. Purchase a light kit when you purchase the fan so you are sure it will fit, or, in a retrofit situation, be sure to ask if the light kit is compatible.

Light kits with arms or branches have fitters, where the decorative glass diffuser slips in around the socket and is held by three small screws. The most common size for a fitter is 2¼ inches. There is a wide array of replacement glass available for this size, but if one piece in a multi-arm fixture breaks, it is not always easy to find glass to match. You could end up having to buy a complete set of new glass even if only one piece is actually broken. To avoid this, you can purchase one extra piece when buying the light kit and hold it in reserve.

If you've inherited your fan and do not know the manufacturer, turn off the electricity going to the fan and take off the bottom cap. Show the cap to the home center or lighting showroom staff. They may be able to tell you what light kits are compatible as well as other electrical requirements (new switches, increased weight of the combined units requiring more support, cost comparison with upgrading to a new unit, and the like).

Controls are necessary to dim the light and regulate fan speed. You can install separate switches for this, or choose models that come with all-in-one switches. These install into an ordinary electrical box and require no special wiring.

Fans can be heavy and may require special electrical boxes or other reinforcement in the ceiling. Check with your local electrical inspector to be sure the product and your application conform to local electrical codes. Additionally, special "rough service" bulbs are designed to withstand vibrations and are recommended for fan lights, although a good fan and light kit, properly installed, should not vibrate or wobble noticeably.

Wall Sconces

Derived from the Latin word "abscondere," meaning to hide, sconces originally were wall brackets holding torches or candles that had a shield protecting the flame. Designs today usually hide the light as well, which can be anything from an incandescent to compact fluorescent to a halogen bulb.

Sconces can direct light up, down, or in both directions.

By design, wall sconces cast flair light towards the wall, diffuse light into a room, or direct light towards the ceiling. Like torchieres, sconces will glare into eyes if they are too low. Mount them high enough to eliminate bulb glare, but at least 8 inches below the ceiling line to avoid ceiling hot spots. Make sure, also, that glare from the fixture's bottom will not bother someone seated nearby.

Wall sconces. Combine these with other lighting for decorative effect and ambient lighting.

Sconces ranging from fanciful to traditional work as wall sculpture as well as lighting.

Styles

Manufacturers often make wall sconces to coordinate with pendant fixtures and chandeliers for a cohesive look. Use coordinated sconces in hallways and stairways to match the larger fixtures in any room like a foyer where they will be seen.

Flank a fireplace with wall sconces. Mount them on the walls of a dining area, or wherever a wall needs a decorative lift. Country variations and contemporary light-sculpture sconces are as much wall art as they are illumination.

In hallways and dining areas especially, install separate dimmers for coordinated wall sconces and pendants or recessed lights.

Wall sconces will show off the wall around them, and so coordinate their style with that of paneling or wallcovering. Achieve the most efficient lighting by reflecting a sconce's illumination off light-colored walls and ceilings. For drama or to create a cozy feeling, put small shades on candlestick-style wall sconces. With shades, they will blend into darker walls better.

Wall reading lights. Use these to free up tabletop surfaces. Place them so they will be useful for tasks, not ambient lighting.

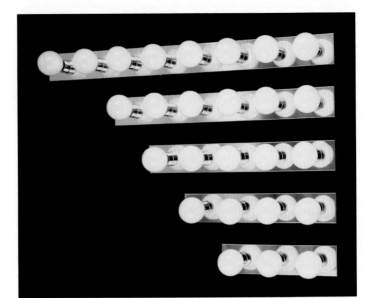

Hollywood style strip lights that take white globes come in various lengths for use around vanity mirrors.

Vanity Lights/ Wall Reading Lights

Unlike sconces, vanity lights and wall reading lights are not primarily for ambient light, but are for task lighting.

Wall Reading Lights

These often are selected to save space on night stands, end tables, or desks. A traditional style has an articulated arm that extends a shaded fixture to be near the person reading or working. Matching lamps flanking both sides of a double bed set an attractive tone. Determine where to place them according to the bed or reading chair height. These lamps work well for desks, too.

Vanity Lights

These traditionally function both for ambient and task lighting, but function must come first. They provide good, strong lighting for applying makeup, shaving, doing hair, and fulfilling other personal hygiene needs. Since they'll be used with mirrors, placement and the kind of fixture need to be carefully planned to avoid reflected glare. Choose vanity lights equal in length to the vanity or center the fixture above sinks. Be sure the fixture is deep enough to extend beyond mirrors or medicine cabinets. For more information on coordinating light fixtures with mirrors, see "Lighting for Mirrors," page 74.

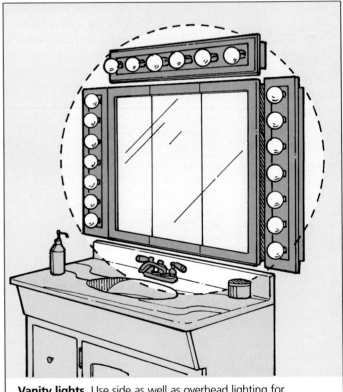

Vanity lights. Use side as well as overhead lighting for grooming tasks.

Bulbs

In some parts of the country, new bathroom lighting must be fluorescent to conform to energy conservation codes. Make sure the fluorescent fixture and lamps provide the best color rendering for makeup and realistic skin tone, within a range of 2700 to 3500 K Color Correlated Temperature (CCT). If you are using incandescent bulbs, use coated or low-wattage clear bulbs or diffusers to eliminate direct glare in front of mirrors. Dimmer controls let users regulate the light level.

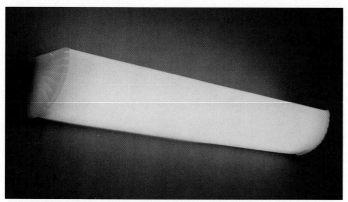

Diffused wall strips that provide even lighting along the length are ideal makeup lights on either side and above mirrors.

Styles

Vanity fixtures tend to be of three general types. The first has one or more arms to hold glass diffusers which point down or up, the second has a row of "Hollywood style" exposed globe bulbs, and the third, a single, long diffuser or cover that hides fluorescent or incandescent bulbs beneath.

The best lighting is from both sides or on three sides of the mirror rather than just across the top, since it eliminates shadows and shading for clear lighting on the face. Center side fixtures at face level, about 60 inches above the floor on average. If you want a single, centered fixture, choose multiple-arm fixtures rather than strip lighting because these provide more even lighting. Position top lighting 76 to 80 inches above the floor for best effect. Mount wall sconces at least 30 inches apart for the best balanced, most even lighting. In any case, a minimum of 120 total watts for mirror lighting should be considered a starting point.

The most common decorative glass diffuser for multi-arm vanity lights fits into a 2 ¼-inch fitter, just as with fan light kits. A wide array of replacement glass is available.

Ceiling Mounted Fixtures

Ceiling mounted fixtures vary from room to room in function and size. In a bedroom, diffused ceiling fixtures may be rarely used except for cleaning, while wall or portable lamps take over the day-to-day lighting. Ceiling fixtures in a playroom, kitchen, or bathroom often are the major sources of ambient light. With such varied purposes, equally varied sizes and shapes are available to accommodate your needs.

Bulbs

Globe fixtures, simple fixtures with glass diffusers, and older models of ceiling-mounted fixtures often are designed for incandescent lighting. Screw-in compact fluorescent lamps will make them more efficient as long as you are not turning them on and off frequently, which cuts efficiency.

Other models are designed from the beginning to take more energy-efficient bulbs, including compact and linear fluorescent. Be sure that the fixture does not produce glare if it is to be used as a major light source, such as a fluorescent fixture in a kitchen or home office.

When you are replacing glass in a ceiling-mounted fixture, be sure you have measured the fitter size, where the glass attaches to the fixture, and the depth of the glass from the fixture outward. This will ensure an accurate fit.

Styles

In some regions, fluorescent lighting is mandated for kitchens and baths, so check the code. Placement is a major consideration in locating a ceiling-mounted fixture that is to provide the majority of ambient light. Styles can echo the furnishings and cabinetry in a room and still provide efficient lighting.

Ceiling fixtures that are especially useful include bathroom fixtures with ventilating fans and perhaps infrared heating. Fixtures that include a dimming feature provide versatility.

Ceiling mounted fixtures. Decide first whether the fixture is to provide ambient light or practical lighting, then select the style.

For large areas, consider more than one ceiling fixture to provide more efficient and even lighting throughout the space. A single fixture may be too bright in the center, leaving walls and corners dark.

Whether you use one or more, coordinate it and fit it into the floor plan. Relate it to furniture or cabinets. Make sure fixtures are set not less than 80 inches from the floor. Normal clearance is about 84 inches.

Track Lighting

Track lighting can provide general, task, and accent lighting through a number of different fixture components all in one flexible lighting system that does not have to be built in. In fact, track systems duplicate the lighting effects of recessed lighting and vice versa.

Track lighting systems usually include track, an electrical feed box, and two or more fixtures that can be slid along the track to whatever position is needed. If you don't want to wire the track directly to an electrical box, check out accessories enabling you to plug the track into an outlet. Most manufacturers offer an extensive variety of fixtures to coordinate with their tracks.

Track lighting's wiring is in the metal track channels. It can be single-circuit, or it can be multiple-circuit to allow two or more sets of lights to be independently controlled. From the manufacturer's specifications, determine the amount of wattage that safely can be installed on that track section's wiring. Add to that any transformers, as well as the combined draw from the individual lamps. A general rule is to keep this within 80 percent of the total allowable wattage.

Tracks come in various standard straight lengths, generally 2, 4, 8, and 12 feet. But you can buy connectors to combine tracks. Connector choices allow you to make track shapes in "T", "L" "X" configurations, or even curves. You can also use flexible connectors. Many also can be cut to size. Some track systems include track units for a single fixture to also allow you to coordinate the lighting look throughout a space.

The tracks usually are mounted on the ceiling, but also can be mounted horizontally and vertically on walls and used on floors as uplights. Special fixture attachments adapt tracks for use on sloped ceilings so the fixtures hang straight down. Tracks can be recessed, surface mounted, or suspended.

Track heads come in a variety of shapes and sizes. They can create all types of lighting effects and take all sort of bulbs. The best thing about track systems is that you can adjust the location of heads, or add or take away heads as your needs change. For example, if you add another chair in a room, you may find you can light it by adding another track head on a nearby track. Suppose you buy a spectacular-looking table lamp and no longer need one of the four track heads on a track. Just remove that unnecessary head.

There are track heads to suit almost all needs. Extensions enable you to extend the lamp down from the track.

Track lighting. Tracks work best when providing indirect lighting, such as bouncing it off the walls.

Floodlights on track can hold efficient fluorescent tubes and reflectors and be adjusted for almost all angles.

Combining track fixtures from different manufacturers may violate the terms of the Underwriters Laboratories listing, manufacturers' specifications and warranty, and local electrical codes. Besides, tracks and track heads from different manufacturers usually just won't fit together. When starting out, select a system that provides a variety of compatible fixtures that can be ordered.

Styles

By nature, most track systems have a modern look. Some are stylish, others are whimsical, and some are designed to be as unobtrusive as possible. The unobtrusive fixtures are usually best in traditional settings, where track is needed to supplement light but other fixtures set the decorative tone. The incredible flexibility of the fixtures offered allows you to customize the track system specifically to your space.

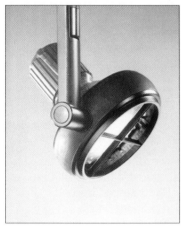

Track heads that not only swivel but are adjustable in a wide arc provide versatility.

Before incorporating a number of different fixtures, make a comprehensive layout of how the system will look when it gets put together. See "Beginning a Decorative Lighting Plan," page 85. Determine your lighting needs first, then select the system and styles that suit your decor. Use them as a decorative feature or disguise them by nesting them adjacent to beams or coloring them to blend into the ceiling or walls. Most track systems are unsuitable where they will come into contact with water or high humidity such as in bathrooms or laundry rooms. Be sure to check on this if you need units suitable for wet locations.

Bulbs

Standard line-voltage track systems use incandescent, tungsten-halogen and compact fluorescent bulbs. The tungsten-halogen's strong, brilliant light is especially effective for accent lighting or to carry from a high ceiling to light areas at more than conventional distances. Compact fluorescent bulbs are the most energy-efficient choice for track heads.

Individual fixtures such as this one are available to match track fixtures, such as shown below.

A truss system makes track a design feature rather than blending the lighting into the ceiling. Heads are adjusted along the truss length.

This cable track system makes the most of low-voltage halogen bulbs by using metal men cutouts to hide thin conductors carrying current from the cable to the exposed bulb.

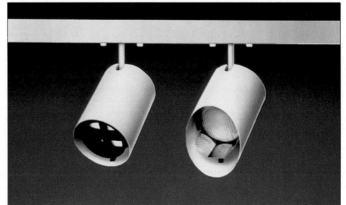

Black cross-baffles reduce spill light and control glare (left), while an internal specular reflector and a spread lens (right) allow for precise light aim without glare.

They can cast either dispersed light or, if the reflector type is used, they can direct light downwards. Low-voltage halogen lamp track systems require transformers either for the entire line or located in the fixtures. Low-voltage track systems require special dimmers.

Most fixtures adapt to more than one lamp type and that adds to a track system's versatility. In your track heads, you can experiment with whatever line-voltage bulbs that will fit, provided their wattage does not exceed manufacturer's recommendations.

Decorative Effects

Track lights excel in providing accent or task lighting. They also provide ambient, diffused lighting when the light is bounced off another surface or spills over from where it is focused. Fixtures outfitted with flood bulbs can provide general lighting, but take special care that you do not produce glare. Most lighting designers recommend bouncing track light indirectly, even for ambient lighting.

For any track lighting, take full advantage of the many accessories, such as filters (including ultraviolet ray filters), baffles, honeycombs, louvers, and shutters that can customize lighting precisely. Other options include clip-on fixtures and pendant fixtures. The choices are ample!

Then, concentrate on the specific effects that are the true advantages of track systems — accent lighting, wall washing, and wall grazing.

Accent Lighting

Tracks often are mounted on the ceiling to accent an object on the wall. The purpose is to confine the light to the object being accented, so that it is well lit without glare.

Generally, fixtures should be aimed at a 30-degree angle from the vertical at normal ceiling height to prevent light from shining in anyone's eyes and to avoid disturbing surface glare. Usually, one fixture is required for each object being accented.

To obtain that 30 degrees, refer to the illustration. Measure the distance from the center of the object up to the ceiling ("A" to "B" on the diagram). Using the "Track Accent

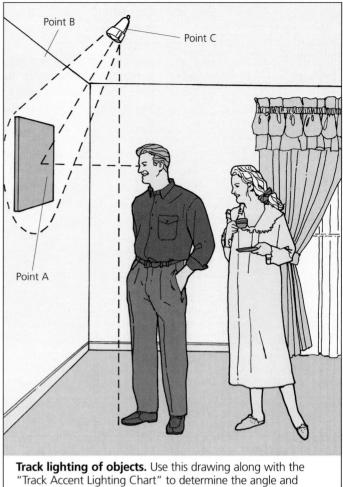

Track lighting of objects. Use this drawing along with the "Track Accent Lighting Chart" to determine the angle and positioning of track lights.

Lighting Chart," mount the track on the ceiling at the ideal location ("C" to "B" on the diagram). This will place it properly at a 30-degree angle. For example, if the distance to the center of a painting is 4 feet, mount the track on the ceiling 27 inches out from the wall.

■ Note that you will want to fine-tune the adjustments depending upon the nature of the object, and how far the fixture suspends from the ceiling.

Wall Grazing

Wall grazing treats the wall itself and its texture as artwork to be featured. In this instance, the idea is to create dramatic shadows to enhance the depth and bas relief on textured surfaces that are interesting, such as stucco, stone, brick, or draperies. Depending upon the texture, fixtures are mounted from 6 to 18 inches away from the wall and about the same distance apart along the track, aimed downward to create shadows and sharp contrast on the textured wall.

Wall Washing

Wall washing lights up the entire wall and can bring out the beauty of wallcoverings, scenic murals or painted effects, grouped artwork, or books. It is another way of producing indirect ambient light.

Track Accent Lighting Chart

If the object is located: A to B distance in feet	Then locate the fixture: B to C distance in inches
2	13
3	20
4	27
5	34
6	41

Track wall grazing. You can dramatically pick up textures by placing lighting close to the wall.

Track wall washing. Even lighting that washes across the entire wall provides soft, ambient light.

For walls up to 9 feet high, mount track fixtures 2 to 3 feet from the wall. For ceilings 9 to 11 feet high, mount track fixtures 3 to 4 feet away from the wall on the ceilings. Space fixtures the same distance apart as the track is from the wall.

General Hints

Many fixtures and lamps have specification sheets detailing the amount of light spread and footcandle levels of light produced at various distances from the fixtures. It is a combination of these and the fixtures that determine the light pattern produced. To position the light exactly, it is critical to make the last-minute adjustments that position the track fixture (sometimes called a track head) exactly where you want it and the baffles or other accessories exactly as they should be.

Before installing a system, check that the lighting will not produce glare when viewed from other rooms, doorways, or through windows. Consider, too, that some kinds of reflective wall surfaces such as marble, high-gloss paneling, paint, or reflective wallcovering can cause hot spots of reflection even with wall grazing or washing. Usually, there is a light fixture that will eliminate the problem with proper location and adjustment.

Also, start with the lowest number of track heads you think you need. If you are not sure whether three or four heads will be adequate, buy three first. You may discover that is enough. You can always purchase more heads later, if you need to.

Recessed Lighting

Many of the effects of track lighting can be achieved with recessed lighting, but with the advantage that the fixtures are discreetly tucked away and psychologically out of sight. Because it can be unobtrusive, recessed lighting often is used in traditional decor to provide additional lighting. It is equally at home in contemporary decor, where broad sweeps of space often need the dramatic lighting effects that recessed systems readily provide. Advances in recessed lighting design enable you to cast light virtually anywhere you wish.

Some recessed systems must be planned and installed before the ceiling is closed, and obviously, it is best to do this if possible. But if that is not possible, check for the systems that can be installed from below in existing ceilings.

Check to be sure that the housing you are considering is compatible with the clearances you have for both depth and proximity to insulation. Low-profile downlights and rectangular fluorescent fixtures called troffers are available that can be used in spaces as shallow as under 4 inches. Manufacturers' data lists applicable depths for specific recessed lighting systems.

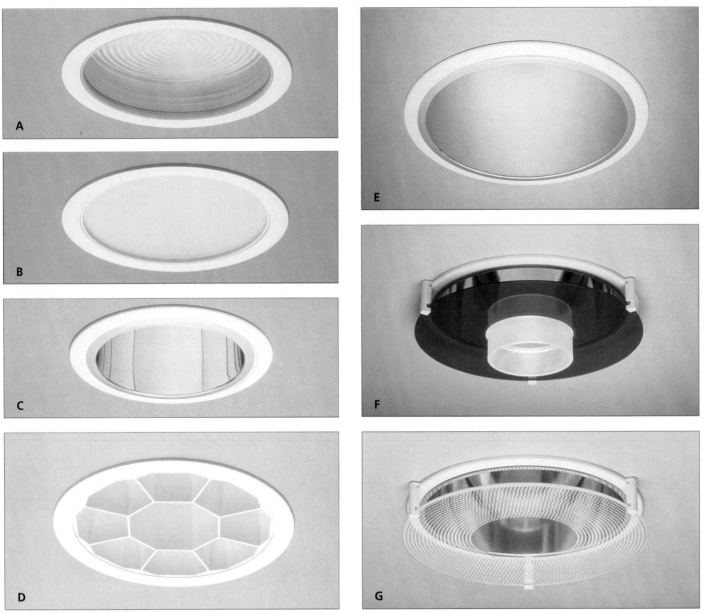

Recessed fixtures come in a wide variety of designs: (A) A recessed fixture with Fresnel lens diffuses the light and prevents glare. (B) A fixture with a prismatic lens specified as a shower light can be used in areas with water. (C) A reflecting interior magnifies the light. (D) A polygonal louver cuts glare from all directions. (E) A fixture with a matte finish inside reduces glare and is often used with recessed bulbs. (F) A recessed fixture can be a decorative addition with a variety of different trims such as this blue surround. (G) A dropped lens with concentric circles provides light and design interest.

Be sure to find out whether you can lay insulation directly around and above the housing. Units specifically for contact with insulation are labeled "IC" for insulated ceilings, and some preserve the integrity of the thermal barrier better than others, as you can judge by reading the manufacturers' literature. A considerable amount of heat can be transferred through recessed lighting fixtures that are not insulated. Units that are not designed for use with insulation usually have instructions for the minimum allowable air space clearance around the fixture. The National Electrical Code requires at least 3 inches. Heat from the fixture can be a fire hazard if these instructions are ignored.

Do not overlook the possibilities of a system already in place. Often, refocussing or repositioning an eyeball, changing the outside part or trim completely, or simply changing a bulb

can create a world of difference. Investigate energy-saving halogen, low-voltage, or compact fluorescent bulbs as well.

Top-grade recessed lighting systems are the most flexible, allowing you to change trims, louvers, diffusers, and other fixture types as your needs change. To add to that flexibility, install systems on separate circuits and use dimmers where feasible. Low-voltage systems also are available. Small openings make systems disappear even more than the larger apertures and are ideal for spotlighting.

Figure out where you need your light, then use the fewest fixtures to provide it. Arrange a pattern that is pleasing, keeping visual clutter to a minimum. For example, line up fixtures in a square, a line, or circular pattern rather than placing them at random.

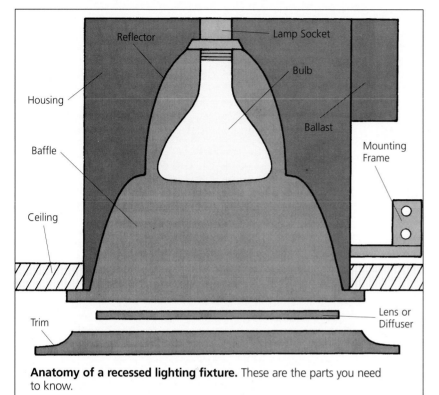

Anatomy of a recessed lighting fixture. These are the parts you need to know.

Anatomy of Recessed Lighting

In The Ceiling

■ Housing—The portion of the recessed light above the ceiling line, which can be the reflector itself on some models. Energy code air infiltration requirements may restrict use of units that allow air infiltration.

■ Mounting frame—A metal support that attaches the housing to the ceiling structure, often designed to attach to rafters. Special frames are designed for plaster and dropped ceilings as well as sloped ceilings. With retrofits into existing ceilings these can be clips.

■ Ballast—The starter for fluorescent lights, which may be located outside or inside the housing (the latter for retrofitting). Some bulbs have built-in ballasts.

■ Lamp socket or lamp holder—The electrical fitting into which the bulb/lamp goes. Replacement lamps that are not the same size or type of base as the original call for socket adaptors in retrofitting.

■ Aperture—The opening through which light is directed, which may be anywhere from 2 inches in diameter on up, and in various shapes including round, square, and rectangular.

Trim

■ Reflector—Typically made of aluminum, silver, gold, bronze, or white finish. It directs light out of the housing, or the housing itself may be reflectively surfaced. Housings without reflectors are designed to incorporate reflector lamps.

■ Baffle—A series of light-absorbing ridges ringing the lower portion of the fixture interior, shielding the bulb's brightness when viewed at an angle.

■ Lenses or diffusers—Glass or plastic coverings that are designed to optically create specific light distribution patterns, often with more than one style for a given fixture.

■ Louvers—Used instead of a lens or diffuser, louvers are made of thin metal or plastic strips in vertically oriented parallel strips, grids, honeycombs, or parabolic shapes to shield the glare from the viewer.

■ Flange trim—This can be a self-trim attached to or contiguous with the reflector. Otherwise, a plastic or metal trim ring that covers and seals the edges of the aperture cut in the ceiling for round fixtures.

■ Specialties—Special trims and adjustable fixtures for use in wall washing and accent lighting are available. Most obvious of these are the "eyeballs" with a partially recessed sphere that can be rotated and tilted to direct light. Partially shielded apertures also direct light.

General Lighting Techniques

General downlighting rarely is accomplished with "A" bulbs, since replacing these with "R" and PAR reflector bulbs, halogens, or compact fluorescent bulbs will be more energy-efficient. To provide a general idea of the amount of light needed, refer to the manufacturer's literature of the lines and bulbs you are investigating. Sometimes, though, the best thing to do is to experiment with different bulbs. A lighting showroom might let you try out different bulbs for a day or experiment with different bulbs in displays.

Lighting coverage in footcandles per fixture is based upon providing 15 to 25 footcandles of light for general lighting. Darker rooms will require more footcandles. Also, manufacturers identify the spread of the light beam as the angle where 50 percent of the light is maintained, as well as the spill light range beyond that 50 percent. The chart "Coverage in Square Feet Per Fixture" provides ranges for estimating the spacing ratio for popular recessed lighting.

Coverage in Square Feet Per Fixture

Fixture Trim	"A" Bulb			"R" Bulb		
	75W	100W	150W	50W	75W	150W
Cone	25	40	50	15	30	65
Baffle	20	30	50	10	25	60
Lens	25	35	55	–	–	–
Diffuser	20	30	45	–	–	–

As a general rule, use one floodlight for every 25 square feet (5 feet by 5 feet) of floor area for general lighting. Investigate energy-efficient substitutes for "A" bulbs that provide comparable light.

Wall Washing

Wall washing uses the entire wall as a giant reflector. For best effect, overlap the light spread for a continuous sweep of light, instead of creating scalloped, separated circles. Even light extending into the corners will keep corners from appearing drab and forbidding. The amount of light you use depends upon the absorption of the wall itself—its darkness and texture—and how much reflected light you want to cast into the rest of the room.

Generally, wall washing light levels and recessed fixture placements can be determined by using the figures from the "Light Level Chart" below.

Determine the light level you require. Divide the length of the wall by the spacing needed, centering the lighting. Place the fixtures the same distance from the wall as from each other. For instance, to create medium light level with wall washers with 100 watt "A" bulbs or equivalent on a 10 foot wall, four fixtures are needed.

Wall washing specialty fixtures and bulbs will provide even more exact estimates for placements in the manufacturer's literature.

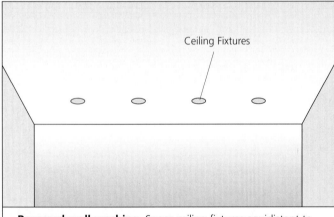

Recessed wall washing. Space ceiling fixtures equidistant to the wall and each other.

Light Level Chart

Lamp and Wattage	Spacing(s) for Medium Level (15-20 footcandles) (in Feet)	Spacing(s) for High Level (30-45 footcandles) (in Feet)
100 Watt "A"	2	–
150 Watt "A"	4	2
150 Watt "R"	3	2

(Use "A" bulbs or more energy-efficient alternatives.)

Accent Lighting

Use accent lighting to highlight architectural features or artwork. To determine your needs, first refer to the "Recessed Accent Lighting Chart" on page 53. Start by estimating the length of the beam and the width of the beam you need for the specific artwork. Keep in mind that a number of specialty fixtures, lenses, and baffles can be used to tailor the light pattern specifically to the artwork to be highlighted, so that this approximate chart can be further refined as needed.

Accent lighting can be tilted from an adjustable range of as much as 45 degrees from vertical and a rotation range of approximately 350 degrees. Selecting accent fixtures that can accommodate a variety of lamp types and trims will let you adjust as needed when artwork and furniture are moved around. Some models also are designed so that bulbs are easily replaced without having to reposition and refocus the fixture itself. Some fixtures even extend down from the ceiling for a more concentrated focus where needed, much like track lighting.

For all recessed lighting, in using the charts always consider upgrading to a more efficient bulb than the one listed. In most cases, lamp packaging offers replacement comparisons for older models so that you can easily see what to purchase, or it is covered in literature for easy comparison. For instance, a screw-in compact fluorescent reflector bulb may be an easy replacement for an incandescent model, and halogen "R" lamps also are efficient replacements for regular "A" lamps. Many low-voltage halogen bulbs offer extremely tight beam control and so are most effective for accent lighting.

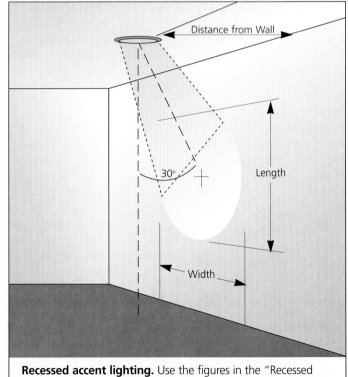

Recessed accent lighting. Use the figures in the "Recessed Accent Lighting Chart" on page 53 to determine placement of the fixture.

Recesssed Accent Lighting Chart

Beam Length	Beam Width	Distance From Wall	Lamp Selection (or equivalent)
5 feet	2.5 feet	2 feet from wall (8 foot ceiling)	50W PAR-36 WFL (12V)
8 feet	3 feet		50W MR-16 FL (12V)
4.5 feet	2 feet		75W R-30 SP
Wall bottom	7 feet	↓	75W R-30 FL
5.5 feet	2 feet	3 feet from wall (10 foot ceiling)	75W PAR-38 FL
2 feet	1 foot		25W PAR-36 NSP (12V)
2 feet	1.5 feet		50W MR-16 NSP (12V)
5.5 feet	3 feet	↓	50W MR-16 NFL (12V)
3 feet	1.5 feet		75W PAR-38 SP

- Lamps aimed 30 degrees from vertical
- Length and width indicate where candlepower drops 50 percent of maximum
- Substitute energy-efficient equivalent bulbs where possible

A diffused ceiling fixture, either singly or in units, provides even overhead diffused lighting.

Recessed Troffers and Luminous Ceilings

Recessed troffers are square or rectangular fluorescent fixtures installed above the ceiling with an opening flush with the ceiling. They are generally 2 feet x 4 feet, 2 feet x 2 feet, or 1 foot x 4 feet to fit between ceiling joists. Some troffers have parabolic louvers that produce a very narrow spread of light. Other troffers have diffusers that create a soft spread of light.

Luminous ceiling fixtures can be recessed or attached to the ceilings, sometimes with the effect of an entire ceiling of glowing light. Reflectors and fluorescent lamps provide energy-efficient choices for this lighting.

Depending upon the strength of the light and placement, both can provide general lighting and good even lighting over specific work/task areas, most often in kitchens and bathrooms. That's why you see this type of light so often in office buildings and other commercial applications. So do not overlook the many advantages of these fixtures for home workshops and home office areas as well.

Recessed luminous ceiling panels. These are an excellent ambient light source for the kitchen or other task-intensive areas.

Architectural Effects

Lighted coves, soffits (sometimes referred to as cornices), and valances make the most of architectural elements by casting them in a new light. Architectural luminaires are specifically designed to create the reflected light. Coves distribute light upwards. Soffits distribute light downwards. Valances distribute light both up and down. A shield hides the light itself from view and can be constructed of metal, wood, plywood, gypsum board, or built-up molding. Baffles, louvers, or diffusers incorporated as needed direct light and reduce glare, especially if the units might be viewed along their length.

A recessed troffer with baffles built into a soffit lights up a large painting while not spilling light into the room.

Cove lighting in a raised ceiling section delineates a dining area effectively while providing attractive lighting.

Do not limit your thinking when it comes to architectural lighting. Units can be effectively used to vertically light the sides of a recessed sculpture niche, along the top of cabinets (with the addition of a trim board), along the base of cabinets, horizontally at the top of a curtain wall to highlight the curtain's fabric, above eye level to highlight an upper wall with special character, or spilling down the surface of textured wood paneling.

Lighted valances can highlight both a vaulted ceiling and a curtain sweep. Often, valances are integrated into window treatments or related to molding heights in a room.

Bulbs

To maintain a complete sweep of light, architectural fixtures stagger fluorescent lamps rather than place them end to end. In this way, there are no dark spots where the ballast ends of the lamps meet; the dark ends are overlapped with light. Methods include staggering the tubes and setting them on the diagonal with the base of one overlapped by the tip of another, side by side. The new T8 fluorescent bulbs are energy-efficient choices for this application, as are other fluorescent bulbs (including compacts), while strip lights are also efficient choices.

Check the effect of whatever lamp you intend to use on the colors it will illuminate. Color quality is especially important when you plan to highlight wood tones or fabrics. Effects can be highly dramatic with architectural lighting. At the same time, it can provide ambient light in an exciting and highly individual way. Even linear fluorescent architectural lighting can be controlled with special dimmers, to further personalize the effects. Here are some questions to ask in determining your architectural lighting needs:

- Is the reflected wall or ceiling smooth enough to be attractive?
- Can I alter the look of the lighting by tinting the surface upon which it reflects?
- Can I increase efficiency by painting the interior of the valance, cove, or soffit white?
- Is there enough distance to the ceiling so that I can cast light across the ceiling without having all light pooling along the wall/ceiling seam? An 8-foot ceiling height is the very minimum required. The top of the cove should be at least 18 inches from the ceiling, with the base of the cove at least 80 inches above the floor.
- How many dimmers are needed for the units?
- How does the reflected light augment the rest of the room's light?
- Will a small soffit, sometimes called "wall slots," solve a lighting problem by providing perfect lighting over countertops?

➤ *Cove lighting above kitchen cabinets wrapping the room makes the room seem spacious, a visual expansion trick.*

5
Lighting Schemes Room by Room

What's your favorite room in the house? The kitchen that always seems congenial? The snug bedroom? The hobby corner that is perfectly outfitted for your favorite pastime?

Impressive front entrances call for lighting that makes the most of them, such as this chandelier scaled for two stories.

Which rooms remain vacant, although you thought everyone would want to use them? While good design elements such as practical use of space and comfortable seating play roles in a room's appeal, the lighting and how it suits the design, colors, and activities often are the deciding factors.

This chapter takes an enlightened tour of a home, room by room. Generally, the ambience and practical needs of room types are similar. Lighting approaches that work in one home probably will work with the same room in another home. Conversely, the unique needs of your special home might best be served by taking tips from all the rooms discussed and applying them where it seems best for you. For instance, if you've turned one living room corner into a book-lover's library space, check out the home office section for lighting ideas.

The rooms covered, in order, include the entrance foyer/front hall, hallways, stairways, living and family rooms, dining rooms and dining areas, bedrooms, kitchens, bathrooms, children's rooms, home offices, and workshop/utility/laundry areas.

While principles for each of these areas/rooms are discussed here, before you begin, consider the versatility of the lighting you want to install. Rooms today often are multi-functional; dining rooms double as libraries or sewing centers. Living rooms also are home entertainment centers. Family rooms may start as playrooms and graduate to a young person's semi-private apartment.

Most designers strongly recommend rethinking space allocation each time you undertake an improvement. While you are at it, rethink the lighting needs not only for today, but for the eventual roles the room may play. The den off the kitchen may need to be converted into a bedroom for an elderly relative. When kids are grown, you may want to convert to single-floor living and create a downstairs bedroom for yourself.

Often, you can design wiring to accommodate future variations and save yourself aggravation and money down the road. Lighting demands may change from activity to activity, from day to night, and from season to season. For instance, a medium ambient light level may be most appropriate in a living room, but to enjoy a fireplace fully, the lighting level needs to be lowered. Exterior lighting during summer evenings also might affect the overall lighting scheme. The same room may need additional lighting in the winter when days are shorter and curtains are more often drawn. Your home has its own unique lighting demands.

Just as runway lights guide a pilot safely home, your lighting from room to room should create pleasing anticipation and safe passage from one space to another. Consider how a room looks when first you enter it and the view (from a lighting perspective) into adjacent areas from the room.

Foyers and Front Halls

Grand entrances begin with great lighting. Lighting defines the entrance space, large or small. Lighting also leads the eye to the spaces beyond. It should fit the tone of the home and the style of furnishings, whatever they may be—dramatic, warm and inviting, imposing, or relaxed and casual. Beyond that, it also should be practical.

Don't scrimp on fixtures here. The quality and beauty of these first fixtures and light usage makes an impression that reflects on your entire home.

Front halls. Combine coordinated light fixtures for the best effect.

Vaulted and Large Entrance Foyers

Two- and even three-story entrance halls call for dramatic hanging fixtures. Halls 75 to 150 square feet can accommodate a single fixture that encloses a bulb or bulbs. The fixture should be a minimum of 12 inches in diameter or it could be a chandelier a minimum of 18 inches in diameter. Hang the chandelier so that it is attractive at ground-floor level, but does not impede doorway functioning.

Match or complement this fixture with wall sconces on the main floor and upper stories. A coordinated ceiling fixture for upper floors can carry the scheme through.

Most large spaces, especially with vaulted ceilings, call for uplighting (as from wall sconces or spotlights) to delineate the ceiling. Decorative wall sconces and brackets with uplighting visually anchor the first floor ceiling line. They should be placed to disperse murky corners that the center fixture's light cannot reach without overlighting and creating glare.

Recessed, track, or accent light fixtures can provide ambient light and add visual punctuation. Most foyers have a decided decorative focal point, such as architectural details, a painting, antique hall tree, center table in traditional design, or plants and trees. Plan wall washing and accent lighting to accommodate these attributes.

Hall mirrors allow for final adjustments of coats, makeup, and the like and should have lighting that illuminates the person at the mirror.

Entryways on a Smaller Scale

Scale a center light to a small space (20 to 75 square feet) by selecting a fixture that is no smaller than 8 inches in diameter and that has an interesting look. Complement the central light with wall fixtures or recessed lighting.

Small entryways. Use a surface-mounted wall ceiling fixture along with wall sconces to take up the least visual space.

For small foyers or entrances, use ceiling fixtures or chandeliers that add style while taking up little floor space.

Mirrors often are used in small spaces to visually expand the space as well as for last-minute clothing adjustments. Be sure that lighting does not glare from the mirror itself. If another object is the focal point of the entry, bathe it in accent lighting.

Special pointers in lighting large or small entrances/ foyers include:

■ Check that no lighting glares into another room or directly out the front door, blinding visitors.

■ Provide foyer lighting even in daytime if exterior light is in extreme contrast to the foyer's natural light level. This will help eyes adjust to the difference.

■ Illuminate any steps down or other changes in level leading from the foyer. A recessed ceiling spot that casts a shadow to delineate the stair riser is a simple solution.

■ Install switches so they are accessible from the front doorway, such as on the opening, not the hinge side of the door. See that they are controlled by a switch near the interior doorway(s) that lead into the foyer.

■ Use separate dimmers for different kinds of lighting to individually control the center fixture, recessed lighting, or accent lighting.

■ Anticipate the need for indoor switches for outdoor lighting (both entrance lights and pathway lights), and plan your wiring accordingly.

Interior Hallways

Hallways may branch off the foyer, extend from a ranch house living room, or provide access to second-story bedrooms. No matter where they are located, hallways rely heavily on lighting for both safety and style. Even the smallest hallway can be made attractively stylish through the choice of handsome lighting fixtures. If the fixture is used alone, it in effect becomes the "furniture" of the hallway and it sets the style. Alternately, you can use lighting to illuminate other design elements such as paintings that decorate a hallway.

Repeat a fixture at least every 10 feet to provide relatively even lighting. Combine ambient lighting from indirect lighting sources for a timeless quality and glow. For interior hallways that receive no natural light, consider using energy-saving fluorescent lighting if the lights will be on for long stretches.

Balance the lighting in a hallway to relate to the levels in the main rooms that lead into it. You may want dimmers to vary the adjustment from night to day.

Safety. Install switches where light can be controlled from either end of the hallway. Consider using a motion sensor that automatically turns lights on when a person enters this space. Install a simple night light or dimmer to provide the minimum energy-conserving light level needed without assaulting sleepy eyes.

Good lighting is essential for a windowless interior hallway. Here pendants and torchieres make the lighting so interesting you don't miss the daylight.

Closets

At the very least, a hall closet should be illuminated by light directed from a nearby hallway fixture. Better still is to put a fixture in the closet. The National Electrical Code is very specific about requirements for lights in clothes closets. See "Requirements for Fixtures in Clothes Closets" below. A simple, inexpensive solution for lighting infrequently used closets is to install a battery-operated fixture.

Requirements for Fixtures in Clothes Closets

The National Electrical Code allows you to use either incandescent or fluorescent fixtures in a closet. Both types can be either surface-mounted or recessed. The code does not allow pendant fixtures.

If you use an incandescent fixture, the bulb must be completely enclosed; no bare bulbs or baffled fixtures are allowed. This restriction doesn't apply to fluorescents, which don't get nearly as hot as incandescents.

According to the code, surface-mounted fixtures can be mounted on the wall above a door. If the fixture is incandescent, there must be at least 12 inches between the bulb and the closet's storage area. If the fixture is fluorescent, there must be at least 6 inches between the bulb and storage area.

If the fixture is recessed, whether incandescent or fluorescent, it can be installed in the closet ceiling or above the door as long as it is at least 6 inches from the storage space.

As shown in the illustration, the electrical code defines storage space as the area within 24 inches of the closet walls from the floor up to the highest clothes-hanging rod, or 6 feet, whichever is higher. Above the highest rod, or 6 feet, whichever is highest, the storage area is 12 inches from the walls. If the closet has shelves that are wider than 12 inches, then the entire area above the shelves is considered storage area.

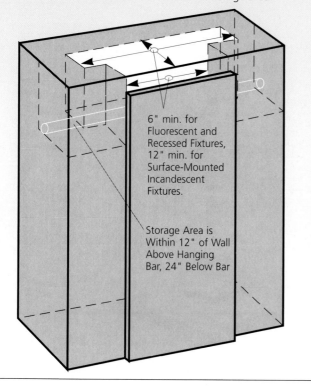

6" min. for Fluorescent and Recessed Fixtures, 12" min. for Surface-Mounted Incandescent Fixtures.

Storage Area is Within 12" of Wall Above Hanging Bar, 24" Below Bar

Stairways

Fixtures both top and bottom, operated by three-way switches, are the old-time solution to most stairway lighting. Other inventive options described here make the most of the beauty of stairways and provide additional lighting along the way for increased safety.

Light stairways both bottom and top. Manufacturers often have matching wall and ceiling fixtures to unify the design.

Stairways. Light both ends and any landings in between.

Safety

A stairway should have a fixture near the bottom and one at the top landing. Make sure the lower fixture bulbs are shielded from the view of people descending the staircase. Be sure the upper and lower light sources provide good delineation of the stairs themselves. A strong downlight installed near the top of the stairway illuminates the edges of each stair and reveals the height of steps. To define the depth of the riser, a soft light source at the bottom will illuminate its surface, or you can position lighting just below the step. This can take the form of strip lighting along the risers or individual fixtures at each step. Do not light the riser with the same intensity as the tread so that they blend into one another. In any case, make sure the top and the bottom step (where most accidents occur) are both well lit.

Further step definition also can be achieved through use of side lights, mini-lights across the step, or worked into the molding, soffited lighting along the stairway walls, or carefully recessed lighting that overlaps pools of light ascending the stairway.

Treat a landing as you would a top step, providing extra lighting to define it in contrast to a continuation of stairs. Often, you will want a decorative object on the landing and will need to provide accent lighting for this object in addition to safety lighting.

Use strip lighting along the stairs to clearly define each step.

Psychologically, a conventional stairway registers as a "proceed carefully," while a single or two-step level change can go ignored until someone has stumbled. For this reason, light any level change with as much care as you give an entire staircase.

Open Stairways

Factor in the ambient lighting from adjoining areas in creating safe stairway lighting. You may need to increase downlight to create sufficient contrast on the stairs. If the stairway is beautiful, you can use it as an accent wall by bathing it in light. A more subtle approach is to have a spill of light coming from above, subduing the stairway when not in use but keeping it as a decorative room element.

Living Rooms and Family Rooms

Like the great halls of castles of the past, living and family rooms are centers of activities. Each activity requires its own lighting, and at times may conflict with the activity needs of others. For instance, half the family may want to watch television, which requires a low light level, while the rest may want to read or do needlepoint, which calls for bright task lighting. The trick of the lighting director (you) is to orchestrate these needs into a harmonious whole. The other goal is to provide various kinds of flexible lighting to adjust to the family's various wants at various times.

Start by defining your probable furniture layouts and task lighting demands. Make a simple list of what lighting you need. It will serve as a cross-check when you are developing your lighting plan. A sample list below can get you started.

Lighting Needs List	
Furniture/Activity	**Lighting Needs**
Reading chairs	Intense task lighting
Crossword/card table	Moderate task lighting
TV, video games, computer	Low general lighting free of reflection

That low general lighting for TV may be compromised by the intense task lighting for reading, unless both are selected to work with one another.

Using traditionally-shaped table lamps anchors the design of this room, while recessed lighting highlights the raised ceiling and accents walls.

While changing the lighting often is the easiest answer, sometimes altering the furniture arrangement proves to work best. Consequently, your lighting plans need to be integrated into the overall decorating scheme.

Solutions can include selecting a reading lamp that is totally opaque so it creates no reflection on the TV screen. Place reading chairs off to the sides of the television, out of the line of reflection to others seated in the room.

There are some general guidelines for selecting fixtures or table and floor lamps and placing them in relation to common activities. Select those that fit in your specific family/living room. Light levels are given in conventional incandescent watts, but energy-saving substitutes such as fluorescents can be used in most cases.

Activity/Task Lighting Requirements

Reading. Table lamps, wall or swag lamps, hanging fixtures, floor lamps, and small supplementary bright lamps such as halogens all are good reading sources.

■ Table lamps are portable, decorative, and contribute to general and task lighting. Three-way or dimmable lamps allow for a higher level of light for tasks that call for prolonged use and lower light level for casual use. You will need 150 watts for casual reading and up to 250 watts for prolonged reading or close work.

In general for reading, experts recommend shades that are moderately luminous to provide background lighting with bottom dimensions of 16 to 18 inches, top dimensions of 8 to 17 inches, and depth of 10 to 20 inches. For corner tables, use a shade whose bottom dimension is at least 18 inches. The bottom edge of the shade should be about 40 to 42 inches from the floor. Place these so the base is in line with the reader's shoulder, 20 inches to right or left of the center of the book. On a corner table, be sure to select a lamp rated for bulbs from 80 to 250 watts or 100 to 300 watts, and center the lamp on the table. The shade bottom should be at least 18 inches in diameter. Position very tall table lamps behind the shoulder in floor lamp position.

■ Floor lamps provide a generous light spread and often can be adjusted to suit your chair. The best height is 40 to 49 inches from the floor to the shade bottom. Some are adjustable, to direct light specifically on the reading surface. Wattages required for reading are the same as for table lamps.

Standard shade sizes are 12 to 18 inches at the bottom, 8 to 17 inches across the top, and 6 to 15 inches high, depending upon lamp size.

Place low lamps (40 to 42 inches from floor to shade bottom) in line with the shoulder, 20 inches right or left of the book center. Position taller lamps 15 inches left or right of book center and 12 inches back.

■ Floor lamps with tables in their bases should be restricted to a height of not more than 42 inches from floor to

Reading table lamps. The bottom of the lamp shade should be just below eye level. This means that lower tables will require taller lamp bases than will higher tables.

Reading floor lamps. Place taller lamps to the side and 12 in. back from the book or project.

shade bottom, because this lamp must be used beside the seat. The best position is when the shade bottom lines up with the seated eye height.

■ Wall or swag lamps and hanging fixtures free up table surface space and are good for end tables of uneven height, since you can hang the lamps at the same level no matter how tall the table. Bulb wattage and types are the same as table lamps.

Shades may need top shielding and a diffuser across the bottom if glare is a problem. Usual shade dimensions are bottom 14 to 18 inches; top 6 to 12 inches, and depth 6 to 10 inches. Center lamps in line with the shoulder 20 inches to one side of the book center, with the lower edge at eye level. If the fixture is substantially behind the shoulder, center it 15 inches to the side, with the lower edge 47 to 49 inches above the floor (which is high enough to warrant selecting a lamp with a diffuser to prevent glare to others seated nearby).

■ Pharmacy or arc lamps produce intimate pools of directional light. Shades are either opaque, metal, or translucent glass and when the shade is cylindrical, the lamps are called "banana lamps." Since bulbs are usually in the 40- to 60-watt range, these lamps are suitable for casual reading but not for prolonged reading or close eye work.

Position the lamp so that the light pool falls on the book surface without glare to the reader or others in the room, no more than 15 inches above and 12 inches to the side of the task.

■ Bright supplementary lamps are ideal for extra-fine detail work because they employ an extra punch of high, intense white light. Add these to the functional lighting used above for intensely visual tasks such as doing needlepoint, fly-tieing, or quilt stitching. Older models were called "high-intensity" and are still available. However, modern halogen models provide even more light with less energy use, and are good choices for supplementary lighting.

Music Making

Whether it's classic piano playing or folk guitar, musicians need proper lighting to read music and see their instruments.

Ceiling Fixtures. Sheet music on a piano or music stand can be given evenly distributed light top to bottom with a ceiling-mounted unit. A recessed, semi-recessed, surface- or track-

Downlighting in this room keeps glare away from the frequently used video center.

Supplementary lamps. Powerful small lamps are useful additions to regular lighting for demanding tasks.

Recessed lighting for performing. Adjust fixtures for good lighting evenly distributed on performers and sheet music.

Lighting for keyboards. Provide extra lighting for complicated scores or musicians who spend considerable time reading scores of any kind.

mounted adjustable spot fixture each perform well, as long as they do not create glare for others.

Place a single unit in line with a point 24 inches behind the center of the music rack so the fixture will be behind the user's head. Aim at the music rack center. For advanced players reading complicated scores or those playing for prolonged periods, provide stronger light by using two fixtures, 24 inches behind the rack position and 30 inches apart, centered on the rack.

Floor Lamps. An adjustable articulated arm is best, especially if the floor lamp is used by more than one family performer. Select a light-colored, semi-translucent shade with an open top. The bottom dimensions of 16 to 18 inches, top 10 to 15 inches, and depth 8 to 12 inches will provide ambient as well as task light. Use bulbs ranging from 150 to 250 watts.

Place the center of the shade 13 inches in front of the bottom of the music rack, 22 inches to the left or right of the center. The bottom of the shade for an adult standing musician usually is best about 47 inches from the floor, but adjust to a lower height for younger, smaller musicians.

Specialty Lamps. "Piano lamps" are so named because they were designed to rest on the piano and extend an articulated arm to illuminate both the music rack and piano keys. These often are Victorian styled, and add great charm to piano/music areas in Victorian or other traditional homes.

Downlighting washes the bookshelves in this contemporary living room, while a properly located reading lamp is perfect for the chaise longue.

Games People Play

Billiards in the living room may not be your style, but in a family room/great room, billiards or other table games are becoming increasingly popular. It's always nice to have a bridge-sized table for family tournaments with Scrabble, Monopoly, or other favorites. No matter what the table, it calls for even and adequate lighting.

Game or Card Tables. If the table is in a permanent location, permanent lighting options include hanging fixtures such as pendant lamps like those used in dining rooms. Also useful is a flush or recessed, centered ceiling fixture that diffuses light over a wide area, providing the equivalent of 60- to 80-watt fluorescent bulbs. Use four, 75-watt flood recessed or surface mounted fixtures, each placed diagonally about 24 inches beyond each table corner as an alternative.

Billiards Tables. Traditional shaded pendants equipped with either incandescent bulbs or compact fluorescent tubes are one solution. Or you might prefer a single, long traditional pool table light. The important thing is to place the lighting 36 inches above the playing surface so it is high enough to be out of the way, but low enough not to shine in the players' eyes.

Ping-Pong Tables. Louvered or lens-shielded two-tube fixtures centered over each side of the table will provide strong, even light. Be sure the bulb is protected from breakage. Recess lights if the ceiling is 90 inches high or less.

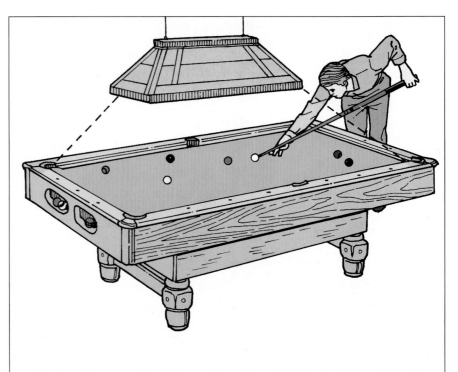

Billiards tables. A pendant is the traditional fixture for billiards tables, which call for lighting directly overhead.

- A collection of indoor house plants or trees.
- Paintings arranged in an attractive grouping.
- A single, magnificent painting.
- Sculpture, either freestanding, or in niches.
- Wall built-ins with artfully arranged decorative objects.
- An entertainment unit containing decorative aspects as well as the television/electronic equipment.

Focal Points and Accent Lighting

Once necessary task lighting is determined, turn your attention to the room's attributes and how lighting can make the most of them. Various methods such as spotlighting and grazing are at your command.

Focal Points. The most effective decorating features one main attraction in a room and then other less impressive elements. Called a focal point, the main attraction provides the overall character of the room and seems to unify the furnishings around it. Even an architecturally undistinguished room can be given a focal point. By definition, the focal point should be impressive enough to grab your attention immediately. Creative lighting is the final touch to bring a natural focal point, such as a fireplace, to life. It is absolutely essential in creating a focal point in a relatively unexciting room.

Nonarchitectural focal points to highlight include:

- Shelving with artful displays.
- An impressive piece of furniture such as an antique armoire with fine surface detailing.

Judiciously placed lighting brings out paneling details and the painting above a fireplace.

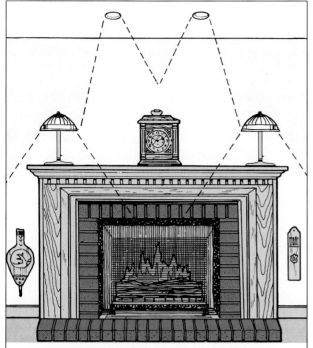

Focal point lighting. This lighting emphasizes the most impressive aspect of a room.

Strip lights above a bar center and neon artwork show off the glassware, while a traditional table lamp makes the design a mix of old and new.

Multipurpose living rooms such as this combine cabinet lighting for accent, task lighting, and wall washing lighting for soft drama.

Other Special Elements. Many of the furnishings just mentioned can function as secondary players if not the focal point themselves. By lighting them well, you provide a sense of visual excitement as eyes travel around a room.

Other elements to consider include interesting molding, a magnificent view (here, the trick may be to avoid glare on the windows at night rather than light them up), a raised or otherwise interesting ceiling, overhanging balcony, skylight (which can be given outline lighting), or even the view into another room, such as a foyer showcasing an attractive chandelier.

Use discreet lighting when a fantastic view is really part of the scheme, as here. Note the adjustable contemporary table lamp, picture light, and hidden lighting above the media center.

General Ambient Lighting

After determining task and accent lighting, turn attention to ambient lighting. The amount you need will depend upon how much ambient light is provided by the other lighting and where it is placed. The light level you want to achieve is no less than one-third of the intensity of the task lights, and about one-fifth of the intensity of accent lights.

By using dimmers to control lighting, you can vary the intensity of ambient light and the drama within the room. For more on layering lighting, see "Total-Room Control Systems," page 137. This is one of the newest trends in sophisticated lighting installations.

Dining Rooms

Romantic dinners start with soft lighting that simulates candlelight. A 10-year-old's birthday party might take place in the same room. And a family reunion can find this same room the center of activity. Add to this the possibilities that the dining room table may be used for hobbies, sewing, sketching, and the like, and planning of lighting takes on great importance.

Assuming that you will want to have a conventional layout with a dining table and sideboard or serving counter of some sort, here are the successful lighting combinations that have worked through the years. First, you will want a

Use an old-fashioned lighting fixture to keep in tone with a room that's decorated in country style.

Augment a chandelier in a dining room with additional lighting, such as the picture lamp and the side lighting reflected in the mirror shown here.

Mirrored cabinet lights show off a priceless china collection and provide ambient lighting to augment a chandelier.

A lowered ceiling section can hold special lighting as well as defining a dining area. The unique antler chandelier is dramatically lit with spotlights, as are the scupture and plant.

Custom side-lit torchieres and a flexible light strip used in a recessed cove provide timeless lighting for this dining room.

pendant or chandelier over the table or even a fan with a light kit. Second, you will want directed accent lighting or task lighting on the serving counter. Third, you will want enough ambient light so that the entire room is cheerful and easy to see. You will want to be able to adjust the lighting with independent dimmers so that you can create the most appropriate light level and emphasis.

Finally, if you will be using the room for other activities, such as making it a mini-library or even a guest room, incorporate the additional lighting you need.

For the chandelier, do not assume the table will be centered in the room. Once a sideboard or other

Dining table lighting. Place furniture first to see where you want the chandelier and other lighting.

150 watts is desirable. For uplighting, experiment with lovely decorative bulbs; clear or frosted bulbs are handsome with rustic materials such as wood or wrought iron, while iridescent or amber bulbs give traditional fixtures the illusion of candlelight.

Pendants, such as Tiffany styles, should have open tops to provide upward light. Underneath, a diffusing bowl, disk, or specialty semi-opaque globe bulb will help eliminate glare. The bulb should not, however, extend below the edge of the shade.

A word of caution: If your table has glass, or lacquer, or a highly polished surface, make sure your fixture's reflection

Pendant table lighting. Check that any fixture will not glare off a highly reflective furniture surface, such as glass, mirror, or lacquer.

elements are considered, you may want to move the table off-center. Therefore, plan your furniture placements first, then your lighting.

Lighting Over the Table

In rooms with a conventional 8-foot ceiling height, the bottom of the fixture should be 27 to 36 inches above the table. Raise the fixture 3 inches for every additional foot of ceiling height. In deciding how high to place a chandelier, consider the height of your dining room chair backs. For example, place the chandelier higher with high back chairs such as ladderbacks; place it lower for low-backed captain's chairs.

Most fixtures look skimpy in average-sized dining rooms unless they are at least 20 inches across. However, allow at least 6 inches clearance on each side of the table so that guests will not bump their heads. For rooms approximately 10 feet by 10 feet square, use a pendant or chandelier 14 to 20 inches; for 12 feet square, use a pendant or chandelier 20 to 26 inches; and for 14 feet square, a pendant 24 to 30 inches.

Chandeliers with downlights bring out the sparkle in table-ware, especially crystal. Bulbs totaling 200 to 300 watts are sufficient to light most tables, and a minimum of

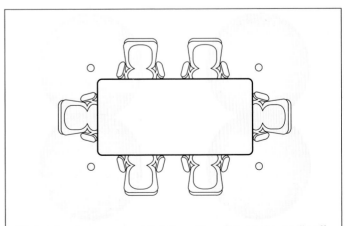

Dining track or recessed lighting. Place fixtures diagonally off the four table corners for subtle lighting.

does not produce unpleasant glare. Augment or replace chandelier lighting with track or recessed lighting. Use a ring of four downlights around the table's edge, or on each side of the centered chandelier on a long table. Smaller recessed housings are especially effective, and low-voltage recessed lighting with pin spot trims can create outstanding effects.

If a chandelier doesn't suit your more contemporary style, replace chandelier lighting with downlights centered over each side of the table.

Buffet Servers

Scrumptious food needs to be presented in the most flattering light. A variety of methods work for buffet servers or sideboards. For example, flank the unit with sconces in a style that coordinates with the table's lighting fixture, mounted 60 inches above the floor. Use recessed or track fixtures spaced 2 to 3 feet apart with 50- or 75-watt reflector bulbs mounted 9 to 12 inches from the wall.

Undershelf Lighting

If you have a china cabinet that's not well lit, now is the time to rectify the situation. If you plan to use the dining room as a library, plan the book display. Add decorative objects to relieve the massiveness of just books alone and plan specialty lighting for the decorative objects displayed. Wash the books in light.

For general lighting, wash the walls or consider some uplights if the ceiling is attractive. Some newer homes today have a two-level ceiling in the dining room. Emphasize this feature with a hidden light source such as mini-lamp strips or a fluorescent staggered strip system.

Kitchens

Good lighting principles from the dining room apply to the kitchen as well. Wherever family meals are eaten, they deserve good convivial lighting. In addition, providing

Elegant lighting touches keep the kitchen/family room bright without fighting with the ocean view. Low voltage pendants over the counter, recessed lighting, and iron chandelier all work together.

good task lighting is critical in the cooking area, where sharp knives, scalding and burning materials, and the subtleties of fine cooking all coexist.

Energy-efficient fluorescent lighting is mandated by code in some states for kitchen remodeling. For example, in California, codes require that primary kitchen and bathroom fixtures be fluorescent. In most kitchens, fluorescent is an ideal choice for at least part of the lighting because these are lights that are turned on for hours at time. Also, fluorescent's reduced heat production is a warm-weather plus in a kitchen where the stove is also producing heat. Select fluorescent lights that are most flattering to foods—warmer tones represented by 3000K to 3500K in the light index.

General Lighting

Close-to-the-ceiling fixtures provide light to see into drawers and cabinets. Depending upon your arrangement of cabinets, these may be most effective if installed near work areas rather than in the center of the ceiling. Two 48-inch tubes in a fixture are sufficient for kitchens up to 120 square feet. For larger kitchens, use fixtures that accommodate four 48-inch tubes.

Recessed incandescent fixtures placed 6 to 8 feet apart also provide general lighting and can be dimmed. Recessed downlight fluorescent fixtures are spaced the same for the best light spread. (Note that they cannot be dimmed with incandescent dimmers, though.)

General Perimeter Lighting

In large kitchens, try perimeter lighting. Use two-tube recessed or surface-mounted fluorescent fixtures in the ceiling, over the front edge of the counter to form a square, "L" or "U" pattern to suit your cabinet layout and provide general illumination. An alternative is to add a soffit 8 to 12 inches from the upper cabinet line, into which you can mount recessed reflector floods or fluorescent tubes shielded with louvers or lenses.

Task Lighting

Augment centered ceiling lighting that would otherwise be the sole light source so that you do not work in your own shadow at the sink, range, and countertops.

Sinks. An individual recessed downlight or fixture that can be outfitted with an energy-efficient reflective compact fluorescent provides adequate task lighting when installed over the sink in the ceiling or soffit. Two reflective downlights placed 18 inches apart on a 2-foot track or recessed and centered over the sink also are effective. Another solution is to use a thin-line fluorescent tube mounted behind an 8-inch deep faceboard.

Rangetops. Most range hoods are equipped with fixtures that accommodate the minimum of 40- or 60-watt incandescent or equivalent that is required for efficiency. For economy in general task lighting, substitute compact fluorescent fixtures

Kitchen lighting. Provide specific task lighting for each chore, such as washing, baking, and rangetop cooking.

or linear fluorescent fixtures for incandescents where possible. Position any task light towards the front of the range to prevent glare, using similar lighting as that for a sink.

Countertops

Undercabinet lighting is ideal for countertop work surfaces. Mount fixtures as close to the front of the cabinets as possible to prevent reflected glare. Choose from slim, energy-efficient fluorescents, miniature track lights, or low-voltage linear systems, all of which are suitable for kitchens. Use an

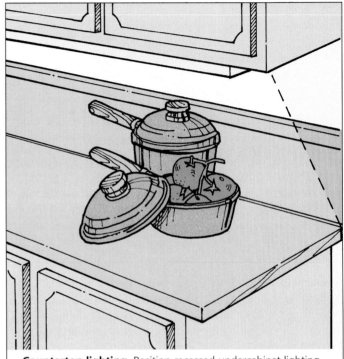

Countertop lighting. Position recessed undercabinet lighting toward the front and 24 in. above the work surface.

A pretty backsplash and strong undercabinet lighting brighten a sink without a view. Undercabinet lighting and recessed both are used for task and ambient in this kitchen.

Accent lighting over the cabinets and task lighting are balanced here, in a sleek modern kitchen.

opaque fixture or shielding on the cabinet bottom to minimize glare. Add a faceboard if necessary. Use fluorescent fixtures (they come from 12 to 48 inches long in regular increments) that cover at least two-thirds of the length of the counter. Lighting that extends into corners and fills the space uniformly is sleek and most attractive.

Peninsulas and Counters Without Upper Cabinets.
In a small kitchen the general lighting fixture located over the counter doubles as a task light. Otherwise, either recess or surface-mount fixtures 20 inches apart, centered over the counter. Use 75-watt reflector floods or equivalent compact fluorescent lamps, or miniature low-voltage pendants.

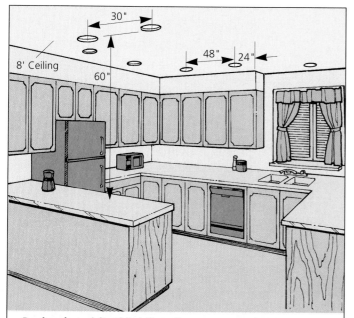

Peninsula or island lighting. Create an attractive pattern with ceiling lighting to tie it to the rest of the room.

Pendants, decorative ceiling fixtures, and recessed lighting are all used to define areas in a working kitchen.

Islands or Dinettes.
Use one or more decorative pendants over islands or dinettes. Antique schoolhouse, country-store, and old-fashioned pool table styles are some fashionable choices. Installed with an appropriate dimmer, this light provides the atmosphere that is perfect for dining. Figure a total of about 120 watts incandescent or 32 to 40 watts fluorescent to light a dinette. Miniature, low-voltage pendants equipped with tiny halogen bulbs add sparkle and atmosphere in a modern vein.

Overhead pendants with diffusers over the bulbs to prevent glare are used here as a unifying solution for small kitchens.

Accent Lighting

Cabinets illuminated with low-voltage mini-lights under, over, or inside provide ambient as well as accent lighting. Do not overlook concealed lighting above the cabinets,

Strong lighting from recessed sources works for tasks and is muted when used over a dining counter. Note the orderly ceiling light pattern.

Cabinet lighting. Install lighting inside glass doors and above cabinets to show off collected treasures and provide accent lighting.

spaces, such as a pantry, lend themselves to fluorescent lighting for energy efficiency. If your kitchen is open to a family room or sitting area, be mindful of the kind of light and glare that adequate kitchen lighting can create.

Undercabinet lighting that's discreetly hidden from a standing cook may produce unsightly glare for those seated nearby. Install cabinet facing low enough to camouflage the light and prevent this. In an open plan combination family/dining room/kitchen, consider these interactions as well:

- Do not position an entertainment/TV center in a kitchen extension so that the kitchen lighting glares on the television screen.
- Do not place the home entertainment unit directly opposite the kitchen.
- Don't hang a pendant so that it blocks the view from the kitchen to either the television or the fireplace. Cooks deserve to see the sights, too.

Even placement of recessed lighting keeps the design of this kitchen clean. Screened undercabinet lighting additions look like built-in additions to cabinets.

especially if you decorate them with baskets, bowls, or other accents. Hanging baskets of food or plants also benefit from spot illumination.

Additional Considerations

Second sinks, desk areas, pantry, and laundry areas in a kitchen require their own specific lighting. Small storage

Bathrooms with Sparkle

It may not be backstage at the Roxy with elaborate strips of makeup lights, but it is the place where most people prepare themselves for the day. The function of bathrooms has expanded in recent years, and chances are that if you

"Hollywood" lights provide ideal surrounding lighting for grooming. Note the lighted makeup magnifying mirror on the right.

In showers, use recessed lighting fixtures designed specifically for water situations. A well-lit shower is safer to use.

want to consider relighting it, you also are contemplating expanding its size, reorganizing its functions, adding a larger bathing area (perhaps a whirlpool or other soaking tub), or perhaps installing a new sauna-style shower stall. Or, you may just be sick and tired of trying to cope with inadequate lighting. Whatever the reason, a switch to good bathroom lighting substantially changes the efficiency, safety, and looks of the room.

Newer, more elegant bathrooms call for more decorative lighting considerations than the conventional older bath. In addition to general and task lighting, decorative lighting where the lamp fixture style itself enhances the decor now finds its place in the bath. Accent lighting, especially if you have installed a focal point as dramatic as a luxurious marble whirlpool, can make the most of the elements that set the bathroom's tone.

General Lighting

In a small bathroom (about 100 square feet) vanity lights may be sufficient to provide general illumination. But even for this size as well as for anything larger, a combination exhaust fan/infrared heat lamp/ceiling fixture is a desirable option.

Recessed lighting often provides general lighting in today's modern bathrooms. But general lighting still needs to be supplemented with side lights to provide balanced, shadow-free illumination at a vanity. Consult with your local building and electrical code inspectors about lighting areas such as whirlpools, linen closets, and showers. Specific require-

Use stronger lighting, here supplied by special recessed fixtures and cornice-style overhead vanity/sink lights, to illuminate dark wood walls.

Unconventional lighting may be the only decorative element you have room for in a small bathroom. But such lighting can be highly effective, as in these lighted mirrors.

ments may vary for both fixtures and spacing. Recessed lighting is a natural choice for niches at various locations such as in the tub/shower area and over the toilet. Fixtures are designed specifically for damp locations, and a variety of trim is available to create different lighting effects.

In larger bathrooms, especially with changes of level, for example leading to soaking tubs, additional lighting is necessary for safety.

Lighting for Mirrors

Even, shadow-free lighting that illuminates both sides of the face, under the chin and the top of the head is best for shaving, makeup, and hair care. Highly translucent milky white plastic or glass diffusers let light through to illuminate your face, while light-colored vanity tops and sinks reflect light up under the chin. Do not aim directional lights at the mirror itself, since that will produce glare back into the room. Use only those fluorescent fixtures that come closest to the color of incandescent lights for the truest renditions of makeup colors and the most flattering reflection for anyone first thing in the morning. You need at least 120 incandescent watts for mirror lighting for these chores. Install separate switches for your mirror lights.

A powder room may need lighting mostly to create atmosphere. Here, a traditional wall sconce appears doubled in the mirror.

Mirror lighting. Center lighting on either side of a grooming mirror at face height.

Small Mirrors

Decorative wall brackets on either side of small mirrors illuminate sides of your face evenly. Do not make the common mistake of mounting wall sconces too high. They should be face height, not above. Therefore, place them no higher than 60 inches above the floor, and at least 28 but not more than 60 inches apart, unless they are combined with another vanity light source. Ideally, combine wall sconces with a matching ceiling fixture or wall mounted fixture above the mirror.

Side lights are wonderful solutions for contemporary bathrooms. They can be linear incandescent or fluorescent lights with special coatings to reduce glare and spread light to eliminate shadows. Often the mechanical fasteners that hold them in place are concealed so that they maintain the clean lines of the mirror, countertop vanity, and other sleek bathroom design elements. They can be placed up to 48 inches apart for efficient lighting, and need supplementing with recessed or surface mounted ceiling lights if more widely spaced.

To rely solely on recessed fixtures for mirror lighting, place them up to 36 inches apart and place them between the person and the mirror, not directly overhead. Select recessed fixtures with lamps that provide a wide illumination spread, such as a flood bulb.

Large Mirrors

A fixture above a 36- to 48-inch-wide mirror is sufficient to provide diagonal side lighting as well as overhead lighting. A series of recessed soffit lights, or even surface mounted lighting, can provide the same efficiency provided they are spaced on either side of the sink and will overlap the light delivered.

Mirrored walls behind double-sink vanities are popular and offer great lighting opportunities. Treat each sink as a task area, and light it accordingly. Depending upon your design, you may want to install a series of side light columns, or span the entire mirrored wall with a fixture that integrates the entire sink/counter/mirror area. The American Lighting Association recommends that a fixture above a solid mirrored wall be mounted 78 inches off the floor.

Theatrical lighting strips around bathroom mirrors provide the highly effective makeup lighting used by actors. But a common mistake is to use too few lights, that are too bright, creating unpleasant glare that makes the lights uncomfortable and inefficient. Avoid this by selecting units that use soft white instead of clear globe lights or exposed bulbs. Since light is magnified by reflection in the mirror, cut glare by lowering wattage — for instance, substituting 15 watts for 25 watts. Another option is using reflector

Use grazing light to make the most of interesting walls. Here, the lighting is recessed in a soffit with architectural molding.

bulbs that direct light back instead of outward towards your eyes, as long as they are not badly reflected in the mirror.

Use a combination of both side and overhead theatrical strips so that individual bulb wattage can be lower. Add a dimmer so that each person can adjust the light level to his own needs.

Recessed fixtures also are highly effective, especially recessed incandescent fixtures with dropped trim such as a glass collar. Center them over the counter and place them 36 to 48 inches apart. They can provide general illumination for baths of up to 100 square feet, but for larger spaces, add another fixture for each additional 50 square feet.

Shower and Tub Lights

Everyone, but especially kids and older adults, needs good lighting in slippery, potentially dangerous areas in and around showers and tubs. Lighting should be bright enough for safety, grooming, reading labels on soaps, shampoos and other products, and adjusting shower heads and water temperature.

Recessed downlights or other fixtures designed especially for wet locations can be used inside a shower or over a tub/whirlpool. Use shielded fixtures so that there is no glare for reclining bathers. Shatter-resistant white acrylic diffusers that eliminate the danger of glass breakage are safest. Put the switch out of reach of those in the tub or shower to reduce risk of electrocution.

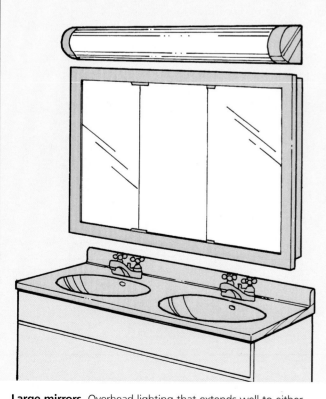

Large mirrors. Overhead lighting that extends well to either side can provide enough sidelight for grooming.

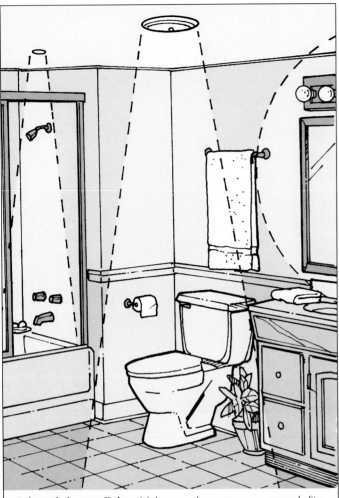

Tub and shower lights. Make sure these areas are properly lit with fixtures designed for wet locations.

Bathroom lighting fixtures to be placed in damp areas such as shower enclosures must be clearly marked "Suitable for Wet Locations" or "Suitable for Damp Locations." They must be installed so that water cannot enter or accumulate in wiring compartments, lamp holders, or other electrical parts.

Lighting fixtures used in other parts of the room have no special physical requirements. Surface-mounted ceiling fixtures should be installed using an octagon box with an offset bar hanger attached, an octagon box on a joist bracket, or a box attached to an adjustable bar hanger with fixture stud. Wall fixtures should be installed on a 4-inch-square box with a raised cover plate. Recessed ceiling fixtures come with built-in boxes.

Toilet Compartments

Provide lighting in this area when the toilet is separated and walled off. A ceiling or wall fixture with 60 to 75 incandescent watts or the equivalent is sufficient.

Special Considerations

Whirlpools and other spa-like tubs make the modern bath the center of luxurious living. For real relaxing, lighting can be adjusted to calming and soothing levels with a number of fixtures in the main room. You can provide such interesting touches as toe space lighting softly illuminating a sumptuous floor or strip lighting safely delineating a step up to a tub.

Many bathrooms-cum-spas feature wide windows and/or skylights that create a modernized version of the Garden of Eden. To transform the look at night, bathe an attractive window treatment in light to keep the scene cozy. Lights can highlight bathroom plants, which usually thrive in the moisture-laden environment. Bulbs will provide the necessary illumination if plants are not exposed to natural light.

Powder Rooms

Fewer lights are needed in the powder room, which generally is smaller in scale and has no tub or shower. However, in the powder room, it is especially important to locate switches logically and in easy reach because the room will often be used by guests who are not familar with it.

Make sure switches are within easy reach and logically placed. Switches placed outside the bathroom often are best. If the powder room or any bathroom will be used as a guest bathroom, install a night light. An illuminated switchplate is another thoughtful and prudent safety feature for bath lighting.

Beautiful Master Bedrooms

Haven, retreat, home office, sleeping chamber, dressing room, television viewing room, many moods and functions define this important space. Lighting for all these activities has to be adjustable, and dimmers will allow the greatest flexibility in setting moods. Start by defining your bedroom's functions and the lighting requirements for each.

Soaring ceilings are a good place for angled recessed lighting as used in this bedroom. Bedside lamps are within easy reach.

General Lighting

Ceiling fixtures, recessed downlights, chandeliers, fan lights, and track lights all have the potential for strong lighting needed for housekeeping, care when someone's ill, and for seeing into drawers and shallow closets. They also pose a potential glare problem for people in bed. If the ceiling fixture is rarely used when occupants are in bed, glare is irrelevant. However, if the fixture is frequently used while you are in bed, check it out for glare when you are lying down.

Wall sconces and illuminated cove lighting are just two indirect solutions that are highly effective in bedrooms. In large bedrooms, consider spacing recessed fixtures about 8 feet apart for even lighting.

Provide a three-way switch beside the bed and at the door to control the general lighting. It is a safety feature as well as a convenience.

Keep lighting from interfering with TV viewing if that's a favorite activity in the master bedroom. Here, main lighting is supplied by modern hanging pendants flanking an armoire that contains a TV.

A properly adjusted low-voltage strip light fixture places light exactly where needed for reading in bed. Meanwhile, ambient light comes through a glass block wall.

Bedside Reading Lamps

Units that operate independently so that one person can read while the other sleeps or watches television can be as casual as miniature lamps that clip onto the books themselves. Other choices include lamps that are bright enough for ambient lighting, but that can be dimmed or switched down to a low light level. In a bedroom, opaque shades or lamps with shields that restrict light distribution may be a better choice than lamps with translucent shades. When installing wall lamps, take into account both the depth of the headboard and the pillows to be used for reading in bed. Otherwise, the reader could end up in his or her own shadow.

Ceiling cove lighting is used for dramatic but calming effects.

Bedside reading lamps. Individual bedside lamps that can be dimmed are most convenient in shared situations.

Table Lamps. Lamps on bedside tables should have a shade with a bottom 15 to 17 inches, top 8 to 15 inches, and a depth of 6 to 14 inches. Use the same bulb wattage as you would in a living room table lamp, but this lamp should be in line with the shoulder, 22 inches to the side of the book's center and with the shade bottom about 20 to 24 inches from the top of the mattress.

Wall or Hanging Lamps. These lamps make the most of tight space, since they free up tabletop surfaces. Position them just as you would table lamps. A lamp with a top shield or diffuser may be needed, since often these lamp shades are not as deep and high as table lamps. Be sure also that any bottom diffuser with a lamp does not extend below the shade bottom and create glare.

Headboard and Wall-Mounted Lighting. Unless the lighting is positioned well away from the wall, it may cast the reader in his own shadow. Better solutions include floor lamps that can be adjusted or pin-spot recessed fixtures that provide very tight beams. They allow a lamp to be adjusted within the housing and tilted up to 35 degrees, so that individual adjustment is easy. Another solution is to use baffled fixtures. They keep a bedmate from being disturbed while you escape away into the night with a favorite page-turner thriller.

Low-voltage MR16 lamps contained in a simple strip fixture that can be squared on the ceiling surrounds a bedroom, grazing light across storage units and lighting the bed.

Accent Lights

In many bedrooms the area just above the headboard holds the major artwork in the room. For these rooms, track or recessed lights that provide framed, tight-beamed lighting aimed at the artwork without overflow are an ideal solution. Usually they are positioned 18 inches from the wall at ceiling height.

Bedside hanging lamps. Positioning for lamp shade lower edge is determined by placing it at just below eye level.

Recessed light over the window washes down across shades or curtains to create a pleasing image from the bed. Carefully selected objects complete the still life.

Grooming double dresser lamps. Use diffused shades and aim for the same lighting as for a bathroom vanity.

Dressers and Vanities

To make dresser and vanity lights effective for grooming, simulate bathroom vanity lighting but with boudoir flair. Position lamps on either side of a mirror and use highly translucent or off-white shades. For large dressers where you stand while grooming, select lamps that are 25 inches measured from the dresser top to the center of the shade. Generally, effective dimensions are a bottom of 11 to 14 inches, a top minimum 7 to 8 inches, and a depth of at least 7 to 9 inches.

Scale down for grooming while seated, as at a vanity or dressing table. Select lamps that are 15 inches from the tabletop to the center of the shade. The best shade dimensions are bottom 9 to 11 inches, top 7 to 8 inches and depth 7 to 9 inches, so that the overall lamp does not take up much dresser top space. The bulb should be at least 2 inches below the top of the shade so that you do not look onto it when standing.

Position shades at least 6 inches from the wall with the center of the lamp bases 36 inches apart. Bulbs that go up to 100 watts are sufficient for most grooming, while different people may need more or less light. Using three-way bulbs or lamps with dimmers suits these lamps to ambient lighting. Check that smaller lamps will accommodate the bulb wattage, since small lamps often take 60-watt bulbs.

Double dressers and large dressing tables require broader lamps that will be in scale and produce more light. These table lamps may take bulbs of up to 100 or 150 watts to make grooming easy to see.

Comfortable Children's Rooms

Children's rooms call for unique lighting. Initially, lighting must work well for both parents and children, as parents spend time in children's rooms dressing and cuddling kids. Over time, the children's requirements become more important, as playing, sleeping, reading, studying, and doing hobbies create their own lighting needs for a child.

Children's room lighting can add fun and flair to the mix, but its greatest contributions are comfort and safety.

Developing eyes should be treated as a precious commodity, not to be abused or strained. Never mind that Abraham Lincoln was reputed to read before the log cabin fire: your children probably will be working at a computer terminal, watching television, and developing hand-motor skills at video games. They need lighting that supports these more highly demanding visual tasks. Children are less aware of vision strains, so it is up to the grown-ups to make sure they see the light!

Any lamp to be used in a child's room needs to be designed so that it doesn't easily tip over or produce dangerously high heat levels that could burn at a careless touch. To combat tipping, look for lamps that are not top heavy and are generally well balanced or that clip securely on to a bed post or desk.

School-age children need areas to display treasures and hobbies, and when lit these provide ambient lighting. Strip fixtures that hold MR16s toplight the shelves and desk.

Make sure a night light or lamp is within easy reach of the bed in a child's room. One that's scaled to child size fits the decor best.

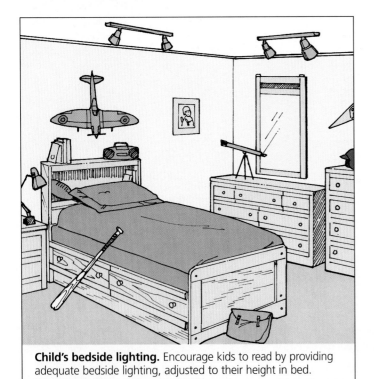

Child's bedside lighting. Encourage kids to read by providing adequate bedside lighting, adjusted to their height in bed.

General Lighting

Track or adjustable recessed lighting is a good choice in the children's younger years. Both eliminate or reduce the need for table lamps that might tip over. Adjustable systems are best because they can be refocussed and redirected as a child's activities change. For instance, you can concentrate more light from the floor to a play table as the child graduates from one to another.

Opt for bright, general lighting that is good for children playing on that floor in early years. Add localized light where reading, drawing, or craftwork takes place, such as in a favorite carpeted corner. A dimmer for one or more lights, adjustable from the doorway, is an invaluable alternative to a bright light to attend to a baby or youngster's nighttime needs.

Reading in Bed

Children are lower to the mattress than adults when reading in bed. Adjustable lamps with articulated arms can be positioned best to meet a child's growing needs.

To encourage children to read, provide comfortable lighting on the bed or wherever reading takes place. Bedside lamps provide safe lighting when a child must get up in the middle of the night. Make sure that bunk beds have lighting that is within easy reach for both upper and lower occupants, whether it doubles as a reading light or not.

Reading Lamps for Chairs

A comfortable chair for reading a toddler a good-night story calls for lighting that makes the book easy to read. You also may want to sit beside your child on the bed to read, so that you can share the pictures and have the child participate. In this case, a lamp with a bottom diffuser would be a good choice. It would be bright enough for the adult without glaring in the child's eyes, which would be at a lower level. Careful positioning of the lamp will also mitigate glare.

Apply the same principles for lighting and reading for children as you would for adults, but factor in children's shorter distances from the chair, mattress, or floor. Children often spend a good deal of time on the floor or bed, reading, playing, doing puzzles, and drawing. Make sure the lighting keeps up with your child's own special routine.

Homework

A desk with good lighting is the command center for studying, drawing, writing reports, and doing artwork. Usually, the same space doubles as a work surface for crafts and hobbies. Follow the guidelines under "Home Offices," page 81. Those guidelines can apply to children's study areas as long as you adjust for height.

Hobbies and Crafts

Model building, working with beads, and other activities that require strong light may demand supplementary lighting over and above good general task lighting.

Computer lighting. Provide both task and general lighting that is compatible with the screen at a child's height.

Provide an automatic night light that goes off at dawn after chasing away monsters after dusk.

Computers/Video Display Terminals

These require both task lighting to illuminate the text and background lighting to mitigate the contrast between the video screen and area behind it. For computers and televisions, follow the same principles described in the section on home offices. Simply adapt these principles to a smaller-sized person.

Shared Rooms

Create a lighting plan that is unique to each individual who shares the room, but that also takes into account its impact on the other person. For instance, if one child wants to read in bed, be sure that his light is shielded from his roommate. In setting up lighting for all tasks, keep glare to a minimum. Try creating desk/hobby areas enclosed within their own miniature dividing walls so that even strong task lighting does not overflow the study area.

Night lights are especially important in shared rooms, where one child can trip over what another child has neglected to put away. Finally, since shared rooms are never large enough, use plenty of ambient light to brighten the walls and visually expand the space.

Home Offices

Home offices have come a long way since the 1700s when they held a cherished writing desk or secretary, quill pen, and inkwell. Secretaries and treasured desks have long been symbols of a well-run home, whether proudly displayed in a living room, in a kitchen, secreted away in a corner of a master bedroom, or removed altogether from the rest of the home to a den or study.

Today's home office can be used every day as the main workstation for a telecommuter. It also can be an occasional place to catch up on the office's overload, or it can be the home's record-keeping center. In any case, today's home office lighting must meet the needs of people using modern equipment that is a far cry from that old-fashioned quill pen. Lighting contributes to the general demand for electric service to a home office. It takes its place with such power drains as electronic surge protectors, fax, computer, copy machine, and other equipment.

Two masters must be served in the arrangement of a modern home office: aesthetics and utility. While good lighting is essential to utility, it does not necessarily limit you to high-tech designs. As long as the light provided is adequate to the chore, the look of the fixture can be as fanciful or old-fashioned as you wish. For instance:

- A funky-styled 1950s gooseneck lamp may be perfect to light copy beside a computer on a modern desk.
- The entire computer can be housed in a traditionally-styled roll-top desk with a bookkeeper's lamp accessory.
- If video editing/viewing is part of your work, the TV and VCR can be housed in a classic armoire of country or French Provincial style, and lighting can be provided by a tole-style candle lamp.

Before embarking on these decorative choices, figure out your practical lighting needs. Consider the following recommendations to set up a well-functioning home office.

Apply whichever principles are appropriate to set up work-stations elsewhere in the house, such as a child's study area or a classic den/library with darkened paneled walls and book-filled shelves.

General Office Lighting

The overall goal of office lighting is to create a comfortable environment free of harsh contrasts and glare. For a home office of about 120 square feet, two large ceiling fixtures, each containing two energy-efficient fluorescent tubes with baffles, will provide well-diffused general lighting while eliminating shadows on the desk. Use fixtures that each take four fluorescent tubes for larger offices.

Place the fixtures to the right and left of the desk, so light comes over the worker's shoulder.

Lighting placed in front of the desk can cause annoying reflections. If a desk must be placed with a ceiling light in front of it, select one with baffles to reduce glare. Or try track or recessed lighting that can be directed away from the desk surface.

Desk Positioning

Placing a desk against a light-colored, non-glossy wall provides reflected but non-glaring light across the desktop surface. Do not place a desk in front of a window facing directly outside, where there's bound to be glare throughout the day. Place the desk at right angles to outside light, and balance the light for daytime use by providing lighting on the side opposite the window.

Recessed fixtures can wash bookcase cabinets and desktop surfaces, while the computer is left without glare.

Lighting can be minimal at desk areas where computers often are used. Here, overhead shelving has space underneath for fluorescent lighting strips for task work.

The desk is an area where a wide spread of light is necessary. Light sources can include office-styled desktop lamps, swing-arm wall or floor lamps, suspended fixtures, or a fluorescent shelf lamp — all for bright, even light over a large area. No matter what the fixture or lamp, position it so the shade or the bottom of the fluorescent fixture is 15 inches above the desktop. Shades for desk lamps should be non-glaring, translucent, and with a white or near-white lining. They need to provide ambient light as well as desktop illumination.

For a single, traditional desk lamp that also provides ambient lighting, select a lamp with a shade that is approximately 16 inches wide at the bottom, 14 inches wide at the top, and has a depth of 10 to 12 inches. Use desk lamps that accommodate 150-watt equivalent bulbs for casual use, 250-watt equivalent bulbs for intensive or prolonged use and for older eyes. Put the lamp to one side of the central work area and 12 inches back from the desk front edge. Place it on the right for left-handed people, on the left for right-handed people.

Adjustable arm wall lamps leave work surfaces free and so are ideal for small or medium-sized desks. Position these with the shades located 15 inches above the desk surface, just as for desktop lamps. If the wall lamps you choose have shades shallower than 10 inches, mount them so that light doesn't glare from either below or above the shades, or use lamps that come with a bottom or top diffuser.

Use a pair of wall lamps to cover a large area and create a shadowless work surface. For shallow desks, 20 to 22 inches deep, center the lamps 30 inches apart and use a 100-watt bulb in each for casual use. For critical sight tasks or prolonged use, use a standard size desk and center lamps 36 inches apart and not more than 17 inches from the desk front edge. Use lamps that take 150 watts or the equivalent.

The same principles in selection of bulb wattage capacity, shade opacity, and lamp positioning apply to suspended lamps or floor-standing lamps.

Desk lamps with fluorescent, compact fluorescent, and halogen bulbs are best used for task lighting. They can produce a good working light level at a desk where the general illumination is high. They also are useful in lighting desks where a computer is to be used, since you want to maintain a low light level surrounding it.

Computers

If there's too much contrast between background lighting and the task at hand, you become fatigued. Light on the keyboard and ambient lighting should be in a ratio of no more than 1 to 3 to the task lighting for reading whatever papers need inputting in the computer. The brightness of the papers should be roughly the same intensity as the computer screen.

Generally, a low level of ambient light is best if your work is computer-oriented. Remember to rebalance the screen brightness control on the display terminal when you readjust the general lighting. Overall lighting systems that can be adjusted depending upon whether you are using the computer or doing other desk work are ideal.

Software programs with white background and black letters are kinder to your eyes and easier to match to the light intensity of paper than programs with dark backgrounds. Screens that have surface glare are extremely hard on eyes, especially since many computer users are unaware of the glare as their straining eyes peer around and through it.

To detect computer or television screen glare, place a mirror before the monitor and see what reflects in it. Locate the terminal so that the images of lamps and windows are not reflected from the screen into the viewer's eyes.

Be as thoughtful in setting up a laptop as a permanent unit. Laptop screens often are harder to read than conventional computer screens, requiring even trickier lighting solutions. The user is the final judge of the light that works best with his or her own computer setup.

Credenza and Shelf Lighting

Install undercabinet fluorescent strips over shelves and credenzas. Mounted close to the front of the unit and shielded from view, the strips will not cause glare to reflect off the work surface. Muted, non-reflective walls below the light strips are essential to keep down glare.

Accent Pieces

Mementos, professional certificates, favorite photographs, inspirational plaques, plants — anything that takes the hard edge off office decor needs lighting attention. Recessed or track lighting can add the appropriate punch without interfering with the workaday lighting needs.

Miscellaneous Considerations

No matter why a home office has been set up, working hours often are not the same as those of conventional 9-to-5'ers. Lighting is even more important if you work at home in addition to a another job, and your eyes have already put in a day's work. Provide relatively even, bright lighting, which will keep strain to a minimum.

Computer lighting. Eyestrain and other problems are best avoided by matching background lighting to the screen and keeping the task lighting within a 3 to 1 ratio.

General office work. Diffused general lighting, accent lighting for special objects, and task lighting are all needed.

In contrast, if you've moved your entire operation into your home, your lighting needs should take into account the ambient light of daylight streaming through windows. Counter it with appropriate task lighting, and reduce any glare with window treatments if the light is just too bright.

Laundry Areas

The laundry area calls for functional lighting for sorting, treating spots, measuring detergent, setting dials, and making sure that last sock makes it out of the dryer.

A large ceiling fixture with energy-efficient fluorescent tubes in warm white tones will provide good all-around color rendition. Center the fixture over appliances, tubs, or a sorting table, whichever is where most sorting and preparation is done. Center a hanging fixture 48 inches above the work surface so that it does not impede folding.

Install spotlights before front-loading washers and dryers, so that you can see inside. Make sure as well that task lighting is available for reading small-print detergent instructions.

Ironing

Touch-ups occasionally are necessary even if the entire family is converted to wash'n'wear. Angled light in front of the ironing board shows up wrinkles best.

With a fixed board such as a foldout, use ceiling-mounted adjustable cans 20 to 24 inches ahead of the board's front edge with 150-watt reflector flood bulbs or the equivalent.

Place a floor lamp or directional light source with a 150-watt bulb close to the center of the movable board on the side opposite the person ironing and nearest the pointed edge of the board. You need to see wrinkle shadows to be able to iron them out.

Workbench Lighting

Similar to the requirements for a sewing or craft area, workbenches and stationary power tools need both good even light and special supplementary light that can be adjusted to where it is needed. A fluorescent utility light centered over the front edge of a workbench and about 48 inches above the work surface is standard. It usually accommodates two tubes providing 40 watts equivalent each. For staining and matching wood grains, select a lamp with true warm color tones. Use strong portable or clip-on task lights that can be positioned properly to illuminate joints and dowels. Extend lighting to any storage areas in the work space.

Adjustable lighting is extremely helpful for both workrooms and sewing rooms.

Workbench lighting. Good task lighting and supplementary lighting are assets for any workbench.

Relating Elements and Relating Rooms

In the main, homes are composed of linked boxes of rooms, each in visual contact with its neighbor. While each room has its functional requirements, the beauty of lighting is in its creative use as a decorative tool in each area.

Decorative elements throughout a home or specific to each living area can be either enhanced or diminished by the choice of flattering or unflattering lighting. Lighting that flattens wood grain and distorts warm, mellow wood tones would be a disaster in a home filled with paneling and cabinets. The same lighting might be perfect for bringing out the serene shimmer and depth of tone in marble or lacquered walls.

Used creatively, lighting brings out the best of the room's elements, whether the features are architectural or the furnishings themselves. For instance, a prized Oriental carpet should not be lost in a pool of darkness when it can set the tone for an entire room. A sweep of modular seating in another space may be the main feature; lighting here should be focussed on the furniture not the floor.

Lighting from one room to another can bring out the intricate relationships of the spaces, planes, and ceiling heights that both unify and entice us to go from space to space, room to room. Transitions of light level should be modulated so that they are easy visually. During the day, just providing more light in the dark interior rooms of a home may make all the difference in its mood. At night, consider how each room looks from the other rooms that look into it. Often, simple lighting adjustments create drama where there was none, bringing out the best in the home's design.

Beginning a Decorative Lighting Plan

Before figuring out the wiring and outlet placement, you need to establish the lighting needs. Using graph paper, do your furniture and cabinet layouts, making provisions for anticipated changes and needs. Here are the steps to take:

■ Draw up house plans (or use existing ones) large enough to show the relationship between the various spaces to be seen, room to room. Mark the position of the windows, doors, and other architectural features such as fireplaces.

■ Add built-in furniture and related items such as kitchen cabinets and appliances. Make tracing paper sketches of changes you might be planning, and add layouts of furniture as you plan to arrange it. Note the activities that are to take place in each area, such as sleeping, TV watching, studying, cooking, and so forth.

■ Check danger spots for safety, such as changes of level, stairs, or places of limited natural daylight. These are easiest to spot when you walk through a house at dusk. This assessment also will help in establishing a nighttime lighting scheme.

■ Keynote decorative aspects to feature, such as color, architectural advantages such as high ceilings, furniture or a wonderful nighttime/daytime garden view.

■ Mark off likely traffic patterns, both to avoid wires and to make sure that adequate lighting is provided where needed.

■ Make a preliminary lighting plan overlay. Use tracing paper to allocate the types of lighting and fixtures that fit both the furnishings and the activities planned in the spaces including task, ambient, then accent lighting.

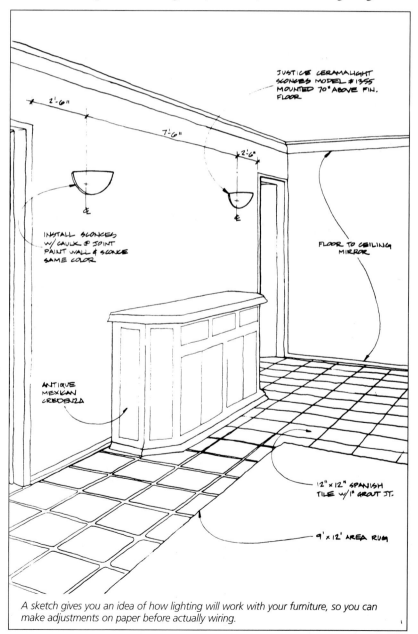

A sketch gives you an idea of how lighting will work with your furniture, so you can make adjustments on paper before actually wiring.

■ Approximate with lamps you have. Use what's on hand to see how lighting changes affect the room by actually positioning lamps where you think you want them. A pragmatic approach often yields the most useful solutions.

■ Start the selection process. Armed with these preliminaries, you are ready to determine which fixtures and lamp types to consider for each area. Keep plans loose at this point. Various systems requiring different kinds of wiring are possible and you want to be open to them all.

■ Determine switch and outlet locations. Add such special details as dimmer switch positions.

■ Check your preliminary plans with retail stores and collect manufacturer's information. Check on any local building codes that may apply.

■ Begin your wiring planning. Now you can determine which additional lighting needs can be served by existing wiring and which will require new wiring. The following chapters will cover the kinds of wiring options available and how to decide which suit your needs best.

You even can take a picture of your interior and then sketch in lighting. See how beautifully the lighting all works together in this space, due to planning.

6
Working With Wire and Boxes

Whether you are refurbishing an old lamp or adding new lighting fixtures to your home, the first step in doing proper and safe electrical work is selecting the right materials for the job. In this chapter you will learn how to select the right wire and how to make safe electrical connections. You'll also learn how to choose the proper electrical boxes for the job at hand.

Types of Wire and Cable

Technically, the metal through which electricity flows is called a conductor. In the real world, it's called wire, cord, and cable. That is how it is referred to in stores that sell it. Most instructions use these simple terms, too.

For practical purposes, a wire is a single strand of conductive material enclosed in protective insulation. You can buy single-strand wire off a roll in any length you want. It is sometimes precut and packaged in standard lengths. A cable has two or more wires grouped together within a protective sheathing of plastic or metal. Cable is normally sold boxed in precut lengths of 25, 50, or 100 feet. Cord usually is a series of stranded wires encased in insulation. Cord is sometimes precut and packaged, but is usually sold off the roll. All conductors are priced by the lineal foot.

There are three different types of wires: copper, copper-clad aluminum, and aluminum. For any project, you should always use the same type of wire that is installed in your home. You can determine this by opening a switch or outlet box, pulling out the wires, and noting the information printed on the insulation. The markings will tell you the voltage, the type of wire or cable, the manufacturer, and the American Wire Gauge size.

Aluminum Wire. You must use special care with aluminum wire. It does not behave like copper wire. Aluminum wire tends to expand and contract, working itself loose from terminal screws. This can cause trouble — mainly electrical fires. If your home uses copper-clad aluminum wire, do not add aluminum wire to it. Use copper or copper-clad aluminum wire.

If your home has aluminum wire, check to make sure that the switches and receptacles are marked CO/ALR or CU/AL. The CO/ALR marking is used on switches and receptacles rated up to 20 amps. The CU/AL marking is used on switches and receptacles rated at more than 20 amps. If the switches and receptacles do not bear these markings, replace them with those that do.

Never use aluminum wire with any back-wired switch or receptacle that requires pushing the wire into the device. Aluminum wire must connect to terminal screws.

Since recommendations for wire sizes are generally for copper and copper-clad aluminum wires, you must readjust the designation to the next larger size when using aluminum wire. Example: If No. 14 (copper) wire is recommended and you are using aluminum wire, you must use No. 12 wire instead.

Wire Size Numbers. You will probably be concerned mostly with No. 14 and No. 12 wire sizes.

The term wire refers to a single conductor. In a cable containing two wires, both wires will be the same size.

Wire numbers are based on the American Wire Gauge (AWG) system, which expresses the wire diameter as a whole number. For example, No. 14 AWG wire is 0.064 inches in diameter, and No. 12 AWG is 0.081 inches. The smaller the AWG number, the greater the diameter and the greater the current-carrying capacity. The National Electric Code requires a minimum of No. 14 AWG wire for house wiring. Exceptions to this are the wiring used in lighting fixtures, furnace controls, doorbells, and other low-energy circuits.

Wire Ampacity. You also must consider the wire's ampacity, or the current in amperes that a wire can carry continuously under conditions of use without exceeding its temperature rating.

If a wire is too small for the job, it will present a greater-than-normal resistance to the current flowing around it. This generates heat and can destroy insulation, which can cause a fire.

No. 12 wire is rated to carry a maximum of 20 amps; No. 14 wire is rated to carry up to 15 amps.

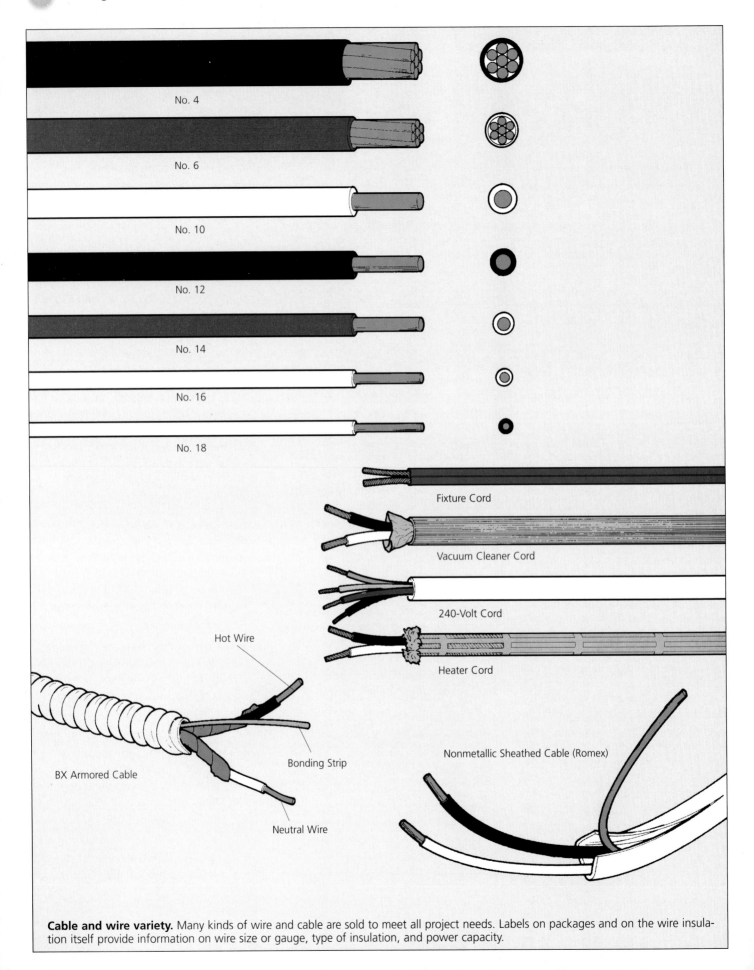

No. 4

No. 6

No. 10

No. 12

No. 14

No. 16

No. 18

Fixture Cord

Vacuum Cleaner Cord

240-Volt Cord

Heater Cord

Hot Wire

Bonding Strip

Nonmetallic Sheathed Cable (Romex)

BX Armored Cable

Neutral Wire

Cable and wire variety. Many kinds of wire and cable are sold to meet all project needs. Labels on packages and on the wire insulation itself provide information on wire size or gauge, type of insulation, and power capacity.

Cable for Circuits. House circuits are usually wired with nonmetallic sheathed cable, with metal-armored cable, or with insulated wires running through metal or plastic pipe called conduit.

For most projects, you will be working with flexible nonmetallic sheathed cable. This cable is often referred to by the trade name Romex. It contains insulated power and neutral wires and a ground wire.

Armored cable is called BX. Inside the flexible metal sheathing are insulated power and neutral wires and a ground wire. Use of BX cable sometimes is restricted by code. Check the local codes where the material is sold. BX also is restricted to use indoors in dry locations. It sometimes is specified for use where power wires need extra sheathing protection.

Conduit, according to code, can be galvanized steel pipe or plastic pipe. Metal conduit comes in three types: rigid — often preferred for outdoor use — intermediate, and electrical metal tubing or EMT, a newer type popular for house wiring. Standard conduit diameters are ½, ¾, 1, and 1¼ inches.

There are fittings to join conduit for straight runs and at 45-degree angles. The material is bent with a tool called a hickey.

Cord. This is stranded wires encased in some type of insulation, such as plastic, rubber, or cloth.

For wiring lamps you'll most likely use zip cord, which is two wires, usually No. 18 gauge, encased in a rubber-like insulation and held together with a thin strip between the wires. You can easily separate the wires by pulling them apart, hence the name zip cord. You zip it apart. Cord is used for lamps, small appliances, and cord sets that have plugs and/or receptacles on one or both ends of the cord.

Selecting Cable

Wire, whether solid or stranded, comes in several types of cable. For house wiring, you'll use solid wire encased in one of the three types of cable described here:

Type NM. NM cable is for use only in dry locations. It is used most often in house circuits. Each wire (with the usual exception of the equipment grounding wire) is wrapped in its own plastic insulating sheath. The hot wire is wrapped in black, and the neutral in white. If the ground wire is insulated, it is wrapped in green. If the ground wire is bare, it is wrapped in paper. The entire cable is wrapped in plastic.

The wire in Type NM cable is either AWG No. 12 or AWG No. 14 for normal house circuits. Larger sizes, such as No. 10 or more, are used for heavy appliances. The National Electrical Code specifies that No. 12 wire must be used for certain household circuits.

In either size, NM cable is available with two or three conductors plus an equipment grounding conductor. This ground-wire system is highly recommended. Use three-conductor NM cable where two hot wires are needed.

Type NMC. This cable may be used in both damp and dry locations. The distinguishing characteristic of this cable is that the individually insulated wires are embedded in solid plastic to provide protection against moisture. As a result, it is appropriate for basement installations where codes permit.

Type NMC is available with two or three conductors plus an equipment grounding conductor and in AWG No. 12 and AWG No. 14.

Type UF. This cable is for use in wet locations, including burial underground. UF cable may be used instead of conduit.

The distinguishing characteristic of this cable is that the individually insulated wires are embedded in water-resistant solid plastic that is heavier than that used in Type NMC cable. The UF cable is available in AWG No. 12 and AWG No. 14 as well as other size wires. It contains two or three conductors plus an equipment grounding conductor.

Abbreviations on Wire

Markings on the insulation, plastic sheathing, and on nonmetallic cable explain what is inside and identify the type of insulation covering. Consider the following designation:

14/2 WITH GROUND, TYPE NMC, 600V (UL).

The first number tells the size of the wires inside the insulation or cable, in this case No. 14 gauge. The second number tells you that there are two conductors (wires) in the cable. There also is an equipment grounding wire, as indicated. The type of cable is given; the number following indicates the maximum voltage allowed through the cable.

Finally, the UL notation assures you that the cable has been rated as safe for the uses for which it was designed. The National Electrical Code requires that wires of types NM and NMC be rated to withstand heat of 90 degrees Centigrade (194 degrees Fahrenheit).

Estimating Wire Needs

To estimate the amount of wire or cable you will need for a project, measure the distance between the new outlet and the power source.

Add an extra foot for every connection you will make. Then, to provide a margin for error, add 20 percent to this figure.

For example, if you measure 12 feet between a new and existing receptacle, add another 2 feet for the two connections, making a total of 14 feet. Then add 20 percent (about 3 feet) to the total. To do the job, start working with 17 feet of cable. The same formula is used for wire, with the exception of lamp/appliance cord.

Stripping off Wire Insulation

You can use a jackknife, but an inexpensive wire stripper is a better tool to remove the insulation from wires. First cut the wire to the right length. About ¾ inch of insulation should be stripped off the wire for the best terminal connection.

1 Match Wire to Stripper. Put the wire in the hole in the handle that matches the wire size. For lamp wire, the hole will be No. 18 or No. 16.

2 Rotate the Stripper. Lightly grip the handles of the stripper in a closed position with the wire inserted in the correct hole. Then rotate the stripper around the wire a couple of times.

3 Pull off Insulation. With the handles still closed, pull the wire out of the stripper. The handles will grip the insulation and the pulling action will strip it off.

Stripping by Knife. If you use a jackknife or utility knife to remove the insulation, be very careful to cut only the insulation and not nick the wire with the blade. Go completely around the insulation with the cut. Then pull off the insulation with your fingers.

Stripping Cable Sheathing. You can buy a stripping tool to slice the sheathing on cable. Once stripped, the sheathing then has to be trimmed with a knife or scissors.

You can also use a jackknife or utility knife to make the first stripping cut. Be extremely careful that you do not cut the sheathing on the wires inside the cable as you slice the sheathing.

For most connections, you will need to strip back the sheathing about 6 inches.

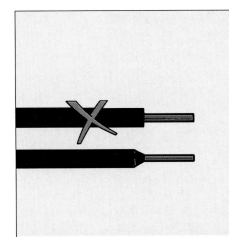

Cut insulation this way. Insulation cuts should be tapered, not square, if possible. Some wire strippers provide tapered cuts.

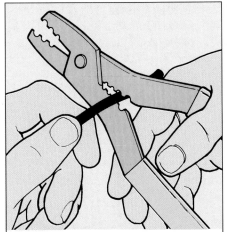

Match wire to stripper. Match the wire to the numbered hole in the handle of the wire stripper. Insert the wire in this hole; grip handles.

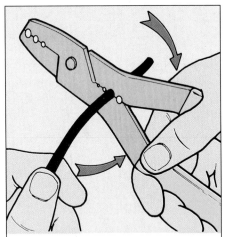

Rotate the stripper. With the wire in the right hole, lightly grip the stripper and rotate the stripper completely around the wire.

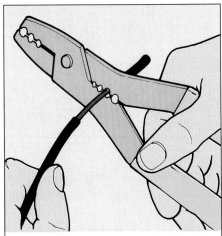

Pull off insulation. Keep the handles closed after the insulation is cut through. Then pull the wire out of the tool to strip off insulation.

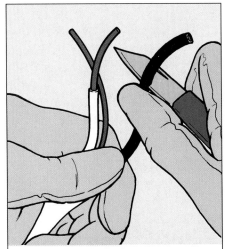

Stripping by knife. Be careful not to cut or nick the wire. A glove or thumb protector is a wise precaution against cuts.

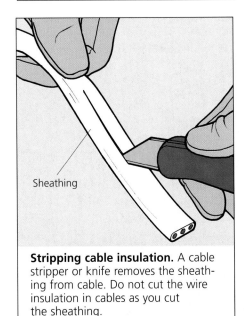

Sheathing

Stripping cable insulation. A cable stripper or knife removes the sheathing from cable. Do not cut the wire insulation in cables as you cut the sheathing.

Making Wire Splices

According to the code, all wire splices must be enclosed in a switch, outlet, fixture, or junction box.

Stranded Wires. Strip off about ¾ inch of insulation. With your fingers, twist each wire individually so the strands are tightly together. Then, with your fingers, twist the two wires together.

Solid to Stranded Wire. Strip off about ¾ inch of insulation from both wires. Twist the stranded wire tight; then wrap it around the solid wire with your fingers. Then, with pliers, bend over the solid wire to secure the stranded wire to the solid wire.

Solid to Solid Wire. Strip off about ¾ inch of insulation from both wires. With pliers, spiral one piece of solid wire around the other piece, making the twist fairly tight, but not tight enough to break the wire.

Twist on Wire Connector. Pick a wire connector that fits the splice. See "Choosing the Right Wire Connector," page 92. Insert the wires into the wire connector with a slight twisting motion. Don't apply too much downward pressure on stranded wire splices; if you do, the wire will buckle and flatten. Just screw the connector onto the splice.

X-Ray View of the Splice. After the wire connector is in place, it should completely cover the splice with a bit of wire insulation seated in the opening of the wire connector.

Wrap the Splice. When you're satisfied that the splice is tight and securely covered in the wire connector, wrap the wire connector and an inch or so of the projecting wires with plastic electrician's tape. The tape is a safety measure that helps to make a stronger splice. However, do not rely on the tape to hold the splice together. If the splice is not tight and covered by the wire connector, remove the splice and start again.

Stranded wires. Twist stripped stranded wire with fingers, making a tight wire. Then twist the wires together as tight as you can.

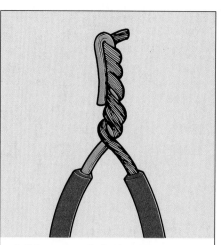

Solid to stranded wire. Wrap stranded wire around solid wire, using the solid wire as a base. Then bend over solid wire to lock the splice.

Solid to solid wire. Twist solid wires together tightly with pliers. Do not overtighten the spiraled wires or you will crack or break them.

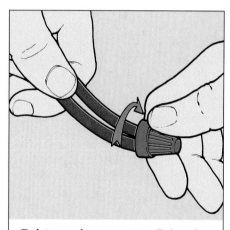

Twist on wire connector. Twist wire connector onto splice rather than twisting splice into the wire connector. If the splice is too long for the connector, trim the wires.

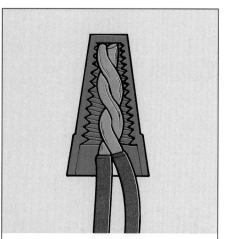

X-ray view of the splice. Here's how the splice looks in the wire connector. The splice should be completely covered and tight with insulation in the flange of the connector.

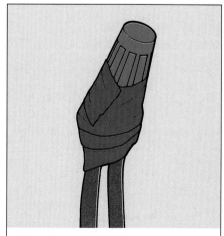

Wrap the splice. To strengthen the splice and connector, wrap the connector with plastic electrician's tape. One spiraled layer of tape is plenty.

Choosing the Right Wire Connector

When you want to connect one cable to another, you splice them using a wire connector. Wire connectors are also called wire caps or Wire Nuts, a trade-marked name.

Wire connectors are typically cone-shaped plastic shells with a coiled-copper or threaded-metal insert. When you twist the plastic cap onto stripped wires you're splicing together, the metal insert grips the wires and twists them tight. Some wire connectors are simply ribbed cones; others have ears or wings to make them easier to tighten. Some are made of hard, brittle plastic; others are softer and more resilient. Some wire connectors are filled with silicone for making water-resistant splices in damp areas like bathrooms.

Wire connectors are made in different sizes and are color-coded for the gauge of cable they'll fit, but the color-coding scheme usually varies with the manufacturer. Tables on the wire-connector packaging explain the color scheme, giving minimum and maximum wire capacity for each size. For example, a medium yellow connector from one manufacturer is listed as joining a minimum of two 16-gauge wires and a maximum of four 14-gauge wires, while a larger red connector will join a minimum of two 14-gauge wires and a maximum of four 12-gauge wires or three 10-gauge wires. Be sure to use wire connectors made for the wires you're splicing.

Working with Aluminum Wire

Most wire that you buy will be copper or copper-clad aluminum wire. You may discover, however, that your home has been wired with solid aluminum and, unless you decide to completely rewire with copper, you will have to work with aluminum wire.

Aluminum wire used to cause problems when it was used in switches, outlets, and fixtures that had not been designed for the characteristics of aluminum wire. The wire tends to come loose by expanding and contracting at terminals. Loose wires can cause electric arcing, which can produce electrical fires.

The industry has solved part of the problem with switches, outlets, fixtures, and equipment made especially for use with either aluminum or copper wire. The products are plainly marked with the letters CO/ALR.

Wiring Procedures. Extra effort must be made when connecting aluminum wire to terminals, as described here. It's also a smart idea to apply the same rules to copper wire when connecting it.

Strip, Loop, and Hook. Remove about ¾ inch of insulation from the wire. Use wire strippers, if possible. Loop the end of the bare wire with needle-nose pliers. Just grip the wire in the jaws of the pliers and wrap it around the jaws, which are rounded. This automatically forms the loop of the size that is required for terminals. Then place the loop around the terminal screw with its opening to the right.

Tighten the Terminal. When the loop is in place, tighten the terminal screw so the screw and contact plate make full contact with the wire.

Give it Another Half Turn. When the wire is snug under the terminal screw, give the terminal screw another half turn.

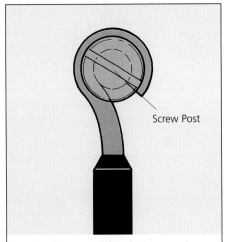

Strip, loop, and hook. Remove insulation from wire and twist end into a loop; hook the loop around the terminal with the opening to the right.

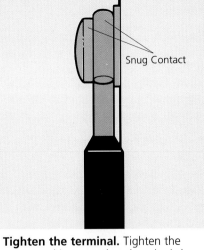

Tighten the terminal. Tighten the screw, making sure that the wire is in full contact with the screw and contact plate. Screw must be tight.

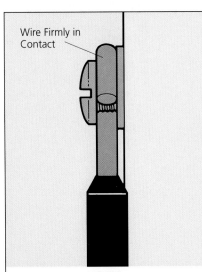

Give it another half turn. Give the screw another half-turn after you have initially tightened it. But don't strip slot or threads with too much force.

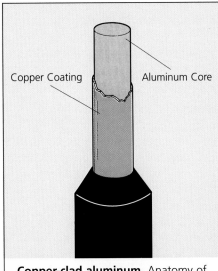

Copper-clad aluminum. Anatomy of copper-clad aluminum wire shows how a copper plating is added to the wire to make the wire safer.

Selecting Nonmetallic Cable

You probably will buy and work with nonmetallic plastic-sheathed cable more than any other conductor or wire. It is often called by its trade name, Romex, which has almost become synonymous with any non-metallic electrical cable. Local codes may allow nonmetallic cable only in certain locations, or may specify that you use another type, such as metallic armored cable, or wires running in conduit.

The outer sheath of nonmetallic cable is usually a moisture-resistant, flame-retardant material. Inside, there are two or three insulated power wires, and perhaps a grounding wire.

For most residential wiring, two types of nonmetallic cable are often used. They will be labeled Type NM or Type NMC on the package or the cable.

Type NM may be used in dry locations and be either concealed or exposed. Type NMC meets the same requirements as NM, but it also is fungus- and corrosion-resistant. It may be used in moist, damp, and corrosive locations; it may be used in hollows of brick and concrete blocks used in building. It may not be used in dwellings with more than three floors.

Both types contain either copper wire in gauges 14 through 2, or aluminum or copper-clad aluminum in gauges 12 through 2.

Two-Wire/Bare Ground. The cable has a hot wire in black insulation, a neutral wire in white insulation, and a grounding wire, which is bare—no insulation.

Two-Wire/No Ground. This old-style cable has just two wires: a hot or power wire covered with black insulation and a neutral wire covered with white insulation.

Three-Wire/No Ground. This old-style cable has one hot wire covered with black insulation and another hot wire covered with red insulation; the

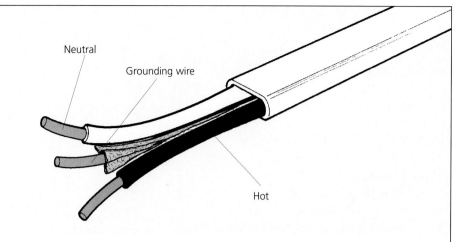

Two-wire cable with bare-wire ground. Two-wire nonmetallic cable with bare grounding wire has a hot or power wire encased in black insulation. The so-called neutral wire has white insulation; the grounding wire is uninsulated. This cable is commonly specified for residential wiring.

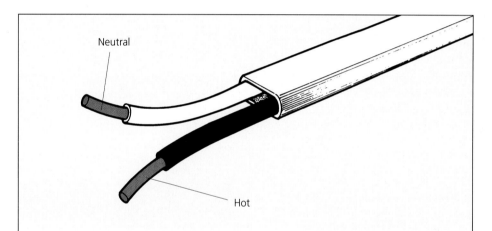

Two-wire cable with no grounding wire. Two-wire nonmetallic cable with no grounding wire has a hot wire in black insulation and a neutral wire in white insulation. Wires in cable are color-coded so they are not mixed when hooking up fixtures along a circuit's entire run. Color matches terminals. This type of cable no longer meets code because it offers no ground protection.

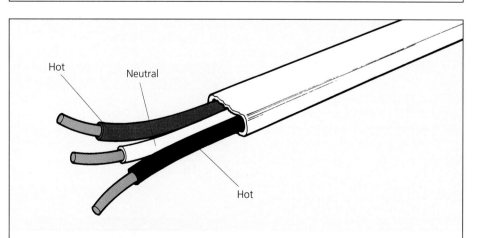

Three-wire cable with no grounding wire. Three-wire nonmetallic cable without a grounding wire has a black-insulated hot wire, a white-insulated neutral wire, and a red-insulated wire that is considered a hot wire. In three-way switch hookups, the red wire becomes the hot switch wire. This type of cable no longer meets code because it offers no ground protection.

neutral wire has white insulation. A three-wire cable is used to connect three-way switches.

Two-Wire/Coded Ground. In this cable, the grounding wire is insulated and often color-coded green or green and yellow stripes. The other color codes are the same: black for hot wires, white for neutral.

Three-Wire/Ground. This cable is commonly used for house circuits in which a grounding wire runs through the complete circuit. The grounding wire may be hooked to a clip or terminal in an outlet box, or it may be connected by a pigtail—a short length of wire—to a grounding terminal in the box or on a receptacle.

Type UF Cable. Type UF cable can be used for interior wiring in wet or corrosive locations where type NM cannot be used. It looks the same as other types of nonmetallic cables but is marked with the letters UF on the package or insulation. Like type UF, type USE cable may be buried underground.

Cable Wire Sizes. It is recommended that all new residential circuits use No. 12 gauge wire. No. 14 gauge wire may be added to an existing circuit of No. 14 wire.

In the store, you will find cable packages and the cable itself marked with the wire size, followed by the number of wires inside the cable sheath. Check the markings carefully so you buy exactly what you need.

For example, a cable with two No. 12 wires will be marked "12/2." If there is also a grounding wire, it will be marked "12/2 with Ground." The first cable has two insulated wires, black and another color. The second has those wires and the ground wire either bare, or insulated in green or green and yellow.

Wire gauge No. 8 to No. 4 designate single wires. No. 6 to No. 2 are multiple wires held together by the insulation. No. 16 and No. 18 contain multiple strands twisted or braided together.

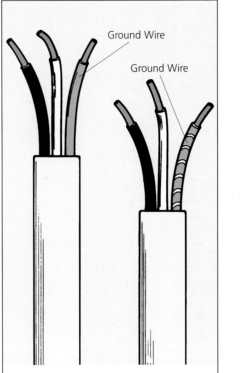

Two-wire/coded ground. Two-wire cable with insulated ground wires may be color-coded with solid green or green and yellow stripes.

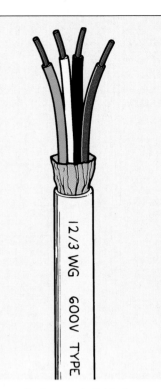

Three-wire/ground. Cable for three-way switches has a black-insulated power wire, white neutral wire, red switch wire, bare or green ground wire.

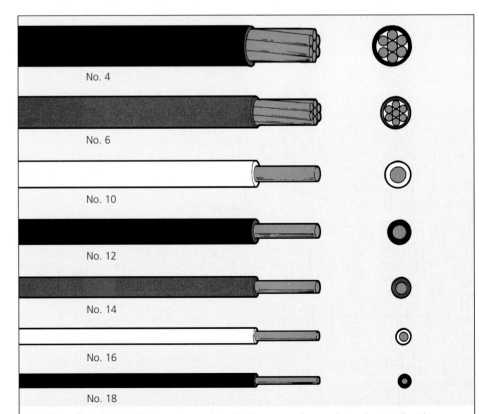

Cable wire sizes. Wire gauge numbers indicate conductor sizes; the smaller the number, the larger the wire. No. 4 through No. 8 have multiple wires and use special connectors. No. 16 and 18 wires are used only on fixtures or as extension cords, never for installed circuit wiring.

Working with Nonmetallic Cable

To prepare nonmetallic or plastic-sheathed cable for installation, you need a sharp utility knife, a wire stripper, and a cable ripper. You can cut the cable with a knife, but a ripper is better in many cases because it protects the insulated wires within the cable sheathing.

Cut Sheathing. Place the cable on a flat surface, such as a workbench. Measure about 8 inches from the end of the cable and make a mark.

Then insert the cable in a cable ripper at the marked point. Press the cable ripper together with your fingers and pull the cable through the ripper to the end of the cable.

If you use a knife instead of a ripper, start cutting the sheath at the mark. Run the knife down the sheathing, being extremely careful not to cut the insulated wires inside the cable. It may take several shallow cuts with the knife to part the plastic sheath. If you damage the wire, cut that part off and start again.

Trim Sheathing. With your fingers, peel back the sheath and then use a knife to trim away the excess sheathing at the first cutting mark.

Cut Wire Insulation. With wire strippers, remove about ½ to ¾ inch of insulation from the black-insulated power wire, the white-insulated neutral wire, and the green or green and yellow grounding wire (if it is insulated).

As you work, check to make sure that you did not cut the wire insulation with the ripper or knife as you removed the sheathing. If you did cut the insulation on the wires, trim off all wires at the cutting mark and start over. The insulation on the wires inside the cable must be completely sound in order to prevent hazards, such as an electrical short circuit or, worse, an electrical fire.

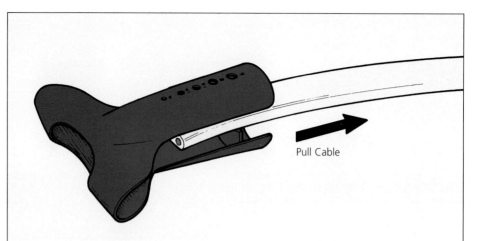

Cut sheathing. A cable ripper makes a clean cut in the outer sheath of nonmetallic electrical cable. Slip the wire into the ripper at the cut-off mark—about 8 inches from the end—and grip the ripper firmly. Then pull the cable through the ripper to make the proper cut.

Pull Cable

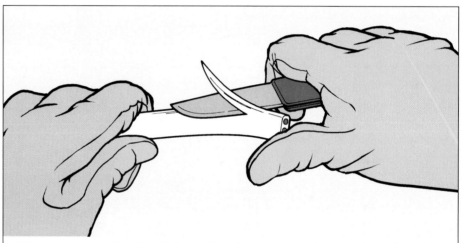

Trim and remove the sheath insulation. Remove excess sheathing insulation with a sharp utility knife or jackknife. Trim it flush with the cut-off mark that you made on the cable. Don't nick the inside wire insulation. With a knife, it is wise to wear a glove or thumb protector to avoid cuts.

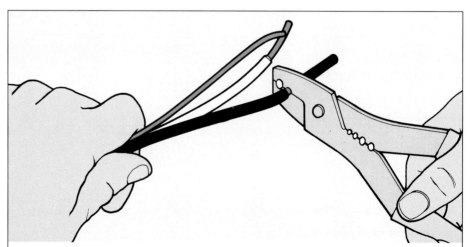

Remove the individual wire insulation. Use wire strippers to remove the insulation from the wires inside the cable. If you have accidentally cut this insulation with the ripper or knife, trim the wire at the cut-off mark and start the process over again. Damaged insulation can cause electrical hazards.

Working with Electrical Boxes

Switches, outlets, and fixtures are mounted in electrical boxes. All wires are terminated, spliced, and stored in electrical boxes. Boxes are designed to serve specific purposes. For example, paneling switch and outlet boxes are extra slim so that they fit between ¾-inch furring strips and the back surface of the paneling material. A standard switch box is too deep for this application. You must specify which box you want by name when purchasing supplies in a store.

Some boxes have special clamps and clips for securing wire and cable; some boxes have special fastening and nailing devices, such as adjustable hangers that go between framing members: studs, joists, and rafters.

Other buying considerations include box capacity — how many wires it can accept — and the number and position of cable entry holes. These are commonly knockout or pryout plugs in general-purpose boxes, but threaded plugs are used in weatherproof boxes.

You can also choose between metallic and nonmetallic (plastic) boxes. Metal boxes may be a bit more expensive, but they are more adaptable. Nonmetallic boxes are not permitted in most large cities, or even in many localities where nonmetallic cable is permitted. Check your local electrical code carefully on this point.

Selecting Electrical Boxes

Electrical boxes fall into two broad categories depending on how they will be used; rectangular boxes are used to house switches and receptacles, while octagonal or round boxes are used to house lighting fixtures. First, let's look at the four most common kinds of switch and receptacle boxes.

Standard Boxes with Adjustable Ears.
This box is a simple rectangular structure with screw openings at the top and bottom front edges. The sides are straight up and down; there are no

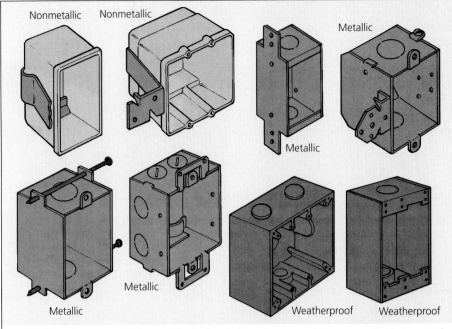

Switch and receptacle boxes. Typical switch and receptacle boxes available in metal and plastic are shown here. Note the different nailing and fastening devices designed to save you time and money.

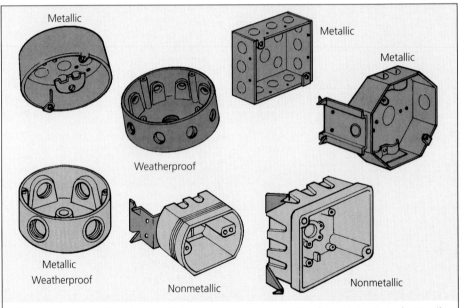

Fixture and junction boxes. Fixture boxes support electrical equipment, such as ceiling lights. Junction boxes are used to splice wires and redirect wiring in long household circuit runs.

brackets or clamps. This type of box is appropriate for plastered walls, since the walls are sturdy enough to hold the box in place. The box is also used for drywall, along with two side brackets that you buy separately. The brackets give the box the support that the drywall alone cannot.

Boxes with Side Clamps.
These boxes have screw-activated clamps on the front side edges. When the screws are tightened, the clamps come forward and spread out to hold the box in place. This type of box is used in paneling or hardboard that is fastened to studs. Both of these wall coverings are sturdy enough to hold the box securely.

Boxes with Side Flanges.
A box with an external flange running along

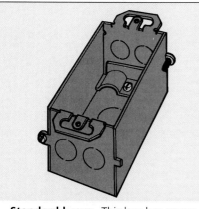

Standard boxes. This box has screw openings at top and bottom front edges. It may be used for plaster walls and gypsum wallboard.

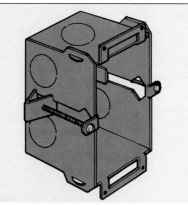

Boxes with side clamps. This design has side clamps that hold the box in position in the wall. When activated, the clamps grip the edges of paneling.

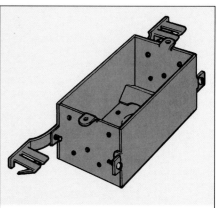

Boxes with flanges. Side flanges with metal teeth are for open construction. The teeth are hammered into the framing members.

one side is used in locations in which you have easy access to a wall stud, such as an unfinished basement or attic. The box is simply nailed to the side of the stud.

This style box may have a mounting flange with metal teeth that are pounded into the stud. Set the box at a depth that will make its front edges flush with the face of the drywall or paneling that will cover the wall.

Paneling Boxes. These shallow boxes hold just one switch or outlet and a single set of wires. They are mounted between ¾-inch-thick furring strips and the back side of paneling materials. Paneling boxes cannot be ganged together.

Selecting Ceiling Fixture Boxes

In stores you will find a huge selection of fixture boxes from which to choose. Your job will be matching the box to the location. The more popular box styles are described here.

Two-Piece Boxes. These are ceiling fixture boxes that are ideal for working with open framing. A bar spans the joists and is connected to the joists either with prepunched nail tabs in the bar hangers or with regular nails. The bar is adjustable to joist widths, and the box mounted on the bar can be moved with a screw clamping device into any position you want.

Offset Bar Hangers. This product is also a two-piece bar combination designed for ceiling fixtures. The difference is that the bar hanger is offset to fit up into the joist openings and the bar is nailed to the edges of the joists. The bar has a box clamp fitting that can be moved to any position across the bar.

Pancake Boxes. This is a flat box,

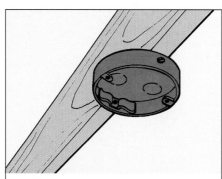

Adjustable Bar

Two-piece boxes. A two-piece box has an adjustable bar hanger. The box can be positioned anyplace along the bar with a screw clamp.

shallow in depth, that is nailed or screwed directly to the edge of a joist. It is designed for open-beam construction, but you can adapt it to covered ceilings or walls.

Flanged Boxes. Another box design is the flanged box. The flange is fastened directly to the edge of the box and it may or may not have prepunched nail tabs to attach the box

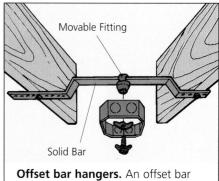

Movable Fitting

Solid Bar

Offset bar hangers. An offset bar hanger recesses the box between joists, although the bar is nailed directly to the edges of the joists.

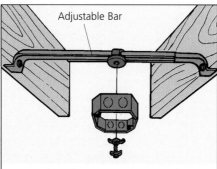

Pancake boxes. If the joist or beam is exposed, or there is little working room between joists, you can use a pancake to nailed to the joist edges.

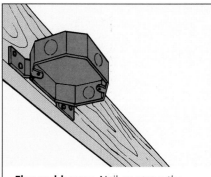

Flanged boxes. Nail or screw the box directly to the joist face. Set the rim of the box flush with the ceiling covering.

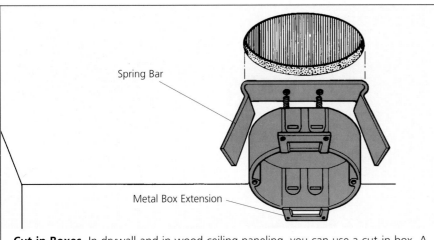

Spring Bar

Metal Box Extension

Cut-in Boxes. In drywall and in wood ceiling paneling, you can use a cut-in box. A spring device holds the box in position against the ceiling. Attachments are installed in the box to handle wires and fixtures. The box can't support extra-heavy fixtures.

to a joist or stud. All boxes, however, will have nail and/or screw holes for mounting purposes.

Cut-In Boxes. These are lightweight boxes that are pushed through a hole you cut in drywall or wood paneling. The boxes have a spring device that hold them in position against the back side of the ceiling or wall material. The boxes also have metal extensions that are installed inside the box to hold fixtures. Observe these boxes' weight limits.

Installing Electrical Boxes

Before you start the project, determine if the existing junction boxes can accommodate additional wiring. Any box can hold only a certain number of connections. These numbers are shown in the chart "Judging Junction Box

Capacity," below. The total number is limited both by physical space and by the provisions of the National Electrical Code.

For safety, don't crowd more wires into a box than the box can handle.

In judging what is and what is not a connection, use these guidelines:

1. Count each conductor (wire) in the box as one connection.

2. Do not count a ground wire that enters the box and is connected directly to the outlet, switch, or fixture.

3. Do not count a jumper wire as a connection.

4. Count a ground wire that is connected to the box as one connection.

5. Count cable clamps or lighting fixture mounting fittings that are

inside the box, such as a nipple or hickey, as one connection for each fitting.

6. Count a receptacle or switch as two connections.

Add the total number of connections and check the chart "Judging Junction Box Capacity" to determine if you can add connections to a box.

For example, a 4x1½-inch ceiling box in which there are two AWG No. 12 wires, one ground wire connected to the box, and a hickey for suspending a hanging fixture has a total of four connections. As the chart "Judging Junction Box Capacity" shows, the maximum allowed for this box is six. So you could add two more if necessary. If more than six connections are needed, buy a new box and keep the old one for future use.

Ganging Boxes

If the box you want to use is too small to hold additional switches, outlets, and wires, you can gang two or more boxes together to provide enough space.

1 **Removing the Box Sides.** With a screwdriver, remove the screw along the right side of one box and from the left side of another, similar box. Lift off the sides.

2 **Reassembling the Boxes.** Put the open sides of the two boxes together. The notch on one box will fit into the flange of the second box. Lock these together. Then drive in the screws to hold the boxes together.

You can gang together as many boxes as you want.

Installing Wires and Cable Inside Boxes

Trim cable to expose at least 6 inches of wire. Remove a round box knockout to use a cable or conduit connector.

1 **Adding a Connector.** Slip the connector collar onto the cable or conduit; let ½ inch of cable insulation

Judging Junction Box Capacity		
Box Size (Inches)	Maximum Number of Connections AWG No. 14 Wire	Maximum Number of Connections AWG No. 12 Wire
Wall Boxes		
3 x 2 x 2½	6	5
3 x 2 x 2¾	7	6
3 x 2 x 3½	9	8
Ceiling Boxes		
4 x 1¼	6	5
4 x 1½	7	6
Major Boxes		
4 x 1¼	9	8
4 x 1½	10	9
4 x 2⅛	15	13

This chart will help you select junction boxes of the proper size for the job.

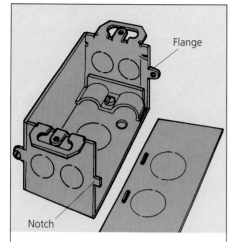

Removing the box sides. Remove left side of one box and right side of another box by backing out screws that hold sides to the boxes.

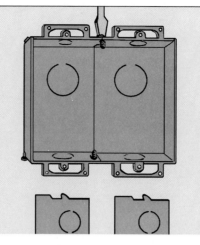

Reassembling the boxes. Put the open sides of both boxes together and lock the notch on one box into the flange of other; replace screws.

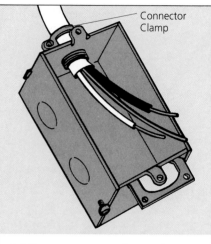

Adding a connector. Fasten the connector clamp over the cable. Let about ½ in. of cable insulation extend past the threaded end.

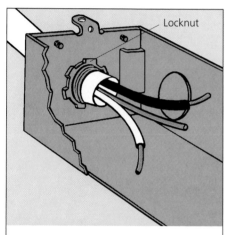

Securing the connector. Put the connector into the hole. Screw on the locknut by hand, then tighten with screwdriver and hammer.

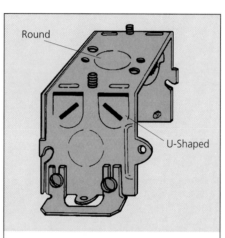

Knockouts for clamps. Remove U-shaped knockouts for saddle clamps. For conduit, punch out round knockouts in metal boxes.

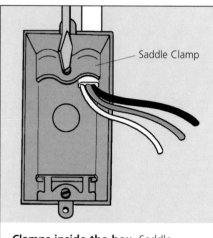

Clamps inside the box. Saddle clamps inside boxes hold wires tightly. Put wires under the clamp. Then tighten the screw to tighten the clamp.

extend beyond the collar. Tighten the collar clamp or setscrew to hold it.

2 Securing Connector. Insert the connector threads through the hole into the box. Screw on the locknut, then tap on its lugs with a screwdriver and hammer to fasten the connector tightly.

Using Box Clamps

To use an interior box clamp, remove the pryout from the U-shaped hole where the cable is to enter. Loosen the clamp screw and insert the cable until about ½ inch of the sheath extends past the clamp. Tighten the screw to hold the cable securely. If

the clamp at the other end is not used, remove it.

Removing Knockouts and Pryouts for Wires

To insert wires into boxes, knockout or pryout plugs must be removed from appropriate holes. To open a hole, tap the knockout with a punch and hammer to break one side free, then twist it off with pliers. Knockouts usually open round holes for cable connectors.

Pryouts are common at the U-shaped holes for interior box cable clamps. Insert the tip of a screwdriver in the slot and twist the pryout free.

Do not remove pryouts or knockouts from any holes that will not be used. Do unscrew and remove unused cable clamps in a box to provide more room for a device and wires.

Cable Connectors. Cables are anchored to boxes either by interior clamps or by connectors. A cable connector is a threaded collar that clamps around the outer insulation and extends into the box, where a locknut secures it. Be sure to get the right connector for the kind of cable or conduit you are using.

Nonmetallic Boxes. Plastic boxes may be used only with nonmetallic cable. They have built-in wire clamps.

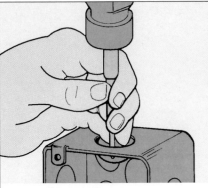

Punching knockouts. A center punch or a nail set and hammer are the best tools to loosen knockouts in electrical boxes. Twist the knockouts off with pliers.

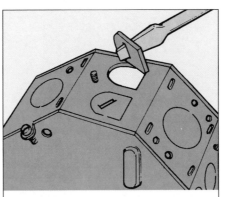

Pryouts. To insert a cable in a clamp inside a box, remove a pryout. Insert a screwdriver in the slot, pry up, and twist out.

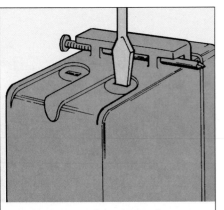

Plastic boxes. Plastic boxes for nonmetallic cable have built-in wire clamps designed to hold non-metallic sheathed cable only.

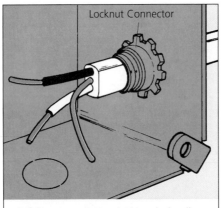

Locknut Connector

Cable connectors. A threaded collar clamped onto the cable extends through a round knockout hole. A locknut secures the collar inside box.

The cable must be help by a fastener within 8 inches of the box. The cable sheath must go at least ½ inch into the box.

Installing Boxes in Walls and Ceilings

Replacing a switch or outlet involves simply turning off the circuit at the main panel, removing the old device, and connecting the wiring to a new one. Replacing a switch or outlet box is almost the same. Turn off the power, remove the faceplate and mounting screws, and pull the device out of the box. Make a diagram of all the connections, then unhook the wires.

Release the fasteners holding the box and work it out of the wall. Undo the cable, insert it into the new box, and

secure it. Then fasten the new box into the wall. That may take some work, for space will be very tight. You may have to enlarge the hole a bit.

With the new box in place, reconnect the switch or outlet, following your diagram, and mount it in the box.

To install a switch or outlet in an existing wall, a hole must be cut in the wall for the box. After the hole has been cut, the power cable has to be fished to the opening and connected to the box and the switch and/or outlet. See "Pulling Wires Through Walls," page 120.

Boxes in Drywall. Plan the location of the box for the new receptacle or switch so it will fall between wall studs. If the outlet is to be placed near the bottom of a wall, position the box 12 to 18 inches above the floor surface. If you want the receptacle at a mid-body height, position the box 10 to 12 inches above the surface of a nearby table or counter.

A switch is normally mounted approximately 50 inches above the floor surface.

Locating Studs. The easiest way to find studs in a wall is to use an inexpensive stud finder. Some finders react magnetically to screws or nails used to hold the wall covering; others sense the density difference between studs and spaces.

Or, measure 16 inches out from a corner and drive a 3- or 4-inch finishing nail partway in. If it hits something solid, it probably is a stud. If not, try a bit to each side until it does. Mark that spot on the wall. You can fill the

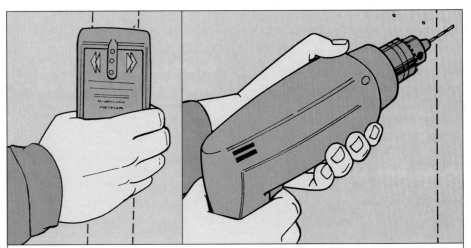

Locating Studs. Locate studs in a hollow wall with a magnetic stud finder (left). To locate studs without a stud finder, drill small holes at 1-inch intervals until you hit a stud. Then measure off 16 inches, the usual space between studs, to find a second one (right).

nailholes with spackling compound or drywall compound, and you will be sure of the stud location.

All other stud locations can be measured from the first stud you find with the nail. The studs will be spaced every 16 inches on center across the wall—or should be.

Another quick method is to pry off the baseboard along the wall in which you want to locate the studs. The baseboard covers the vertical untaped joints of the drywall. These joints are supposed to be spaced 48 inches apart. Then measure from a seam. There should be a stud 16 inches on either side of the seam.

Plaster and Wood Lath. This type of construction was used in older homes; it seldom, if ever, is used in new construction.

To make a hole for an electrical box in this material, you'll have to find a stud as described in "Locating Studs," page 100. Then, if there are no obstructions in the wall, you can use a cold chisel and hammer to remove a layer of plaster from above and below a drilled hole at the box location. This will expose the width of a single wood lath strip and portions of lath above and below it. You probably will have to chip away 1½ to 2 inches of plaster above and below the drilled hole and extend the opening ¾ inch to 1 inch out from the sides of the hole.

Plaster and Metal Lath. Find a stud location first, as described above.

Since you will have to cut through metal, it's best to use the box as a template, drawing an outline of it on the wall where you want the box to be located. Then remove the plaster with a cold chisel and cut the metal lath with a hacksaw blade mounted in a saber saw.

Paneling. Locate the stud positions. Use a stud finder, or look to see where the panels are nailed to the studs. This is not difficult to discover: look closely for the pattern of filled nailholes.

Turn off the power to the room at the main entrance panel, and then drill a small hole in the panel. Check through the hole for any obstructions behind the wall where you plan to locate the junction box. If you find wiring or plumbing, plug the small drilled hole with a piece of doweling and stain the doweling to match the panel so the hole won't show. Chances are good, however, that you won't run into wiring or plumbing. The next step is to use the box as a template and make the necessary cuts in the panel.

In Ceilings. Find the joist locations. They almost always are 16 inches on center and will run either crosswise or lengthwise over the room. Use a stud finder, or start in a corner with the nail test described in "Locating Studs," page 100, and work both ways.

If the house has an attic and the attic floor is not finished, locating the joist positions is very easy. In fact, you can work in the attic, cutting the necessary box holes from above after you determine the location from the room below.

Make sure that you have plenty of support to hold your weight on the joists. Use a sheet of ¾-inch-thick plywood as decking. If the ceiling is tiled, you can remove tiles after finding the joists.

Installing Boxes in Drywall without Stud Support

If you can't locate a stud or joist, use the box as a template and draw an outline of it on the wall or ceiling where you want to install the box. Once the opening is made, you will have to bring the cable to this opening first. See "Pulling Wires Through Walls," page 120. If you do locate a stud or joist, the box is simply fastened to either framing member.

1 **Cut the Paper Covering**. With a sharp utility knife, cut along the template lines that you drew on the wall. Be careful. Make several shallow cuts with the knife, rather than trying to make one single cut through the paper

covering and into the gypsum core of the panel. If possible, cut completely through the panel with a series of cuts.

2 **Knock out the Scrap.** If the piece does not drop out of the hole, the cut may not be complete at every point. Try punching out the scrap with a short piece of 2x4 and a few taps with a hammer—not one blow.

3 **Position the Box**. Before positioning the box in the hole, attach application clips to the side edges of the box. The clips are installed so that the screws are postioned on the outside of the box.

Cut the paper covering. Mark the box location on drywall, and then cut along guidelines with a utility knife. Use a series of shallow knife cuts.

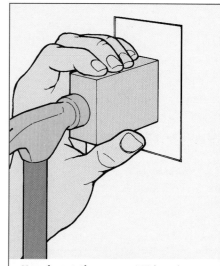

Knock out the scrap. With a short piece of scrap wood and a hammer, tap out the scrap drywall. Let it fall between the studs.

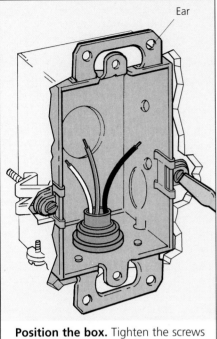

Position the box. Tighten the screws until the box is secure in the hole.

Fit the box in the opening. You may have to trim the hole a bit with the knife, but the box should fit snugly. When the box is in place, simply tighten the screws until the box is secure in the hole.

Installing Electrical Boxes in Plaster and Lath

Many older homes have plaster and lath walls and ceilings. In this construction, lath is nailed across the framing members and then covered over with several different coats of plaster. Cut the hole after you find an unobstructed position for the box. Then, with the hole cut, bring the power cable to the opening and install the box.

1 Chisel a Small Opening. At the box location, chip out a small section of plaster, exposing the width of one lath. Use a cold chisel and hammer for this job.

2 Make and Trace a Template. Make a cardboard template of a standard box. Find the center of the template and mark it. Position the template on the wall and drive an awl or ice pick through the template center point to mark the lath. Then mark the outline of the template on the wall, using the center point as a guide. Drill a hole at the point on the lath.

3 Make the Cuts. Stick masking tape around the guidelines on the wall. This will help prevent the saw from crumbling the plaster. Then score the guidelines a couple of times with a utility knife. Bore ½-inch holes at the four corners of the outlines and where the ears of the box will fit. With a saber saw or keyhole saw, cut out the plaster and lath.

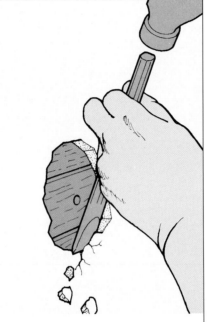

Chisel a small opening. Chip a small hole in the plaster at the box location. Remove just enough plaster to expose one or two lath strips.

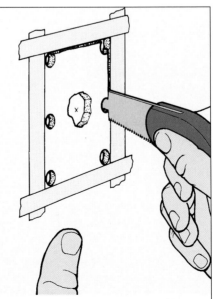

Make the cuts. Bore a series of holes in the plaster inside the guidelines. Then, with a keyhole or saber saw, cut out the opening.

4 Install the Box. Remove the masking tape and push the box into the opening, threading the wires into the box at the same time. Use the utility knife to enlarge the notches for the ears. When the box fits, screw the box through the ears to the lath. The box should be flush with the plaster.

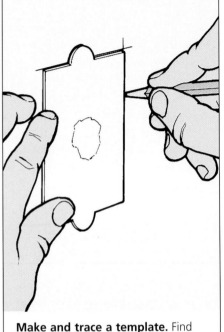

Make and trace a template. Find the center of a box template and mark the center on the lath. Mark the outline of the template on the wall.

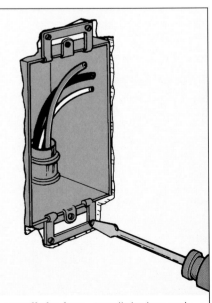

Install the box. Install the box and wires. You may have to trim plaster so the ears of the box fit. Screw the box to the lath flush with the wall.

Installing Boxes in Plaster and Metal Lath

To install a box in plaster laid on metal lath, first determine the box position by drilling test holes to find obstructions. Then make a template, and trace the template outline on the wall. Surround the outline with masking tape.

1 **Remove the Plaster**. With a ⅜-inch metal drill bit, punch holes in the four corners of the guideline and at the ear openings. Then, with a cold chisel and hammer, remove the plaster.

2 **Cut the Metal Lath**. Use a saber saw with a hacksaw metal-cutting blade to cut the metal lath. Or use a keyhole hacksaw.

Fit the box in the opening, making trimming cuts with the utility knife.

Insert wires into the box, push the box into the opening, and use side brackets to hold the box as described in "Installing Boxes in Drywall Without Stud Support," page 101.

Installing Boxes in Wood Paneling

Find the location, mark it, and bring the power wires to the area.

1 **Trace shape of the box.** Place the box on the wall and trace its shape.

2 **Bore Holes in Wall.** Trace the template on the wall. Then bore ½-inch holes at the corners and for the ear brackets. Cut the hole with a keyhole saw or saber saw.

3 **Insert the Box.** Install the wires in the box. Slip the box into the hole, loosening the ear screws if needed.

4 **Tighten the Clamps.** With a screwdriver, tighten the ear screws that hold the box in place.

Installing Boxes on and in Concrete and Concrete Block

Surface-mounting a box on placed concrete or on concrete (or cinder) block walls is easy to do. If you want

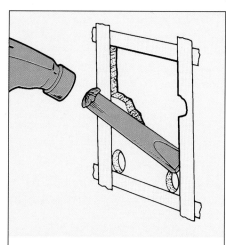

Remove the plaster. Punch holes with a drill within template guidelines. Then remove plaster with a chisel.

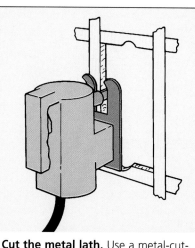

Cut the metal lath. Use a metal-cutting blade to remove the metal lath from the opening. Fit the box in the opening and make any trimming cuts.

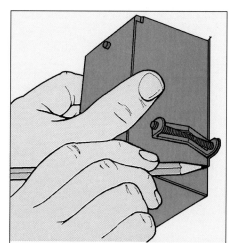

Trace shape of the box. Put the box against the wall where you want it and trace its shape onto the wall.

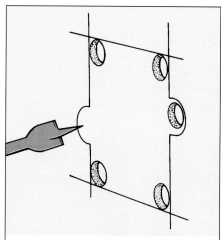

Bore holes in wall. Bore holes in the wood wall at the four corners and where ear brackets fit. Then use a saw to cut out the opening.

Insert the box. Fit the box into the opening and loosen the bracket screws if needed for adjustment. The box should fit with the wall.

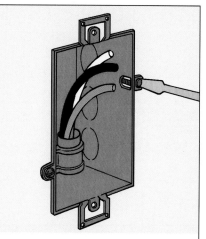

Tighten the clamps. Push the box into the wall and connect the wires to the box. Then tighten the ear screws to hold box in the wall.

to recess the box into a concrete block wall, the technique is simple, but the job is exacting.

In either type of installation, first locate the position of the box(es) and run the wires, probably in conduit, to the location.

Surface-Mounted Boxes. In an extremely damp location, use a water-proof outdoor electrical box. You can mount it directly on the concrete surface with concrete subfloor adhesive.

For a standard box, position the box on the surface and, with a nail or felt pen, make a mark through the screw holes in the back of the box on the surface, locating the position of the mounting screws.

With a carbide-tipped masonry bit, drill ¼-inch holes into the concrete at the marks. The holes should be deep enough to accept lead, plastic, or fiber masonry expansion plugs or anchors. Tap an anchor into each hole.

Place the box with the mounting holes over the anchors and drive in the mounting screws. The anchors expand against the sides of their holes so that the screws hold the box tightly against the concrete surface.

Run the wires into the box and make the necessary connections.

Flush-Mounted Boxes. Use a power drill with a masonry bit, and a cold chisel and hammer to open the block wall to recess both the wiring and the box.

You can use a star drill and hammer instead of the power outfit, but it is time-consuming to do so.

Make a cardboard template of the box and trace the outline of the template on the block wall surface, using a felt pen. Then outline the guidelines with masking tape.

With the pen, trace a channel on the surface where the wires will be

recessed, assuming that you can't fish the wires (cable) through the center holes in the blocks. The channel should be about 1 inch wide. Outline the marks with masking tape.

With the power drill and masonry bit, drill a series of holes within the guidelines. Make as many holes as you can. Then connect the holes with the cold chisel and hammer, cleaning out all concrete debris.

Fit the box and the cable into the recesses. You probably will have to do some trimming with the chisel for a good fit. Run the mounting screws into the box. Then insert the cable in the channel, mount the cable in the box, and put the box in the recess.

With a thick mixture of cement, fill the channel and recess. A small trowel or a putty knife works well. Use ready-to-mix mortar mix that's available at building material stores. Add water and stir.

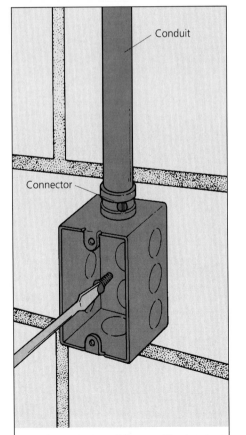

Surface-mounted boxes. The box is mounted with masonry expansion anchors. Drill holes, tap in anchors and drive screws into them.

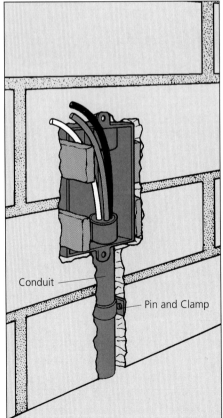

Recessed box in block. Use a drill and cold chisel to cut box and cable recesses. The front edges of recessed box are flush with block wall.

Filling in recesses. When box and cable are in place, fill all the openings around the cable and box with mortar mix tinted to blend with the wall.

When the mortar has set— at least three days or so—remove the mounting screws from the box. The purpose of the screws was to prevent mortar from entering the screw holes.

Working with Ceiling Boxes

To install a ceiling box when there is not access from an attic, you must work entirely from below. Wear goggles for safety.

There are two kinds of installations. An offset hanger bar fastened between joists lets you slide a box to any point across the width of the space, but you must open the ceiling enough to get at both joists. A stud secures the box to the bar. A box with a side flange can be screwed to the side of one joist, if the location is appropriate. This requires a smaller opening in the ceiling.

Box in Drywall Ceiling. Locate the joists in the ceiling and mark the location for the box. You will have to have a 10x16-inch opening in the drywall in order to screw the bar hanger to two joists. Cut along the location marks with a utility knife and break out the drywall.

Fish the power cable through the ceiling to the box site. Then mount the box on the bar hanger between the joists, wire the box, and patch the ceiling with a piece of matching drywall with a cutout for the box.

Access through Attic. If the attic is not finished, you can work from the attic to install a ceiling box. If the attic is rough floored, you can remove a section of the flooring and install the box. Either way, the box has to be mounted on a hanger or fastened to the face of a joist.

Drill a locating hole in the room ceiling. With an 18-inch drill extension and ⅛-inch bit, go through the hole and through the attic flooring. Stick a wire up through the hole.

In the attic, locate the wire and then cut through the rough flooring and remove enough so that you can insert and fasten the hanger or the box to the joists.

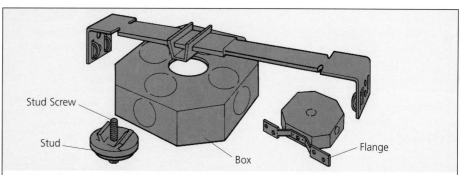

Ceiling boxes. For a drywall ceiling, a bar hanger allows the box to be positioned anywhere between two joists. Stud screws into the hanger through the box. A flange-type box can be screwed to the side of a joist when that is an appropriate position.

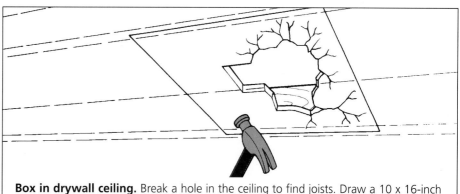

Box in drywall ceiling. Break a hole in the ceiling to find joists. Draw a 10 x 16-inch rectangle around the hole, edges overlapping two joists. Cut the rectangle with a knife or saw. Fish wires; then install hanger and box.

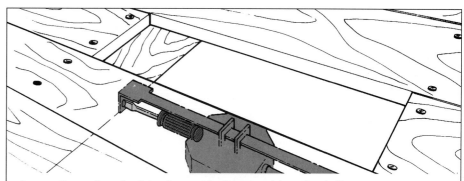

Access through attic. A bar hanger fits between joists. If attic flooring is rough, remove a section of flooring and work from above, saving lots of drywall patching on the ceiling below.

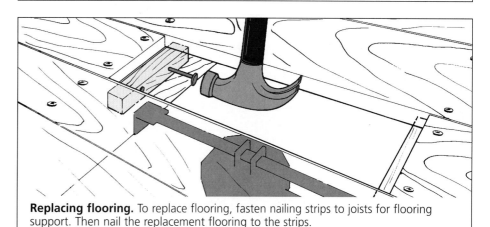

Replacing flooring. To replace flooring, fasten nailing strips to joists for flooring support. Then nail the replacement flooring to the strips.

Use the pilot hole in the ceiling to locate the box. Cut a hole in the ceiling for it. In the attic, connect the cable to the box and replace the flooring.

Installing Boxes in Drywall Ceilings

You'll need a keyhole saw, a drill bit to start the hole into the ceiling material, a tape measure, safety glasses, and the wiring materials. First, find the joists. See "Locating Studs," page 100.

1 Make the Initial Cut. After you locate the joists, cut an 8x8-inch-square opening in the drywall ceiling material.

2 Measure the Joist. Inside the hole you made, determine the exact distances to the joists. Note the measurements; transfer them to the face of the drywall. Add ¾ inch to this mark; this shows you where the joist centers are located.

3 Cut a Square Opening. With a square, mark a 17½-inch-square opening on the ceiling that splits the centers of the joists. Then, using a straightedge and a sharp utility knife, cut out the square.

4 Make a Patch. From a piece of drywall the same thickness as the ceiling material, cut a 17½-inch square patch to fill the opening. In this patch, locate the opening for the box and cut out the opening.

5 Install Box and Patch. Fasten the ceiling box on its hanger to the joists. Then position the box so it fits the hole in the patch. Test it. Then pull the new cable into the box; fit and nail patch in opening.

6 Patch the Patch. With joint tape, a taping knife, and drywall taping compound, seal the patch into the ceiling. Use at least three coats of compound, letting each dry. Sand smooth at the end.

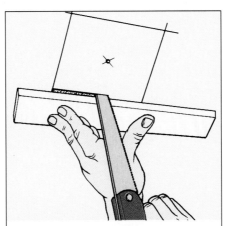

Make initial cut. Locate the joists where you want the box. Then cut a hole about 8 X 8 inches next to a joist or between two joists as a pilot hole.

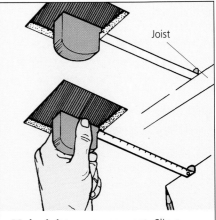

Make joist measurement. Slip a tape measure inside the pilot hole and measure the distance to the joists. Transfer measurements to the ceiling face.

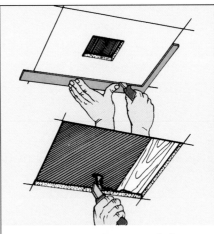

Cut square opening. Cut a hole 17½ inches square. The cut will be in the center of two joists. Trim the cut edges as square as possible.

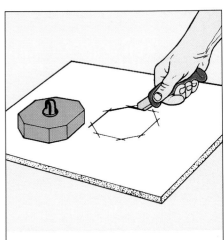

Make a patch. Make a patch to fit the hole in the ceiling. Then locate the box position in the patch. Cut a hole for it. Check sizes as you go.

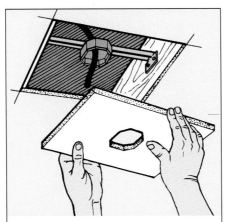

Install box and patch. After you position the box between joists on a hanger and nail the hanger to the joists, pull the cable into the box and fasten it. Test the patch for it.

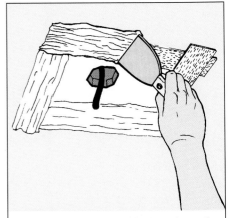

Patch the patch. Cover the edges of the patch with joint tape and taping compound. Use three coats of compound. Sand smooth. Paint to finish.

7
Wiring for Lamps

A bottle filled with scavenged sea-glass, a fabulous flea market find, or a favorite lamp that simply isn't working properly any more, all are candidates for wiring or rewiring.

The effort is small and the rewards are great. Here is a word of caution: make sure that you do not damage the integrity of any antique to be used as a lamp base by wiring it. For instance, you can drill a hole in a ginger jar to accept the electrical cord. However, you also can purchase kits for lamp making that enable you to wire objects without drilling into them. Some kits sit the socket on a cork that fits into the bottle. The lamp cord runs out and down the back of the lamp.

Basics of lamp wiring covered in this chapter include safety precautions and troubleshooting, employing an Under-writer's knot, wiring freestanding lamps, replacing a light socket and switch, replacing a lamp cord, and replacing a multisocket and switch. You'll also learn how to repair a fluorescent ballast and switch.

Trouble-shooting Incandescent Lamp Problems

Heat from bulbs in sockets eventually causes sockets to malfunction, requiring replacement. Plugs and cords get worn out. Switches also break and must be replaced. Here are symptoms and their probable causes:

If the bulb doesn't light:
■ The plug has been pulled from the wall outlet. Push the plug back into the outlet.

■ The bulb is loose and isn't making contact with the socket.

■ The small copper "tongue" inside the socket isn't making contact. Bend the tongue up so that it makes contact.

■ The bulb is burned out. Replace the bulb.

■ The line cord is damaged. Replace the line cord.

■ The switch is defective. Replace the switch.

If the bulb flickers:
■ The bulb is loose and barely makes contact with the socket. Tighten the bulb.

■ The small copper "tongue" inside the socket isn't making contact. Turn off the power to the circuit or unplug the lamp. Bend the tongue up so that it makes contact.

■ There is a loose wire at the socket terminal. Turn off the power to the circuit or unplug the lamp. Then secure the wire.

■ The switch is defective. Replace the switch.

If the lamp blows a fuse or trips the circuit breaker:
First, make sure there is not an over-load or short circuit at the main service panel.

■ There is a short in the line cord. Replace the line cord.

■ The plug is defective. Replace the plug.

■ The socket is defective. Replace the socket.

Spotting Symptoms

How can you tell if any of these problems apply to your case?

Usually, there are signs to let you know if a plug, switch, or line cord is faulty. A defective plug normally has visible damage, such as cracks in the plug housing or loose, broken, or bent prongs.

A bad switch usually feels loose as you turn it on and off, or the bulb may flicker as the switch is jiggled. A damaged line cord often looks frayed.

Checking for Broken Wires
Sometimes there is a broken wire within the line causing problems. You can test it, as explained below. Do not test it if the cord is frayed or a bare wire is exposed.

■ Plug the lamp into a wall outlet and turn on the lamp switch.

■ Flex the line cord back and forth over its entire length. If the bulb flickers, a wire in the cord is broken.

Flexing the cord opens and closes the two ends of the broken wire. When a faulty plug, switch, or line cord has been located, replace the bad part.

How to Solve Lighting Problems

This chapter tells you how to solve a wide range of lighting problems—from replacing a broken cord to repairing a switch to installing new lighting devices, such as dimmer switches, track lights, and fluorescent fixtures.

As in any electrical project, turn off the circuit to the project before you start work. In the case of a table lamp, be sure to unplug the lamp first.

Trouble-shooting Guide to Fluorescent Lights

For the most part, fluorescent fixtures are easy to repair. However, when the cause of the problem is not obvious, troubleshooting can be a hit-or-miss proposition. If you are unsure of the cause, replace one component after another until you find the one that's causing the trouble.

The chart at right lists possible fluorescent fixture failures and their causes and repairs. Causes are listed in the likely order of occurrence, and repairs are listed in the order in which they should be made.

Using Your Senses. Fluorescent troubles you can't see often can be heard and smelled. Here are some examples that may be helpful in finding the problem:

Very Loud Humming. You won't mistake it, although a low hum is normal. Suspect loose wires first, then the ballast, which may be burning out. Or it may be the wrong ballast for the fixture.

Awful Smell. Tubes on their way to permanent darkness can emit an acrid odor. So can ballasts. The smell may persist for several days before the component gives out completely.

No Light or the Bulb Flickers. The fixture seems to work except on certain days when the room is cold. A low temperature—sometimes down to 50 degrees F—can prevent gases in the tube from lighting. A low temperature sometimes can cause the light to flicker until it warms up. Flickering can also be caused by bent and/or corroded tube pins.

No Light. Don't be too quick to blame the fixture. Check the main service panel for a blown fuse or for a circuit breaker that has tripped.

Fluorescent Fixture Trouble-shooting

Type of Failure	Causes	Repairs
Tube fails to light	1. Fuse has blown or circuit breaker has tripped	1. Replace fuse or reset circuit breaker. If problem recurs, check house wiring.
	2. Tube not seated correctly in slots	2. If tube is straight, rotate off and reseat into sockets. If tube is circular, remove and reinstall; all pins should fully engage socket.
	3. Defective tube	3. If starter is independent of ballast, replace starter. If starter is part of ballast replace the tube before you replace the ballast.
	4. Defective tube	4. Replace tube with one of correct wattage, which is marked on old tube. If marking is unclear, check voltage marked on ballast.
	5. Defective ballast or starter in ballast	5. Replace the ballast. Check ballast connections.
Light flickers and swirls around in tube	1. New tube	1. Normal in new tubes; should clear in a short time.
	2. Defective starter or ballast	2. Replace starter if it is independent of ballast; if problem remains, replace ballast.
Light blinks on and off	1. Low room temperature (below 50°F)	1. To eliminate, install a low-temperature starter and ballast or replace entire unit with one designed for low temperature locations.
	2. Tube not seated properly	2. If tube is straight, reseat securely in sockets. If tube is circular, remove and reinstall. All pins must fully engage socket.
	3. Tube pins bent	3. Examine the tube pins. If bent, straighten with long-nosed pliers. Sand pins lightly; wipe away foreign matter. Insert pins securely into sockets.
	4. Sockets deformed or dirty	4. Turn off circuit. Socket contacts of a long fixture should lean inward. If deformed, try repairing them by bending with long-nosed pliers. Sand contacts lightly; blow foreign matter from sockets with an ear syringe.
	5. Loose connections	5. Turn off circuit; remove fixture cover. Remove wire nuts and check all wire splices. Reinstall wire nuts securely.
	6. Defective tube	6. Replace tube.
	7. Defective ballast	7. Replace ballast.
Ends of tube light; center does not glow	1. Defective starter	1. Replace starter.
Tube seems to burn out rapidly	1. Fixture turned on and off at frequent intervals	1. Avoid turning fixture on and off so frequently.
	2. Incorrect ballast	2. If short tube life occurs after replacing ballast, ballast may be incorrect type for the fixture. Check ballast and fixture types. An electrical parts dealer can help you.
	3. Incorrect ballast wiring	3. Turn off circuit. Remove fixture cover and trace wire connections.
	4. Mating tube failure	4. Replace a burned-out tube immediately, especially in some rapid-start fixtures holding two or more tubes.
	5. Defective starter or ballast	5. Replace starter; if condition continues, replace ballast.
Discoloration at tube ends	1. Normal condition	1. Brown or gray bands about two inches from tube ends are normal.
	2. Worn out tube	2. Gradually enlarging black bands at tube ends indicate tube is going bad. Replace tube.
	3. Defective starter or ballast	3. If black bands develop on new tube, replace starter; if condition continues, replace ballast.
Humming	1. Normal	1. Some humming is normal.
	2. Loose ballast wires	2. Loose wires can cause humming. Turn off circuit. Remove wire nuts and check connections. Secure wire nuts.
	3. Incorrect ballast	3. If humming started after installing ballast, it may not match the fixture type. Check ballast and fixture types.

Fluorescent fixture trouble-shooting. Match the fluorescent fixture problem you're having with the trouble-shooting chart above. Tubes and starters usually go bad before ballasts and other parts of the fixture.

Rewiring Freestanding Lamps

Table lamps, pole lamps, pedestal lamps, and others that are freestanding and individually wired, are all assembled in almost the same way: a cord running up through a base is connected to a socket.

Heat from the bulb in the socket eventually causes the socket to malfunction, requiring replacement. Wear and tear on the plug end of the cord requires replacement of the plug and cord. Switches also wear out and must be replaced. The procedures for replacing individual sockets, switches, and plugs are explained in this chapter.

The procedures for rewiring a lamp from start to finish are shown here and on the following pages.

First, unplug the lamp and set up the rewiring project on a workbench or table surface with tools and materials handy. Materials that you will need include cord, sockets, switches, glue, and plastic electrician's tape. Tools include a screwdriver, pliers, wire strippers, and a sharp utility knife, pocketknife, or paring knife.

Remove Harp Assembly. Remove the lamp shade, which is held by a decorative nut called a finial either at the top of the shade or where the shade joins the body of the lamp. If the shade is supported by a harp, slide up the small finger nuts at the base of the harp bracket with one hand and lift off the harp with the other.

Remove Base Covering. Most table lamps have a felt pad covering the bottom of the lamp. The covering usually is glued to the bottom of the lamp. Remove this covering by first breaking the glue seal with the blade of a utility or pocket knife, and then peel back the covering so you have access to the cord and/or switch in the base of the lamp.

Most pole and pedestal lamps don't have this covering; the cord runs directly into the lamp housing.

If the lamp has a nut that holds the lamp cord secure in the bottom of the lamp, remove it. This is a flat nut and washer assembly, and the nut turns counterclockwise to loosen.

Some pole lamps have a cord locking nut, which is removed the same way. However, in other pole lamps, the cord may be simply threaded into the housing. Most pole lamps have a cord locking nut just under the shade. Remove this nut to remove the shade and loosen the cord when you want to replace the socket/switch.

Removing Wires from Single Sockets. Lamp sockets have a thin brass housing. To remove the outer shell, squeeze in on the sides, just above the base cap. (Pry with a thin blade if necessary.) Pull up to expose a cardboard insulating sleeve. Remove that, loosen the terminal screws, and unhook the wires. The copper lamp cord wire always goes to the brass socket terminal, or to a switch lead (see page 110). The silver wire goes to the silver terminal.

Lamps with Multiple Sockets. The wires are connected to the sockets the very same way as on single sockets. However, to replace the cord, you will

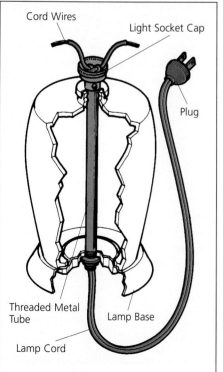

Anatomy of table lamp. A cord runs through the base of a lamp, sometimes completely through a metal tube, and attaches to socket terminals.

Cord Wires
Light Socket Cap
Plug
Threaded Metal Tube
Lamp Base
Lamp Cord

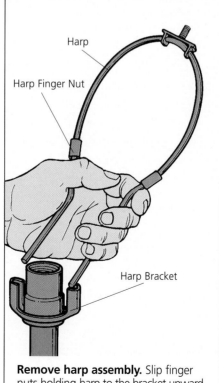

Remove harp assembly. Slip finger nuts holding harp to the bracket upward. Then squeeze the harp in your fingers and lift it out of the harp bracket.

Harp
Harp Finger Nut
Harp Bracket

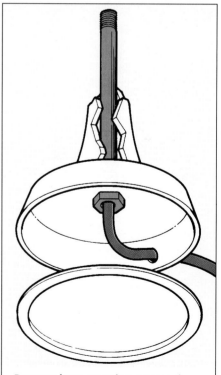

Remove base covering. Loosen the edge of the felt pad with a knife and then peel back the pad. This will reveal the locking nut securing the tube.

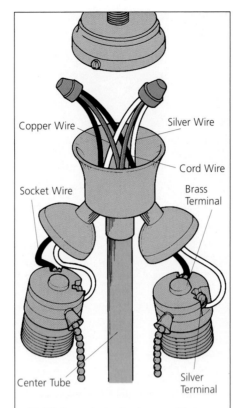

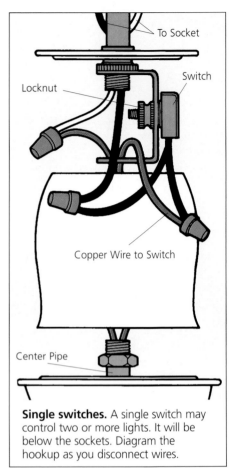

Single-socket wiring. Remove the brass socket housing from the cap to expose socket terminals. Then remove wires by loosening terminals.

Multiple sockets. For lamps with two or more sockets, remove brass housing and wires from terminals. Then remove switch wires.

Single switches. A single switch may control two or more lights. It will be below the sockets. Diagram the hookup as you disconnect wires.

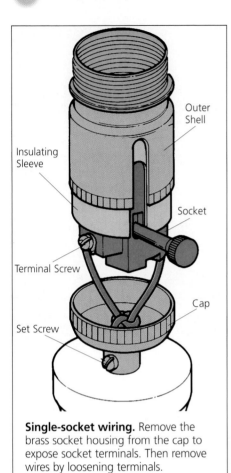

Base switches. If a lamp has a base switch, disconnect the wires here and at the socket(s). Note the wiring plan for hookup later on.

also have to disconnect the wiring connections in a storage housing near the sockets. The connections are spliced with wire connectors; remove these connectors after you note which wires are connected to each other. You can identify them by the color of the insulation.

Sockets with Single Switches. The lights may not be controlled by switches on the sockets. Instead, a single switch controls the lights.

In order to remove the sockets and the cord, you will have to disassemble the connections, which are made with wire connectors. Make a careful diagram of how the wires are joined.

Lamps with Base Switches. If the lamp has a base switch that controls the light sockets, the wiring connections will be located in the base. Make a wiring diagram.

On pole lamps, the lights may be controlled at the socket. Or a single switch may turn on all lights at the same time. In this case, you will have to disconnect the switch assembly in order to remove the cord. Note the connection, which usually is black wires connected to the switch with the white wires bypassing it.

Soldered Connections. When you take a lamp apart you may find solder connections between wires and brackets

or tabs. The best way to disconnect these is to heat the solder, not the wire, with a soldering gun until you can pull the wire free.

When you reassemble the connection, you may be able to reheat the solder the same way and reuse it. If not, heat the older solder, scrape it off, and then use rosin core solder (noncorrosive) for new connections.

Removing the Cord. Temporarily attach the new cord to the old cord at the socket connection. Strip a bit of insulation from the new cord to make a tight joint, and then wrap the joint with a couple of layers of electrician's tape so the connection won't pull apart.

Untie any knots or loosen any setscrews in or around the cord on its route through the lamp.

Then pull the old cord out of the lamp base and thread the new cord into place. Disconnect the old cord and discard it.

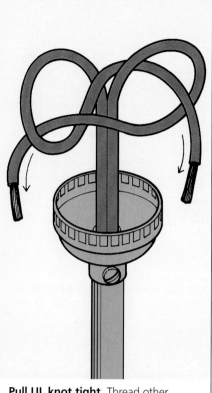

Soldered connections. Heat the solder, not the wire, until it melts and pull the wire out. To reassemble, use noncorrosive solder.

Underwriters' knot. Split the wire or divide the wires and make two fairly large loops. Thread the end of one wire through the opposite loop.

Pull UL knot tight. Thread other wire through the opposite loop, forming a loose knot. Pull wire ends apart, making a tight knot.

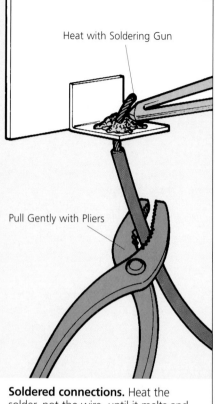

Labels: Brass-Plated Upper Section; Cardboard Insulation; Plastic Switch and Socket Base; Zip Cord; Brass-Plated Base

Socket connections. Hook bare wire ends around terminals clockwise and tighten screws firmly. Reassemble socket.

Underwriters' Knot. Most lamps are wired with zip cord, which has a thin section between the two insulated wires so it splits down the middle. At the socket end, split the cord and tie an Underwriters' knot in it, leaving approximately 3 inches of loose wire at the end of the knot. Make a loop in each wire and thread the end of each wire through the opposite loop. Pull the knot tight. The knot prevents the wire from pulling loose from terminals in the socket.

Socket Connections. Strip about ¾ inch of insulation from each wire. With your fingers, twist the stranded wire as tightly as possible. Then wrap the bare wire around the socket terminals in the direction the terminal screws turn down—clockwise.

When you replace wire connectors, twist the wires together as tightly as you can, insert the wires into the base of the wire connector, and twist the wire connector. Then wrap the nut and wires with a couple of layers of electrician's tape.

Replacing a Light Socket and Switch

This project applies to a brass lamp socket that has a rotating, push-button, or chain switch attached to the socket. Do not attempt to repair the switch or socket; replace it with a new one.

Be sure to disconnect the light from the power source before your start working on the socket.

1 Remove the Harp. The lamp-shade is attached to the lamp with a frame, called a harp, that fits into a bracket below the socket. Slide up two finger nuts on the harp as you squeeze the harp.

2 Remove the Socket Housing. To remove the metal housing from the socket, squeeze in on the sides of the upper sleeve just above the base cap and work it upward, out of the cap. Slip both the brass and cardboard sleeves off to expose the socket and terminal screws.

Labels on first image: Heat with Soldering Gun; Pull Gently with Pliers

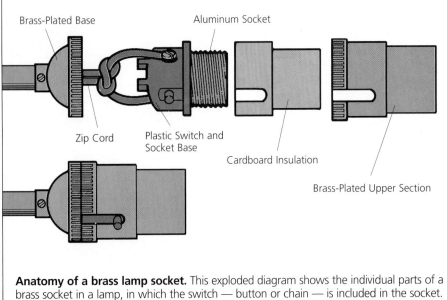

Brass-Plated Base

Aluminum Socket

Zip Cord

Plastic Switch and Socket Base

Cardboard Insulation

Brass-Plated Upper Section

Anatomy of a brass lamp socket. This exploded diagram shows the individual parts of a brass socket in a lamp, in which the switch — button or chain — is included in the socket. Don't try to repair a defective socket switch or the socket. Replace it with a new socket.

Harp Nut

Remove the harp. To remove the harp, pull up on the small finger nuts while you squeeze the harp lightly. Lift the harp from bracket.

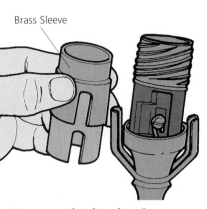

Brass Sleeve

Remove socket housing. Squeeze the brass sleeve just above the base cap and slip it off along with the insulator inside.

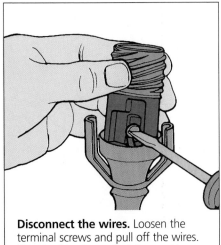

Disconnect the wires. Loosen the terminal screws and pull off the wires. If inspection shows that the cord is damaged, replace the cord.

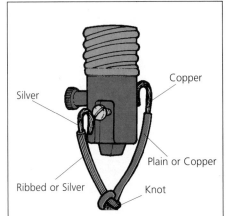

Silver

Copper

Ribbed or Silver

Plain or Copper

Knot

Wire the new socket. Attach the copper wire to the brass terminal and the silver wire to the silver terminal. Reassemble socket.

3 Disconnect the Wires. Turn the terminal screws counterclockwise to loosen the wires connected to the screws. At this point, check the cord. If it is damaged, it should be replaced. See "Replacing a Lamp Cord," page 113.

4 Wire the New Socket. Twist the stranded wire as tightly as you can between your fingers. Then connect the hot copper wire to the brass terminal and the silver wire to the silver terminal. The wires should fit under the terminal screws. If not, disconnect the wires, twist them tight once again, and reconnect them to the terminals.

Place the cardboard insulation over the socket and install the brass-plated upper section. Tighten the screw holding the cord in the socket, if the socket has one. Replace the harp.

Replacing a Lamp Plug

Most lamps are wired with zip cord. If the plug is damaged replace it with a quick-connect plug as described here. As the name suggests, these plugs are very easy to connect. They have spikes that pierce the cord insulation, eliminating screw terminals.

1 Remove the Old Plug. With a knife, cut the cord in back of the plug you're replacing. Replace a worn or damaged cord.

2 Disassemble the Plug. Squeeze the prongs together and pull the plug cover from the plug casing. Don't strip or split the end of the cord. Thread the cord through the hole at the top of the cover.

3 Assemble the Plug. Spread the plug's prongs and insert the cord in the core opening. Squeeze the prongs together so that the spikes inside the core pierce the cord. Push the core into the cover.

Polarized Plugs. If the cord is polarized, the insulation over half of it will be ridged. Alternately, if the insulation is clear, the wire on one side will be

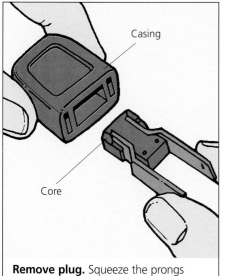

Remove plug. Squeeze the prongs together and pull the plug from the casing.

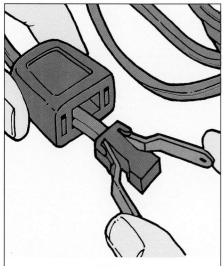

Insert new cord. Spread the prongs and insert the cord in the core opening.

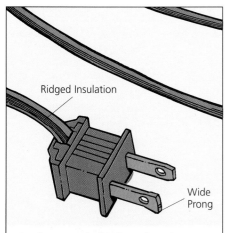

Replace a polarized cord. Make sure that the ridged or silver wire lines up with the wider prong on the plug.

copper and the other will be silver. Use a polarized plug with polarized cord. Make sure that the ridged or silver wire lines up with the wider prong on the plug.

Replacing a Lamp Cord

If you notice that the cord on a lamp is damaged (with or without a damaged switch or socket), replace it.

Removing the Cord. The simple procedure for removing the cord is described and illustrated here:

1. Unplug the lamp from the power source.

2. Remove the harp from the base of the socket. See "Replacing a Light Socket and Switch," page 111.

3. Remove the brass shell and insulation jacket from the socket.

4. Unscrew the terminals holding the wires. Then loosen any screws holding the wire in the cap of the socket. Untie the knot at the cap, if there is one.

Rewiring the Lamp. With electrician's tape, join the new wire with the old wire at the socket connection. Make a tight joint.

Then carefully pull the old cord out of the lamp and the new cord into the lamp at the same time. When the new cord appears, unwrap the tape. It's a good idea to install a new plug on the new wire. See "Replacing a Lamp Plug," page 112. Then rewire the brass socket as described in "Replacing a Light Socket and Switch," page 111.

Cord with Polarized Plug. If your home is equipped with polarized outlets, replace the lamp cord with a polarized plug and cord set. Buy at least one foot more cord than the total you need. The UL-listed polarized cord should be the same size as the cord already in use: No. 18 gauge wire.

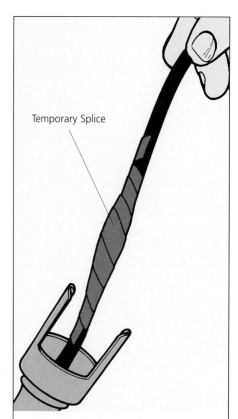

Rewiring the lamp. Splice the new wire to the old wire and pull both through the lamp at the same time after wire is unscrewed.

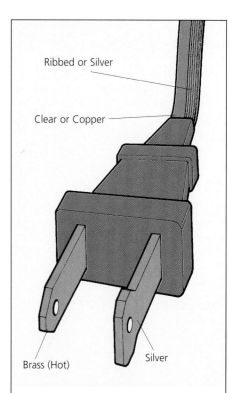

Cord with polarized plug. The large prong of a polarized plug goes to the silver wire; the small prong goes to the hot copper wire. Plug and wire are a unit.

Replacing Multi-socket Lamp Switches

Two-socket lamps usually have one on-off switch that controls both sockets. Three-socket lamps may have individual switches or a single on-off switch.

Soldered Two-Socket. The sockets are molded together. Wire connections run internally between the sockets. The switch turns both sockets on or off at the same time. If one socket won't light, undo the wire connectors holding the switch and the power wires together. Detach the switch wires from the power wires. Connect the new switch.

Separate Sockets. In this two-socket lamp, the sockets are wired separately and can be replaced individually. The switch turns both bulbs on or off at the same time. The wiring arrangement is more complex, because jumper wires connect sockets. With the exception of the jumpers, the replacement is the same as above.

Sockets with Switches. Three-socket lamps with individual switches are repaired this way: Remove the wires from the socket's terminal screws, withdraw the old socket, and reattach the wires to the terminal screws of the new socket. Since three sockets receive current through one power cord, there are jumper wires from the line cord to the terminal screws of each socket.

One-Switch Sockets. A three-socket lamp having one four-way switch is shown at right. The first position turns on socket No. 1 only; the second position turns on sockets No. 2 and 3. The third position turns on all sockets. A black wire connects the switch to the line cord, a black wire connects the switch to socket No. 3, and a black wire connects the switch to socket No. 1. Remove the switch by disconnecting wire connectors. Then reconnect them to new switch wires.

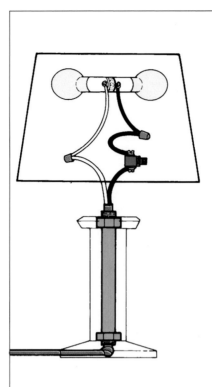

Soldered two-socket. To replace a soldered double socket, remove wire nuts and release splices. Rewire as shown, following color code.

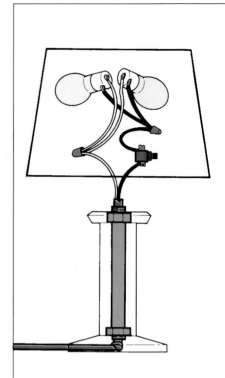

Separate sockets. If lights work independently, replace either socket separately. Release wire nuts; install the new socket or switch.

Sockets with switches. If each socket has its own switch, each is replaced separately. Just release wire from nuts and rewire with nuts.

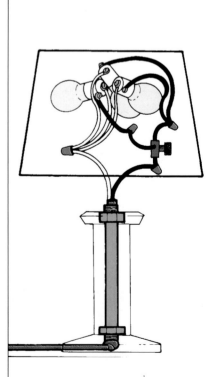

One-switch sockets. To replace single-switch on a multisocket fixture, attach a white wire to each socket; then attach hot wire to each.

All About Fluorescent Fixtures

The three main parts of a fluorescent fixture are the fluorescent tube, which may be straight or circular, the starter, and the ballast. Defects in these components cause most fluorescent fixture problems.

The Tube. A fluorescent tube produces light in this way: Inside a tube, the electric current jumps or arcs from a cathode at one end of the tube to an anode at the other end. The tube is filled with mercury and argon gases. As the arc passes through the gases, it causes them to emit invisible ultraviolet light. To make the light visible, the inside of the tube is coated with phosphor powder that glows when hit by ultraviolet light.

The Starter. The starter is a switch that closes when activated by electric current. After a momentary delay, the starter allows current to energize gases in the tube. There are two types of starters: replaceable ones, which are about ¾ inch in diameter with two contacts protruding from one end. The other is a rapid-start fixture. The starter is built into the ballast and can't be replaced independently of the ballast.

The Ballast. The ballast is a box-like component usually about 6 to 7 inches long. It is a kind of governor that holds electric current to the level required to provide proper light operation. There are two types of ballasts. Choke ballasts limit the amount of current flowing through the tube. Fixtures that hold long fluorescent tubes have thermal-protected ballasts that incorporate transformers and choke coils. When the light is turned on, a transformer steps up the voltage to deliver a momentarily high surge of electricity to get the tube to glow.

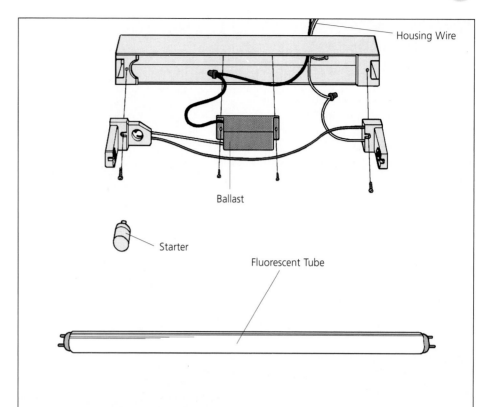

Standard straight-tube fluorescent fixture. The wiring for a separate ballast and replaceable starter is illustrated. The starter fits into a contact seat in the fixture housing.

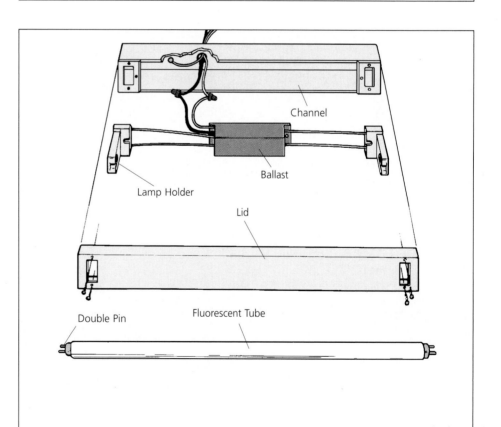

Rapid-start fixture. This fluorescent fixture has a rapid-start ballast and starter in one unit.

Replacing a Fluorescent Ballast

Turn off the circuit breaker or remove the fuse that supplies power to the circuit. Then remove the tube(s), and take off the cover. Jot down the number codes on the old ballast and take them to the store with you, just to make sure you buy the right ballast replacement.

1 Disconnect the Wires. Remove the wire connectors or loosen the terminal screws to disconnect the ballast wires. Notice that ballast wires are color-coded. A ballast wire of a given color is always connected to the fixture wire of the same color.

A thermally protected ballast must be connected in the same way. If the complexities of the wires confuse you, make a simple color-coded diagram before you disconnect any wires.

2 Remove the Ballast. The ballast you are removing is heavier than you might think. Be careful. Have a helper hold the ballast while you remove the fasteners that attach it to the fixture.

Note carefully the alignment of the ballast in the fixture and then take it down.

3 Connect the New Ballast. Again with a helper holding the new ballast, line up the ballast so that it is in the same position as the old ballast was. Screw the new ballast to the fixture.

Match the color codes of the wires and twist these wires together with your fingers or pliers. Then thread the connected wires into wire connectors. Wrap the wire connectors with a couple of layers of plastic electrician's tape.

As a final step, before you replace the cover, turn on the power and test the light.

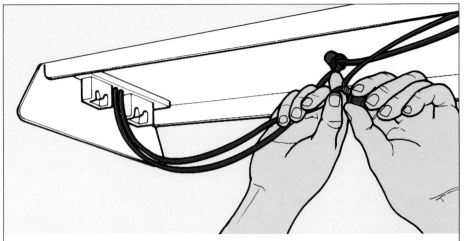

Disconnect the wires. When replacing a ballast unit, first make a color-coded diagram of the wiring. Then remove the wire nuts from all connections and disconnect the splices. Note color-coding of wires and numbers on ballast for purchasing purposes.

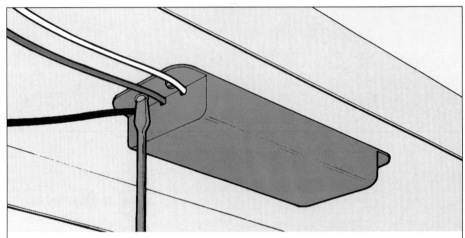

Remove the ballast. Loosen the screws that hold the ballast in the fixture. Have a helper hold the heavy ballast while you do this. Then remove the ballast from the fixture, noting its exact position.

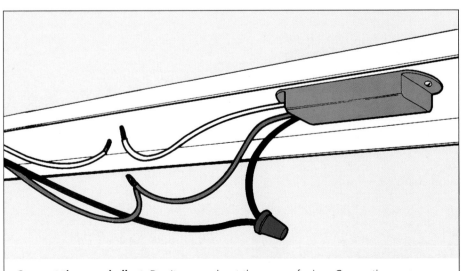

Connect the new ballast. Don't worry about the maze of wires. Connections are made by matching colors, splicing wires, and securing splices with wire nuts wrapped with plastic electrician's tape.

Installing Fluorescent Fixtures

To replace a fluorescent fixture, first turn off the power to the circuit and remove the old fixture from the ceiling. To add a new fixture, install a ceiling box; run in the cable. The techniques are explained in "Working with Electrical Boxes," page 96.

Circular Fixtures. In the center of the ceiling box, add a threaded stud, if one is not present. The fixture hangs on this stud. Add a reducing nipple to the stud. Have a helper hold the fixture while you connect the power wires: black to black, white to white. Wire nut the splices and wrap them with electrician's tape.

Push the wires into the box, thread the nipple through the hole in the center of the fixture, and secure the fixture with a cap nut.

One-Tube Fixtures. You will need a hickey and nipple if the box has a stud. If not, you can attach the fixture to a nipple and strap screwed to the ears in the box.

First splice the fixture wires to the house wires, put a wire connector on the splices, and wrap the splices with plastic electrician's tape. Then attach the fixture to the ceiling box with the nipple, a washer, and a locknut.

Have a helper hold the fixture while you assemble and fasten it to the ceiling box. When the fixture is stable, drive a couple of sheet-metal screws through the fixture housing into the ceiling at each end.

Large Fixtures. Fixtures with more than two tubes usually have a center cutout that is used when hanging the fixture from an octagonal box. The fixture uses a stud, hickey, nipple, and a mounting strap inside the housing. The assembly is held with a locknut. Connect the wiring with wire nuts. Then push the wires into the box and secure the fixture.

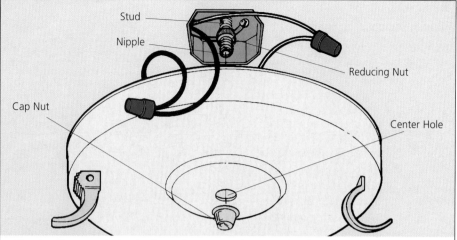

Circular fixtures. A circular fixture is connected to a stud and nipple inside the ceiling box. Complete the wiring first with wire nuts, then hang the fixture with a cap nut on nipple. Install the tube.

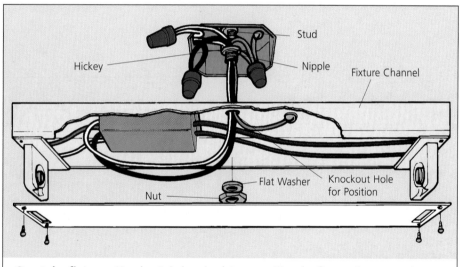

One-tube fixtures. Knockouts in housing let you position the fixture almost anywhere over the box. Punch out knockout. Connect wiring. Fasten to ceiling. Add screws through housing at ends to support fixture.

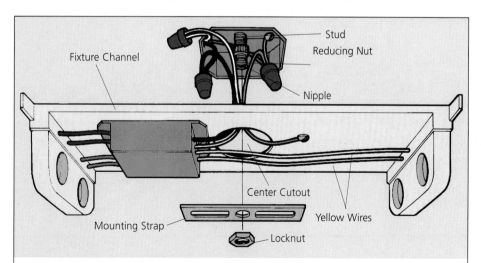

Large fixtures. A trap inside the fixture helps support its weight. The assembly order is: stud, reducing nut, nipple, fixture, strap, and locknut tightener. A cover plate slips into channels along the sides of the fixture.

Replacing Defective Fluorescent Switches

Most fluorescent lights are wired integrally with the housing wiring and are controlled by wall switches. Some fixtures have built-in switches that can fail. Here's how to replace them:

Pull-Chain Replacement. With pliers, loosen and remove the knurled nut and locknut that hold the switch in the fixture housing. Disconnect the switch wires. If they can't be disconnected, cut them, leaving a couple of inches for reconnection.

Lift out the entire switch. Make wiring connections with wire nuts. Tape the nuts, then set the new switch in place. Secure it with locknuts.

Toggle Switches. The technique is the same as for chain switches, except that power wire terminal screws are attached to the switch. Remove the wires, install a new switch, and rewire it.

Replacing a Push Switch

1 **Remove the Switch.** With a wrench or pliers, remove the nut holding the switch in the housing. Then slip the switch out of its socket.

2 **Disconnect the Switch.** When the push switch has been loosened and removed, disconnect the wire nuts and break the splice.

3 **Reconnect the Switch.** Install the new switch, connecting the electrical wires with wire nuts. Wrap the wire nuts with a couple of turns of plastic electrician's tape. Then set the switch in the housing and locknut it tight to the housing.

Flickering Problems. If a tube has the flickers, remove it. Straighten bent pins with pliers. Then burnish the pins lightly with fine-grit abrasive or steel wool.

Pull-chain replacement. To replace a pull-chain switch, remove the knurled nut and locknut. Break the splices. Put in the new switch and reconnect the splices.

Toggle switches. To replace a toggle switch, release the locknuts on the old switch. Attach wires to the terminal screws of the replacement switch.

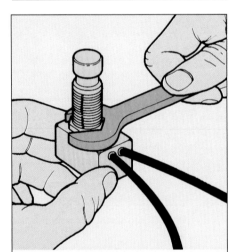

Remove the switch. At the fixture housing, remove the locknut holding the defective switch in place. Then slip the switch out of its socket.

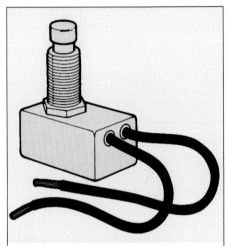

Disconnect the switch. Break the splice by removing the wire nuts. Note the wiring pattern: it usually involves two wires, but it could have three.

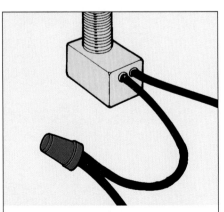

Reconnect the switch. Install the new switch with the same wiring pattern as the old one. Twist the wire nuts tightly over the splices and wrap with tape.

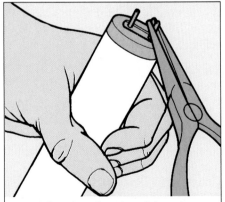

Straightening the pins. If the tube flickers on and off, the pins, not the switch, may be the trouble. Straighten the pins and then polish them with abrasive.

8

Wiring for Light Fixtures

If you are planning to install fixtures where none existed before, you'll need to extend existing circuits or add new ones. In the first part of this chapter you'll find specific instructions for mapping your circuits, snaking wires through your walls and ceilings, and installing surface wiring for new fixtures and connecting your new fixtures to existing and new circuits.

If you are lucky, you already have fixtures in the places you want them and you are just looking to update and/or upgrade them.

In the second part of this chapter you'll learn how to eliminate pull-chain lights, hang new fixtures including a new chandelier or ceiling fan, and install track lighting and fluorescent overhead lights.

If you are simply changing lighting fixtures, you won't need a permit from your local building department. But before embarking on any projects

that involve new wiring, check with your local building inspector to ascertain whether you need a permit for the work you intend to do, and what work, if any, must be performed by a qualified electrician. *Undertake no work until your are sure that all circuits are turned off.*

Mapping Electrical Circuits

If your project calls for installing new wiring, the first thing you'll need to do is map out the wiring circuits you already have. You'll need this information to determine if you can add to an existing circuit or if you need to add a new circuit.

Work with a helper. One person works at the main service panel; the other person tests switches, outlets, and appliances.

1 Make the Working Sketch. Draw a floor plan of each room.

Mark every receptacle, switch, and light fixture. Sketch in heavy equipment that is connected to the service panel. If this equipment has its own separate circuit, so note it.

2 Number the Circuits. At the main service panel, number each circuit breaker or fuse with a stick-on or glue-backed label.

3 Set up the Test. Work on one room at a time. Turn on all lights and appliances in that room. Plug in any lamps. If the room has a double receptacle, plug a light into each receptacle. Do not turn on heavy equipment.

4 Record the Circuit. The person at the main service panel now turns off the first breaker or fuse. On the floor plan, the helper records the number of the circuit or fuse next to each affected switch, light fixture, and receptacle.

5 Identify Other Circuits. Turn on the first circuit breaker or fuse

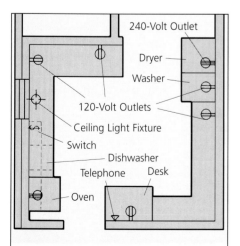

Working sketch. On graph paper, make a plan of each room, drawing in the electrical components. Use your sketch to compute available watts.

Number the circuits. At the main service panel, number each breaker or fuse. When a circuit malfunctions, you'll know the faulty circuit.

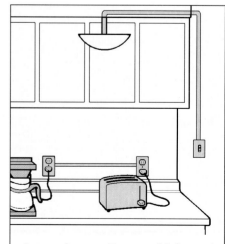

Set up the test. Turn on all lights and appliances in the room being tested. Do not include heavy equipment in this test.

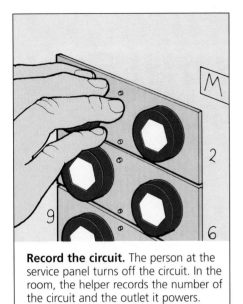

Record the circuit. The person at the service panel turns off the circuit. In the room, the helper records the number of the circuit and the outlet it powers.

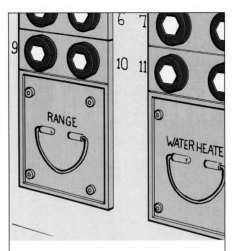

Identify other circuits. The circuit is reactivated; the next one is turned off. Continue until each switch, light, and outlet has been correctly labeled.

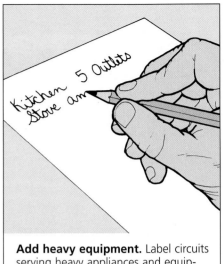

Add heavy equipment. Label circuits serving heavy appliances and equipment in all rooms. Mapping shows where power is available.

and turn off the next one. Continue the recording procedure until every switch, light fixture, and receptacle in the room has been labeled with its circuit number. Do this in every room.

6 Add Heavy Equipment. When the circuits controlling all lights, switches, and receptacles have been identified, identify and label the circuits serving the heavy appliances.

Pulling Wires Through Walls

Stringing wire and cable through existing walls and ceilings is akin to fishing in a muddy creek: you can't see where the line is going, and you have to have lots and lots of patience. While fishing wire and cable through walls and ceilings is time-consuming, and sometimes a bit frustrating, it doesn't require any special skills or expensive tools. In this chapter, we'll show you some tricks of the trade to make the job easier.

Anatomy of a Wall. Whether your walls are covered with drywall or plaster, the framing inside almost always consists of stud construction.

The studs are the vertical wood members, most often 2 X 4s spaced 16 inches from the center of one stud to the center of the next. All wall materials are fastened to studs. The best electrical installations are those in

which junction boxes are mounted on the side of a stud, although this is not required and may not be possible.

The joists are the horizontal wood members, again usually spaced 16 inches on center, in ceilings and floors. Ceiling materials and flooring are nailed to joists.

In new construction, it's easy to run cable either across or parallel to studs and joists. When running parallel, the cable is attached to the side of joists, when running across, the cable runs through holes drilled through the joists. When working with existing construction, however, running cable across

joists or studs means tearing up a lot of wall and ceiling. Usually, you can avoid this by taking the long way around.

From Top or Bottom. If you have access to walls from a basement or attic, you can get power into walls and ceilings by fishing the cable down or up instead of across.

Take time at the beginning to examine and study the different routes that might be open for the cable. Then make a rough sketch or map of the route the cable will take. A little work early on can save you plenty of time and money later.

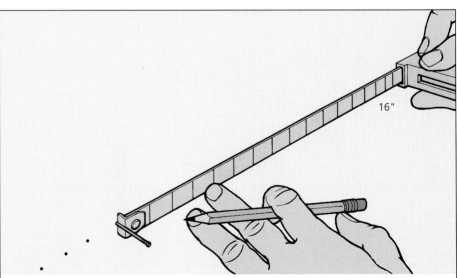

Locating framing. A sure way to find framing members is to start at a corner and measure out 16 in. Then drive a small finishing nail through the wall covering until you find the framing member. Mark this spot and measure out 16 in. for other framing locations.

Opening Walls and Ceilings

Usually the first step in running cable is to open a wall or ceiling where the switch, outlet, or junction box will be located. Then you route or fish the wire or cable to this point.

In Drywall. Cut openings in drywall with a keyhole saw or portable electric saber saw with a drywall blade.

Trace the outline of the junction box onto the drywall. Score the outline with a utility knife, making several passes. Drill holes in the corners of the outline so you can insert the saw. Make the cut on all four sides and either remove the scrap or knock it back between the framing members.

In Plastered Wood Lath. Trace the outline of the junction box onto the wall. Score the outline with a utility knife, making several passes until the knife hits the lath. Then carefully knock the plaster loose by tapping it gently with a hammer. You may not be able to score some very hard types of plaster. In this case, remove the plaster within the outline with a cold chisel. Finally, cut the lath with a key-hole saw or saber saw after drilling a hole to start the blade.

Through Metal Lath. Outline the opening and chisel out the plaster. Use a mini-hacksaw or a hacksaw blade in a saber saw.

Through Wood Paneling. Outline the opening, drill a series of holes along the outline, and then connect the holes with a keyhole saw or saber saw.

In Hollow Block. Put on gloves and safety glasses. Outline the opening and drill holes inside the outline using a masonry bit in a portable electric drill or a star drill and baby sledge hammer. Clean out waste with a cold chisel and sledge.

On Solid Masonry. You can't open this material. The wiring and boxes must be surface-mounted on the material. Drill holes for masonry anchors and insert the anchors.

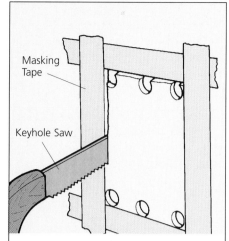

In drywall. Outline the opening, using the box as a template. Mask these lines. Drill holes to start the saw, and connect the holes.

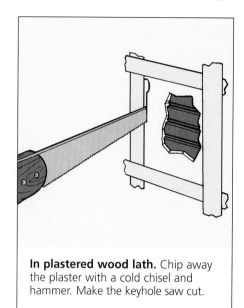

In plastered wood lath. Chip away the plaster with a cold chisel and hammer. Make the keyhole saw cut.

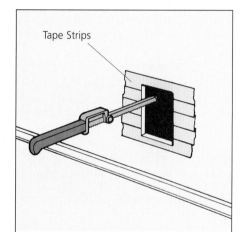

Through metal lath. Cover the area with strips of tape; mark the hole. Open it with a chisel and hammer, cut the metal lath with a hacksaw.

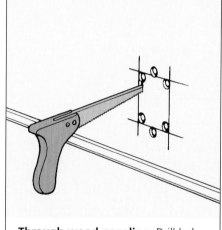

Through wood paneling. Drill holes at the corners of the outline marks and for the box ears. Then connect the holes with a saw cut.

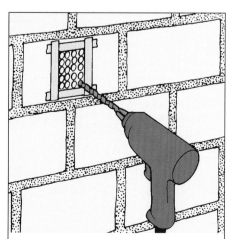

In hollow block. Drill holes in hollow block walls with a masonry bit. Then chisel out the waste material within the outline marks.

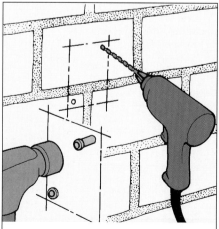

On solid masonry. Outline the box on the surface and mark screw holes inside the box. Drill holes for masonry anchors; drive in anchors.

Fishing Cable at Floor Level

In this situation, you are stringing cable or wire through a basement or crawl space up through the floor into the room above, for example, from an existing receptacle to a new one.

The tools that you need include a drill, long electrician's bit and/or wood bit assortment, fish tape, keyhole saw, electrician's tape, tape measure, and equipment to cut through the walls for boxes.

Start with a Hole

After you have made the opening for the new receptacle or switch in the wall, follow this procedure:

1. Remove the baseboard below the existing receptacle.

2. In line with the receptacle, drill a ¹⁄₁₆-inch hole at an angle through the floor at the base of the wall. Insert a thin wire down through the hole.

3. In the basement or crawl space, find the wire.

4. Next to the wire, locate the bottom plate, which is the support for the wall studs. The plate will be about ½ inch in from the wire directly under the wall.

5. In line with the wire, use a spade or wood bit to drill a hole up through the bottom plate large enough for a cable connector to pass — at least ¾-inch diameter, but check with your connector to be sure. The hole will extend into the empty space between wall studs.

6. Repeat the locating and drilling procedure below the opening for the new box or boxes.

Going Fishing

You now have a route for the cable to follow up through the floor.

1. Thread an electric fish tape, which is hooked on the end, through the knockout opening of the old box

and into the wall space. Have a helper in the basement push another fish tape up into the wall space through the hole that was drilled in the bottom plate.

Maneuver the tapes until they hook together. Then draw the end of the upstairs tape down through the hole in the bottom plate and into the basement. Unhook the tapes.

2. Strip off 3 inches of plastic sheathing insulation from the cable and remove the wire insulation.

If you are using two-piece cable connectors, install the piece that will be outside the box onto the cable. Then strip away about 3 inches of insulation from the cable wires.

3. In the basement or crawl space, thread the bare wires through the fish tape hook. Bend back the ends of the bare wires over the hook and wrap masking or electrician's tape around the cable wires and the fish tape to join them.

4. Pull the fish tape and cable up through the wall, into the box. Secure the cable connector box.

5. At this point, connect the new cable to the wiring in the old box. Box and fixture hookups are explained in "Working With Wire and Boxes," page 87.

Back in the Basement. In the basement or crawl space, run the cable along the joists to the area below the new opening. Repeat the procedure detailed above to bring the cable up through the new receptacle location.

When the cable is fished up into the new box, you can connect it to the receptacles or switches that you have planned.

If you have to run cable at right angles to the joists, drill a ¾-inch hole through each joist and thread the cable through the holes. If you have to run cable parallel to a joist, fasten the cable to the faces of the joists. Use staples or clamps spaced about 48 inches apart.

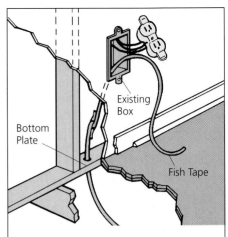

Connecting fish tapes. Push one tape through the knockout and into the wall; push the other up through the plate hole. Join both tapes.

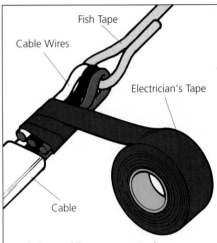

Joining cable to tape. To fasten cable to fish tape, remove 3 in. of sheathing and insulation. Loop wires through hook and tape.

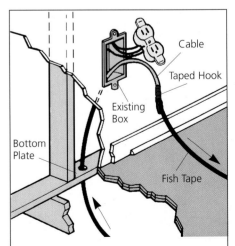

Pulling cable. Pull fish tape and cable up into the room. Remove tape. Strip 8 in. of outer insulation from cable for hookup.

Fishing Cable Along a Wall

In this situation, the room is on the upper floors of the house or there is no attic, basement, or crawl space. You will have to cut access openings along the walls. The process requires extensive repairs, so you'll want to make sure there is no other choice. See "Lath and Plaster Walls" on this page before you start.

Outlet, Then Access

Locate and cut a hole for each new box. Then:

1. Remove the baseboard so you can find the stud position.

2. Locate each stud lying between the boxes you want to join. Once you have located the first one, the process should be fairly simple. In standard construction, studs are 16 inches on center.

3. At each stud, mark off a rectangle centered on the stud that is 2 inches high and 4 inches wide. The width is needed so you can insert a drill. Once the rectangle has been cut out, both sides of the stud should be exposed.

4. Cut out the holes. Techniques for cutting holes in drywall or plaster and lath are described in "Opening Walls and Ceilings," page 121.

5. With the studs exposed, drill a ¾-inch hole through the side of each stud. You may need an angled drill chuck for this.

6. Fish the cable from the first box to the access hole in the wall. Then thread the cable through the hole in each stud until you reach the opening for the next box.

7. Make electrical connections to the outlets, switches, or light fixtures.

8. Now make patches to cover the access holes in the wall. This involves cutting out appropriately sized rectangles from a panel or drywall. This procedure is explained on page 125, "Closing Walls and Ceilings."

Lath and Plaster Walls

If you are working on a lath and plaster wall, you can extend the cable behind the baseboard. This keeps the work hidden from view.

1. Remove the baseboard from under the existing box to the opening(s) for the new box(es).

2. Just above the floor and aligned with the existing outlet, chip out a hole that is 1 inch high and deep enough to break through the plaster and lath.

3. Continue chipping out until you form a channel that extends from the existing box to the position(s) of the new one(s). This channel should be 1 inch high and ½ to ¾ inch deep.

4. Drop one fish tape into the wall through the knockout hole in the box and push another fish tape up into the wall through the channel opening just below it. Hook the two together.

5. Fish the cable down through the knockout hole to the channel. Run the cable along the channel to the area of the new box(es); push the cable into the wall. At the opening for the new box(es), use fish tape to pull the cable up the wall into the opening.

6. When the new box(es) have been installed and the wiring completed, cover the channel with a ¹⁄₁₆ inch-thick metal plate fastened in place with small screws. Attach the baseboard with subfloor adhesive, or nail into studs well above the cable notches.

Going Around Doorways

If a doorway is in the path of the cable, you will have to run the cable up and around the door frame.

1. Remove the trim or molding from around the door. Carefully pry it up and off and pull the nails from the trim through the backside using pliers.

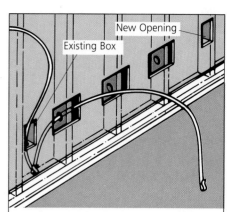

Cable across walls. To route cable across a wall, cut out rectangles to expose studs. Drill holes in the studs for cable; fish it through holes.

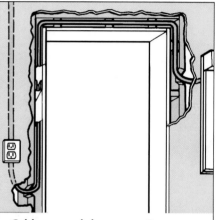

Cable around doorways. Remove the trim and make a patch to route cable around a door frame. Notch out channels for the cable in framing.

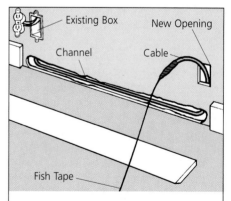

Cable behind baseboard. You may be able to go across with cable by removing baseboard and cutting notches in the framing for it.

2. Notch out door frame spacers with a chisel. Then string the cable in the spaces and fasten it with staples.

3. Replace the trim.

Fishing Cable in Ceilings

If the ceiling is open framing in an attic or crawl space, you can fish the cable up through the wall and work unobstructed from above. If the ceiling is not open, you will have to cut openings to fish the cable up the wall and along between the joists.

Cutting Plate Holes

To get access for working:

1. Follow the joists from the ceiling fixture opening to the place where the cable will turn to come down the wall.

2. At that spot, mark and cut adjoining 2 X 4-inch openings in the ceiling and wall to expose the wall top plate.

3. Use a keyhole or saber saw and a chisel to cut a notch ¾ inch wide and 1 inch deep in the top plate.

Fishing the Cable

With two short fish tapes, feed one into the wall at the ceiling and one from below. When their ends hook, draw the upper tape down, hook on the cable at floor level, and pull it up to the top of the wall. Unhook and secure the cable temporarily. Repeat with the two tapes through the ceiling openings, ending with the cable pulled to the fixture opening.

With a long fish tape, the following is easier. Feed the tape in through the ceiling fixture opening and along between joists until you can grab it at the top of the wall. Tie a weight on a stout cord (or use a plumb bob) and drop it down through the wall to the lower opening. (If it is stopped by a cross brace between wall studs, mark the cord, pull it out, and measure down to that point on the outside. Cut a small opening in the wall and notch the brace for the cable.) When it does hit bottom, tie it to the fish tape above and pull the tape down and out the lower opening. Fasten the cable to the tape and pull it up the wall, across the ceiling, and out through the fixture opening.

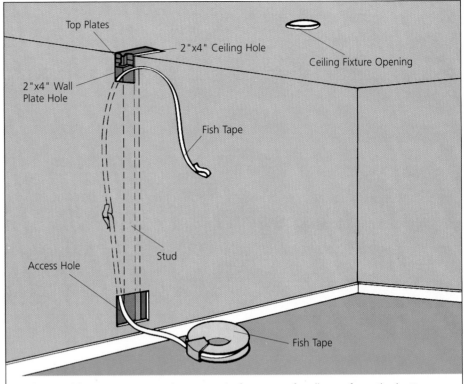

Fishing with two tapes. Feed one tape in from top of wall, one from the bottom. When they hook, draw top tape down, hook on cable, pull it up to top opening, and secure temporarily. Repeat across ceiling to get cable to fixture opening. Staple cable to framing at openings.

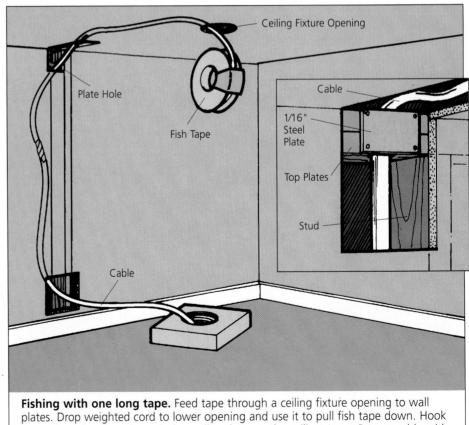

Fishing with one long tape. Feed tape through a ceiling fixture opening to wall plates. Drop weighted cord to lower opening and use it to pull fish tape down. Hook on cable and pull up through the wall and across the ceiling. Inset: Protect cable with a steel cover plate over the notch.

Closing Walls and Ceilings

Once the boxes are installed in drywall or plaster walls, the ragged edges of the holes usually are covered by faceplates over the boxes. However, you may have to do some small patch work along cable routes and around boxes and fixtures. And you may discover that you cut the hole in the wrong place and have to repair it.

General patching procedures for drywall and plaster are illustrated below.

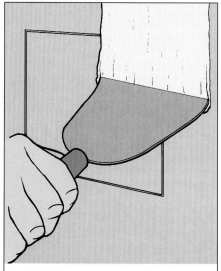

Fill area with patch. Fasten drywall patch in the opening. Embed and cover joint tape in thin layers of taping compound.

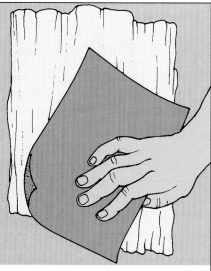

Sand patch smooth. When second layer of compound is dry, sand it smooth. Do not rough up the surface of the drywall patch.

Patching Large Areas

If you have to run cable through the wall studs and must patch them over, follow this procedure:

1. Whether the wall is plaster or drywall, cut patches from a piece of drywall. Fasten them to the studs with drywall nails or screws.

2. With a 6-inch taping knife, spread a thin layer of drywall compound around the cracks and embed joint tape in it, covering the cracks. Cover with a thin coating of compound. Let dry overnight. Cover with a second coat of compound; feather out the edges smoothly onto the patch and the surrounding wall.

3. Let the finish coat dry 24 hours, then smooth with medium-grit abrasive paper. Use a sanding block, and do not rough up any exposed paper surface of the patch. Finish with paint or recover with wallcovering.

Nailhole Repairs

Fill any small holes you made to find framing members, as follows:

1. Mix a small amount of spackling compound to the consistency of thick mud, or use ready-mixed drywall taping compound.

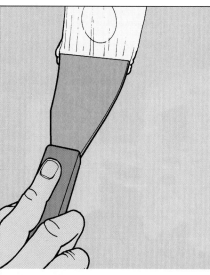

Small hole repairs. Fill holes with taping compound. When dry, sand and spot-paint with a small brush or cotton swab.

2. Press compound into each hole with a putty knife and level it.

3. Let dry for an hour or so; sand; spot finish with a dab of paint.

Installing Surface Wiring

Surface wiring, or more specifically, installing wires in a raceway, eliminates behind-the-wall cable fishing and all the work that goes with it. Raceways are like protected extension cords: the wiring is enclosed in a protective plastic or metal casing. The casing is permanently attached to walls, baseboards, ceilings, or floors. Raceway wiring can include outlets, switches, or ceiling fixtures.

Special connectors turn corners or provide intersections for extending branches from the basic pathway. A raceway is grounded with an equipment grounding conductor, a metal casing, or both.

Raceways and the Code. The National Electrical Code limits raceway use to dry locations not subject to physical damage. The sections must form a secure mechanical and electrical coupling to protect wires inside the raceway. Screws that hold the raceways against surfaces must be flush with the channel surface to avoid cable abrasion. Plastic raceway must be flame-retardant, resistant to moisture, impact, and crushing, and be installed in a dry location.

Before you purchase any materials, be sure to check local codes for special restrictions concerning their use.

Window Shop, Then Plan. It's a good idea to first take a look at a raceway system in a store, paying attention to all available parts.

Then at home, sketch out on graph paper a plan of the route that the raceway will take, carefully measuring and marking distances, box locations, junctions, and so on. Then go back to the store and purchase the materials needed.

The Components. Measure the total distance that the channel will travel, and purchase channel lengths to equal that plus an extra 5 to 10 feet to allow for possible breakage and miscuts.

At the same time, buy the housings for the receptacles, switches, and fixtures. All these pieces must be compatible with the raceway.

You also may need a raceway elbow connector and T-connector junction box. The elbow is used to connect two pieces of raceway that join at right angles. The T-connector box is used for new middle-of-the-run receptacles. You will need reducing connections to connect larger junction and fixture boxes to smaller raceway openings.

The wire used is two-wire with ground: black-, white-, and green-insulated. Install Type TW with the same amperage rating as the wire to which you will connect it. Connections are usually made to an existing switch or outlet, although the raceway system may be on a circuit of its own. Add about one third more wire to your total for hookups and general waste. You will need wire nuts and plastic electrician's tape.

Tools Required. You'll need a screwdriver and masonry or wallboard anchors. Wear gloves.

To cut the raceway to size, use a hacksaw with a fine-tooth blade that has 40 teeth per inch. You will need a wire cutter and stripper to finish the wire connections. To pull the wires through the raceway, use a fish tape.

The Power Connection

Raceway can connect with an existing fixture, switch, or outlet. Wiring connections are the same as in other installations. A backing plate and extension fit over the box; the switch or outlet mounts on them.

New installations use plates that mount directly on the surface. Raceway channel ends slip over tongues on the plates; unneeded tongues are removed. Outlets and switches mount on protruding arms. Deep covers enclose all components.

Channel Connections. The ends of channel sections slip onto surface-mounted extension (straight-line), elbow, and T plates. The joints are covered with snap-on covers.

Large T-Connectors. These connectors receive wires from opposite directions and provide room to house connections between them. The middle leg takes a reducing connector.

Receptacle Installation. A middle-of-the-run installation needs a large T plate. At the end of a run only one elbow or one extension connector is needed. Screw the receptacle back plate to the wall. Mount the connector plates. Slip the raceway channels onto the connectors and the appropriate tongue of the wall plate, and fish the wires through. Wire and mount the receptacle. Twist out the required opening in the cover and mount it. Snap on the connector joint covers.

Fixture Installation. A fixture plate mounts on an existing fixture box or directly on the surface. The fixture mounts onto an extension cover of the plate. A reducing connector cover joins a twist-out opening in the extension to the raceway channel.

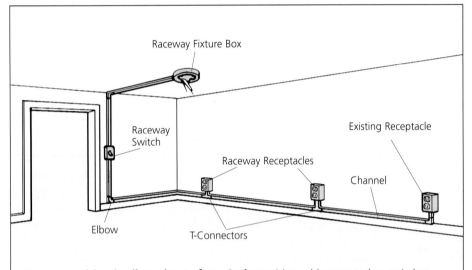

Raceway wiring is all on the surface. Surface wiring adds receptacles, switches, and fixtures without breaking into walls or ceilings. A metal or plastic channel holds two or more individual insulated wires, not cable; special housings and fittings couple with the channel.

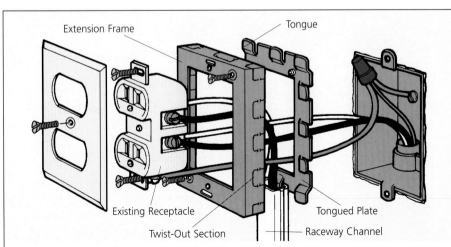

Raceway receptacles are conventionally wired. The existing outlet box is extended with a plate and extension frame to accommodate the raceway channel. Once the raceway channel is in position, you can connect the wires. If using an existing switch box, the same extension parts are used for hookup.

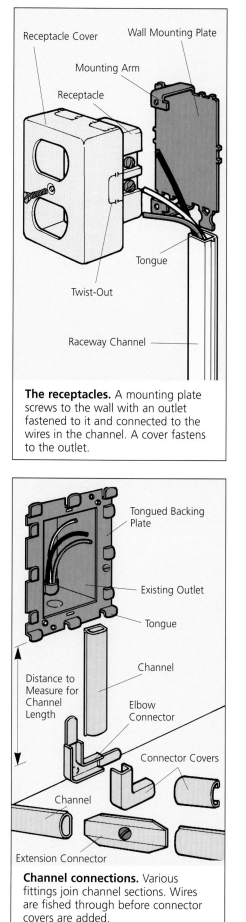

The receptacles. A mounting plate screws to the wall with an outlet fastened to it and connected to the wires in the channel. A cover fastens to the outlet.

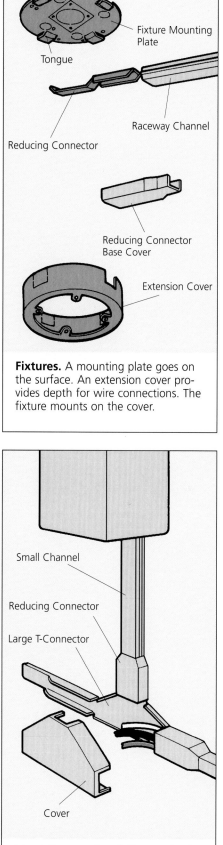

Fixtures. A mounting plate goes on the surface. An extension cover provides depth for wire connections. The fixture mounts on the cover.

Channel connections. Various fittings join channel sections. Wires are fished through before connector covers are added.

Large T-connector. A T-connector is large enough for wires to turn or be joined. Set all devices, then wire.

Hooking Cable to Existing Circuits

Any new wiring can be connected to an existing circuit, provided that the circuit will handle the additional power load. You can figure this according to the formula below; you should do so before adding the new wiring. If you find that the existing circuit will not handle the extra load, you can connect it to the electrical panel, creating a new circuit.

Wattage Ratings. To calculate the wattage (power) available in a circuit, first determine its amperage (amp rating). It will be marked on the circuit breaker or fuse for that circuit in the service entrance panel—15 or 20 amps for most room circuits, 30 or 50 amps for most heavy-duty circuits. Then, Watts = Volts X Amps. Thus, a 15-amp circuit with 120 volts carries (15 X 120 =) 1,800 watts; a 20-amp circuit carries 2,400 watts.

The wattage of any one appliance should not be more than 80 percent of a circuit's total wattage capacity. See chart "Typical Wattage Ratings" on the next page. Appliances with large motors, such as air conditioners or refrigerators, should not exceed 50 percent of circuit capacity. To operate properly and safely, each such appliance must have a circuit to itself.

Joining New Cable to Existing Circuits

Once the new cable is fished through, hook up the wires to the existing circuit. **Turn power off first.** Most situations will require at least one wire splice. Splices can be made only in a box using wire nuts and electrician's tape.

At an End-of-Run Outlet. This is the easiest hookup to complete. Attach the black wire of the new cable to the unused brass screw. The white wire goes to the unused silver-colored screw. With a wire connector, splice the bare wires together.

At a Middle-of-Run Outlet. This hookup requires three wire connectors and four jumper wires—one black, one white, and two bare—each

Typical Wattage Ratings

Appliance	Rating
Room air conditioner	800 - 1500
Central air conditioner	5000
Electric blanket	150 - 500
Blender	200 - 400
Broiler (rotisserie)	1400 - 1500
Can opener	150
Clock	13
Clothes dryer (240-volt)	4000 - 5000
Clothes iron (hand)	700 - 1000
Coffee maker	600 - 750
Crock pot (2 quart)	100
Dehumidifier	500
Dishwasher	1100
Drill (hand)	200 - 400
Fan (attic)	400
Fan (exhaust)	75
Floor polisher	300
Food freezer	300 - 600
Food mixer	150 - 250
Fryer (deep fat)	1200 - 1600
Frying pan	1000 - 1200
Furnace (gas)	800
Furnace (oil)	600 - 1200
Garbage disposal	500 - 1000
Hair dryer	400
Heater (portable)	1000 - 1500
Heating pad	50 - 75
Hot plate	600 - 1000
Hot water heater	2500 - 5000
Microwave oven	650
Radio	10
Range (per burner)	5000
Range oven	4500
Refrigerator	150 - 300
Roaster	1200 - 1600
Sewing machine	60 - 90
Stereo	250 - 500
Sunlamp	200 - 400
TV (color)	200 - 4500
Toaster	250 - 1000
Toaster-oven	1500
Trash compactor	500 - 1000
Vacuum cleaner	300 - 600
Waffle iron	700 - 1100
Washing machine	600 - 900

4 inches long. Identify the black and white wires of the power source cable and unhook them from the outlet. To determine which cable comes from the power source, use a voltage tester. Disconnect the wires to the outlet. Then, and only then, have a helper turn on the circuit at the service panel. Put one probe of the voltage tester against the metal box. With the other probe, touch one of the exposed black wires. If it is the feed wire (the one coming from the power source), the bulb of the voltage tester will light. If the bulb does not light, test the other black wire. The one that lights the bulb is the one you want.

Then turn off the circuit again before you continue work.

Splice the black power wire together with the new black cable wire and the black jumper. Attach the jumper to the brass outlet terminal. Splice the two white cable wires with the white jumper and connect the jumper to the silver outlet terminal.

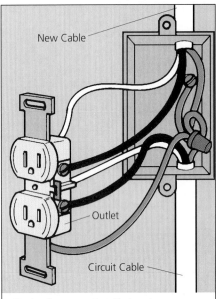

End-of-run outlet. To hook up new cable to an end-of-run outlet, attach the black and white wires of the new cable to the unused brass and silver terminals.

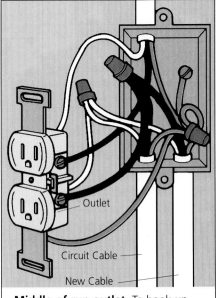

Middle-of-run outlet. To hook up new cable to a middle-of-run outlet, add jumpers from black, white, and bare wire. Cap the splices with wire connectors and tape.

Middle of-run switch. Identify the incoming circuit cable. Connect it to the new cable as shown.

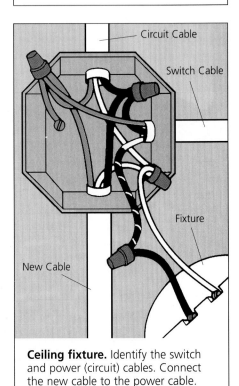

Ceiling fixture. Identify the switch and power (circuit) cables. Connect the new cable to the power cable.

Finally, splice the three bare grounding wires together with jumpers to the outlet and to the box terminal.

At a Middle-of-Run Switch. There will be two sets of existing wires in a middle-of-the-run switch. One set comes from the power source. The other set runs to the fixture or outlet that the switch controls.

Before you can hook up the new cable, you must find out which set comes from the main service panel. Otherwise, your new outlet will have power only when the switch is on. Use a voltage tester as described in "At a Middle-of-Run Outlet," page 127.

Make two 4-inch-long jumper wires—one black and one bare. Splice together the black wire that lit the bulb, the new cable's black wire, and the black jumper. Fasten the black jumper to the brass terminal on the switch. Fasten the black wire that doesn't light the tester bulb to the other terminal of the switch. Splice together the bare wires with one end of the bare jumper, and secure the other end of the bare jumper under the screw at the back of the box. Finally, splice the three white wires.

At a Middle-of-Run Ceiling Fixture. You must first find which of the black wires in the existing cables is live and is not controlled by the light switch. This black wire comes from the service panel. Turn off the circuit at the service panel. In the fixture will be at least two splices that connect black wires. The black wire coming from the power source will not be in the splice holding the black wire coming from the light fixture. Look for the other black wire splice.

Disconnect this splice and separate the wires. Make sure the bare ends do not touch anything. Turn on the circuit at the service panel and use the voltage tester. The black wire that turns on the test light is the one to connect to the black wire of the new cable. Turn off the circuit.

Splice together the black wire from the new cable and all black wires contained in the original splice. With the circuit still off, take apart the white wire splice and add the white wire from the new cable.

Finally, splice all bare wires and one end of a 1 ½- to 2-inch bare jumper. Fasten the other end of the bare jumper under the box screw.

Tapping Junction Boxes. Several circuits may pass through a junction or major box. Have a helper turn off the circuits one by one, as you use a voltage tester to determine which cable controls the circuit you want to tap.

Once you have found the source, turn off the power and then splice the wires together: black to black, white to white, ground to ground.

Tapping Power for Ceiling Fixtures. You have three choices: a middle-of-the-run ceiling box, a wall switch, and an end-of-the-run outlet.

If a ceiling fixture has a built-in switch, the easiest way to get power to it is to connect to an existing middle-of-the-run ceiling box. If the new fixture requires a switch, connect from the power wire in the existing box to the switch, then up to the new fixture. Connect fixture white to existing white.

A Middle-of-Run Wall Switch for a Fixture. If the new ceiling fixture requires a wall switch, it's best to get power from an existing middle-of-the-run switch in the same room. Run two-wire cables from the old switch and the new fixture to the new switch box. Connect the switch to the two black wires, and connect the whites together. At the old switch, connect the new white and black to the power cable white and black.

A Switch Loop for a New Fixture. Tapping into power is no problem in this situation, but if you want a separate switch control for a new

fixture you have a choice of wiring.

If you are tapping a ceiling fixture, add the new cable into the splice containing the feed hot wire. If you are tapping a switch, cut a 4-inch black jumper wire. Splice together the jumper, the feed hot wire, and the new cable wire.

Attach the loose end of the jumper to the brass terminal on the switch. Then wire the switch as for an end-of-the-run switch.

Adding a Circuit Breaker

If you find you need to add a new circuit you'll have to install a new breaker in the main panel. Working on a panel is dangerous, so take all safety measures. If your installation is special in any way or if you are not confident of completing the hookup correctly, have a licensed electrician do the work at the panel after you have done the room wiring. If you do work on your panel, it's a two-hand job so you'll need a helper or some kind of stand to hold your flashlight while you work with the house power off.

1 Shut off Main Breaker. Using your flashlight to see, turn off the power to the house with the main breaker switch, which is mounted at the top.

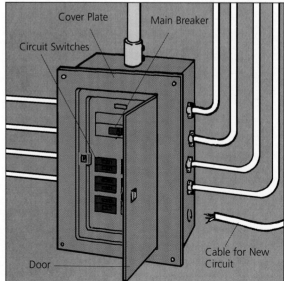

Cover Plate
Main Breaker
Circuit Switches
Door
Cable for New Circuit

Shut off main breaker. Open the door on the panel box, turn the main breaker to the off position, then unscrew the screws at the corners to remove the cover plate.

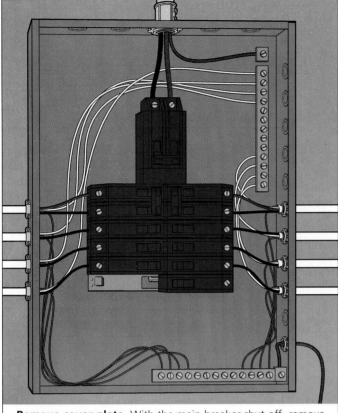

Remove cover plate. With the main breaker shut off, remove the cover plate and note the breaker arrangement. Check to see if there are any breakers not in use (spares) or if there are spare slots for additional breakers.

Bring cable into panel. Pry out a perforated knockout from the side or top of the panel box with a screwdriver. Then thread the cable through a locknut and into the box.

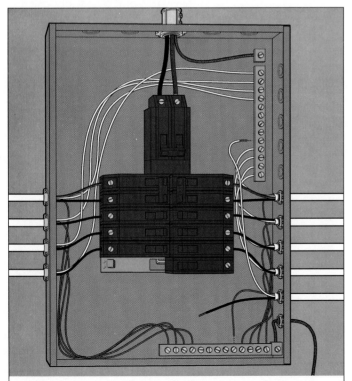

Connect neutral and ground wires. Connect the end of the white wire to the neutral bus bar (where the other white wires are connected). Then connect the ground wire to the ground wire bus, usually near the bottom of the box.

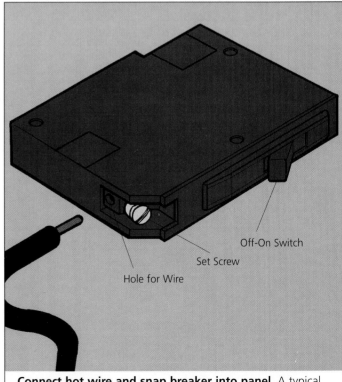

Off-On Switch

Set Screw

Hole for Wire

Connect hot wire and snap breaker into panel. A typical 120-volt circuit breaker comes with a clip in the rear that plugs into the hot bus of the panel and a hole in the side for inserting the black wire of the cable.

2 Remove Cover Plate. With the house power shut off, remove the panel's cover plate and note the breaker arrangement. Each breaker in use is connected to a circuit cable. A label on the cover plate should identify each circuit. Check to see if there are any breakers not in use (spares) or if there are spare slots for additional breakers. If there are no spare breakers but there are empty slots for breakers, you can add a new circuit. If all slots are in use, you may be able to add a double breaker, which is a device that puts two breakers in the space of one. Or you may have to add a subpanel. In any case, if you don't see a spare breaker or slot, it's a good idea to get an electrician's advice.

3 Bring Cable into Panel. Here's how to connect a 120-volt circuit cable to a spare (or new) breaker. Use a screwdriver to pry out a perfo-rated knockout from the side or top of the panel box. Attach a locknut and thread 12 or more inches of the cable through the locknut. Tighten the two screws against the cable with a screwdriver. Remove about 8 inches of the outer sleeve of the end of the cable and strip the wire ends.

4 Connect Neutral and Ground Wires. Insert the ends of the white (neutral) wire and the bare ground wire into holes along the bus bars intended for these wires at the side or bottom of the panel (note how the other circuits are connected) and tighten the setscrews.

5 Connect Hot Wire and Snap Breaker in Panel. Loosen the screw of the breaker and insert the black wire of the cable into the hole below. Then retighten the screw to secure the wire end. Snap the breaker into its slot on the panel board.

6 Replace Panel Box Cover. Screw the cover plate back onto the panel box and record the new circuit on the panel door. Flip the new breaker to the "on" position and turn the main breaker back on.

Eliminating Pull-Chain Lights

Owners of older homes often want to replace a pull-chain ceiling light with a light operated by a wall switch.

You will need to run new two-wire with ground cable from the ceiling light to a wall switch, which requires fishing the wire through the ceiling and down the wall. Besides the cable, you will need a new switch, switch box, wire connectors, electrician's tape, fish tape, wire stripper, needle-nose pliers, and perhaps, voltage tester. To install the box, you will need a keyhole saw and drill bit for holes to start the saw. You can install a new fixture or leave the old.

At the Ceiling. Turn off the power to the light and remove the fixture.

If you find only two wires, the job is simple. If there are more than two wires, you will have to determine which wire is hot and which is neutral. If the wires from the power source are connected to fixture wires, unscrew the wire nuts to bare the wires. If the wires are connected to fixture terminal screws, do not loosen them.

Hold one probe of a voltage tester against the box. Touch the other probe to the bare ends of one of the wire connections or to one of the fixture terminal screws. Have a helper turn on the current. If the bulb in the tester lights, you have located the hot wire. If not, touch the probe to the bare ends of the other wire connection, or to the other fixture terminal screw, to verify that it is hot. Tag this hot wire.

Fishing the New Cable. Run the new two-wire with ground cable between the ceiling fixture and switch. The procedure is to cut a hole for the switch box, then fish the wire from

Replace panel box cover. Screw the cover plate back onto the panel housing and record the new circuit on the panel door. Turn the main breaker back on.

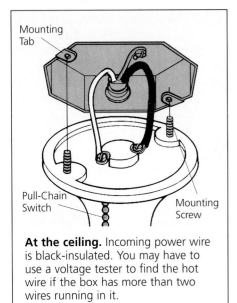

At the ceiling. Incoming power wire is black-insulated. You may have to use a voltage tester to find the hot wire if the box has more than two wires running in it.

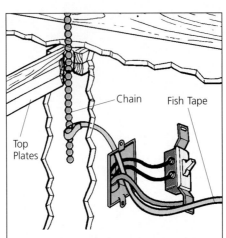

Fishing new cable. To fish through a box knockout, drop a chain from above and snag it with a fish tape. Draw it into the box, hook on the cable, and pull up to the ceiling.

Hanging a New Chandelier

Replacing a ceiling light, such as one over a dining table, with a chandelier, is a very simple job—one some pros call a "change-out."

The procedure involves removing the old fixture, modifying the ceiling box to handle the weight of the chandelier, and making the necessary electrical connections.

1 **Remove Old Fixture.** Turn off the power to the circuit. Remove the fasteners holding the old fixture to the ceiling box. If the old fixture is heavy, have a helper steady the fixture for you while you disconnect the wires at the terminal screws on the old fixture.

2 **Making the Connection.** If the new chandelier weighs more than

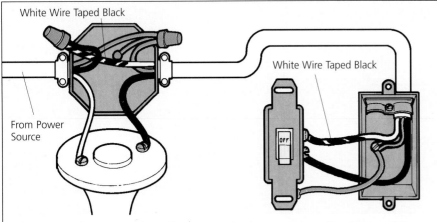

The connection. Here's the wiring connection between the ceiling light and the switch. The incoming power wire bypasses the fixture (tag white wire black) and goes to the switch. The black wire from the switch terminates at the fixture. Ground wire is connected to both boxes and to the switch.

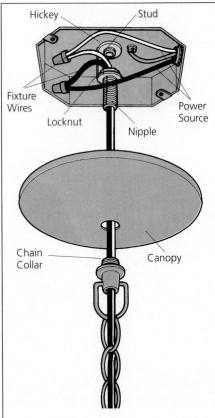

Chandelier-hanging hardware. This hardware includes a stud, hickey, and nipple that supports the extra weight of the fixture. A box knockout accommodates the stud. Wires are spliced black-to-black and white-to-white with wire connectors. Make sure the box is secure to framing.

the ceiling box to the switch box and connect the switch, as shown.

The easiest way to fish the wire may be from the ceiling to the switch. Run the fish tape through the channel formed by parallel joists. See "Fishing Cable in Ceilings," page 124. Where the joists meet the wall, cut a small hole in the ceiling and wall so you can turn the tape downward. You may have to notch the framing members to accept the cable. Hook the cable to the tape at the switch and pull it up the wall, around the wall-ceiling corner, and into the ceiling box.

The Connection. The new cable you have added is for a switch loop. This means that the white wire will be hot as well as the black wire. To identify

the white wire as hot, wrap black electrical tape around the wire where it comes into the fixture box and the switch box. At the fixture, connect the black wire from the power source to the white-taped-black going to the switch. Connect the power cable white wire to the silver fixture terminal. Connect the black wire from the switch to the brass fixture terminal. Pigtail the grounding wires to the fixture box.

At the switch, connect the black and white-taped-black wires to the switch terminals. Connect the grounding wire to the box and to the switch.

Complete the project by patching the holes cut in the wall and ceiling. Then install the ceiling fixture and the switch faceplate.

10 pounds and the fixture you are removing weighs less than 10 pounds, you will need to fasten the new one with a stud, a nipple fitting, and a hickey. A stud is a short piece of threaded tubing that screws into the center of the box. A hickey screws onto the stud, the nipple screws into the hickey, and the collar of the chandelier screws onto the nipple. You may need to replace the ceiling box for this arrangement.

3 The Wiring Connections.
Chandeliers are prewired. Splice the black-insulated wire to the black-insulated wire in the ceiling box. Do the same with the white neutral wires. Cover all the splices with wire connectors and wrap the connectors with plastic electrician's tape.

The chandelier canopy or ceiling escutcheon fits over the ceiling box and is held with a collar nut that screws onto the threads of the nipple in the box.

Installing Track Lighting

Track lighting creates a theatrical mood. It can be formal and informal at the same time, and it can be installed in open ceilings and on finished ones.

If you install track lighting in an open ceiling, you can spray the joists and sheathing above the same color and the track lights will seem to float on the ceiling surface.

You can add local lighting with track lights, which, in many ways, are similar to raceway lighting. The basic part is a length of surface wiring that can be tapped anywhere for a fixture. Because of its flexibility, you can place it in almost any room. The track comes with various adaptors that enable you to add outlets or, in some cases, even a fairly heavy chandelier.

The Power Sources. Track lighting is connected to the house wiring, like any other ceiling fixture. You probably will have to add a ceiling junction box to install this style of raceway, since the existing boxes will not be close enough to the track.

Lighting Suggestions as You Go Shopping. Track lighting installation procedures vary according to the manufacturer and model. Be sure to read all the instructions carefully before you buy the system. You can start with the basic system and add to it as your budget or decorating scheme dictates. Make sure that the brand of track lights you buy will accommodate your plans for the future.

If the track lighting channel is attached to a ceiling, use toggle or Molly fasteners to ensure stability. If the track is mounted on open framing, you can attach the track to edges of joists or along a joist edge. In some situations you can recess the track and the lights between the joists in a straight line.

Connecting Track Lights to House Power

Turn off the circuit on which you will be working. Roughly plot the position of the track on the ceiling. Install a ceiling junction box, if none exists, at one end of the track's location and fish cable to the box. The technique involved is explained in "Fishing Cable in Ceilings," page 124.

If you are using a plug-in track lighting system, install the track as described below and simply plug it into an existing wired outlet.

1 Connector Plate.
The track adaptor plate covers the junction box and holds the track connector and the electrical housing. Assemble these pieces. Splicing like-colored wires together, hook up the track wires to the cable wires. Then fasten the adaptor assembly to the junction box ears with the screws provided.

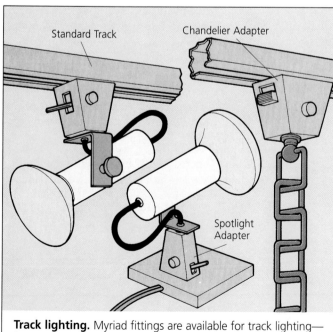

Track lighting. Myriad fittings are available for track lighting—from standard lights to spotlights to chandeliers. The lights also come in different designs to match most decors.

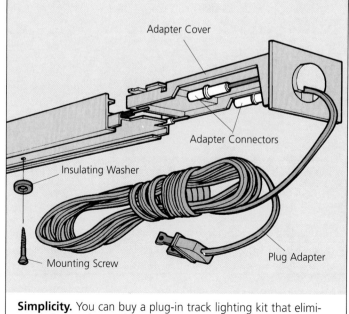

Simplicity. You can buy a plug-in track lighting kit that eliminates the need to make wiring connections. Or you can buy track that must be connected to a wired ceiling or junction box.

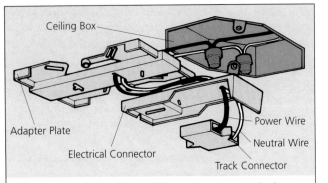

Connector plate. Connect the track wiring to the house wiring using the metal adaptor plate. Wire nut the splices and wrap them with plastic electrician's tape. Fasten the assembly to the ceiling box.

Labels: Ceiling Box, Adapter Plate, Electrical Connector, Track Connector, Power Wire, Neutral Wire

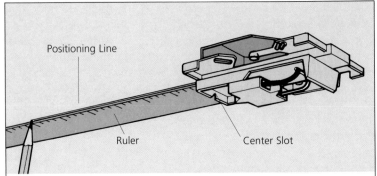

Plot the track. To plot the line for the track itself, align a ruler with the center slot on the track connector. Draw the line straight across the ceiling to the location of the opposite end of the track.

Labels: Positioning Line, Ruler, Center Slot

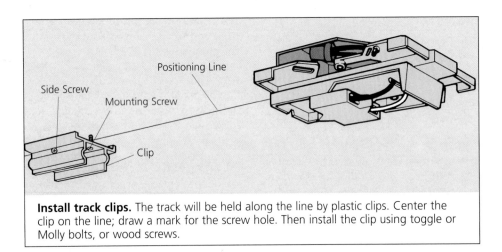

Install track clips. The track will be held along the line by plastic clips. Center the clip on the line; draw a mark for the screw hole. Then install the clip using toggle or Molly bolts, or wood screws.

Labels: Side Screw, Mounting Screw, Positioning Line, Clip

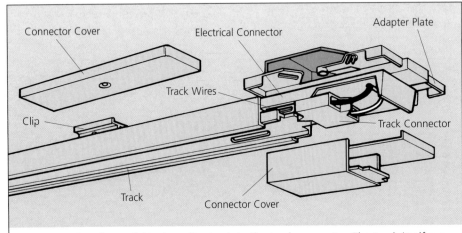

Connect the channel. Hook up the track to the track connector. The track itself supplies power for the track lights. Make sure that the track connection joints are butted tightly together. Then attach lights.

Labels: Connector Cover, Clip, Track, Electrical Connector, Track Wires, Connector Cover, Adapter Plate, Track Connector

2 Plot the Track. The track is held in position by special clips spaced evenly along the track. Hold the clips in place on your line, and mark pilot holes in the ceiling.

Drill the pilot holes and attach the clips with toggle or Molly bolts to a drywall surface or with screws to a wooden surface.

3 Connect the Channel. Connect the track channel solidly to the electrical connector; slip the channel into the track connector. Snap the track channels into the clips. Then tighten the setscrews along the sides of the clips to hold the channels firmly in position.

To complete the project, install the raceway cover and attach the track lights anywhere you wish.

Replacing a Light Fixture with a Ceiling Fan

A ceiling fan can cool a single room simply by keeping the air moving. In winter, a fan mounted in a high ceiling enhances comfort by pulling warm air to the floor. Ceiling fans are available in a wide assortment of fixtures from basic fan units to fans that contain built-in light fixtures. Before purchasing a new fan, make sure the proposed location offers ample space. There must be at least 24 inches between the tip of the fan blade and a nearby wall, and the bottom of the fixture must clear the floor by at least 84 inches.

Usually a light fixture can be replaced by a ceiling fan entirely from inside the room. Codes prohibit hanging the fan from the electrical box however, so a separate support that is capable of holding up the fan will have to be used (some fans weigh as much as 30 pounds). Support brackets are available in kits sold separately from the fan fixture.

1 Remove Old Fixture and Box. First turn off the power to the light fixture at the electrical panel.

Remove the fixture, disconnect the wires, and put a piece of tape over the two wires that were connected to the light fixture to identify them. Remove the box by unscrewing the center fastener and cable clamps. Displace insulation found near the box and bracket temporarily. (For blanket insulation, use a stick or wire to prop up a tent over the area. It can be pulled down after the new bracket is in place.) Use a mini-hacksaw to sever the old support bar and then bend the bar out of the way.

2 Install the New Hanger Brace Bar. Feed the new brace bar into the cavity along the direction of the

joists. Then rotate it 90 degrees so that it spans crosswise in the cavity and the feet rest on the ceiling board. Turn the bar on its axis, allowing it to unscrew and extend until the legs are snug to the joists. Before tightening it make sure the bracket is centered over the hole. (Since you will not be able to see into the hole, these last two actions have to be done by feel only. Be patient and take your time).

3 Attach the New Box. Remove knockout tabs from two holes in the new box. Attach wire clamps to the holes. Feed one cable through each clamp and tighten the clamps inside the box to secure them. Next,

refer to manufacturer's instructions to attach the new hanger assembly to the bracket and box.

4 Attach the Fan Hanger Bracket. Mount the fan hanger bracket on the junction box according to the manufacturer's instructions. Pull down the wires through the bracket.

5 Connect the Fan. Follow manufacturer's instructions for mounting the fan onto the bracket and connecting the wiring to the appropriate fan and light wire leads. Finally, attach the light or cover plate.

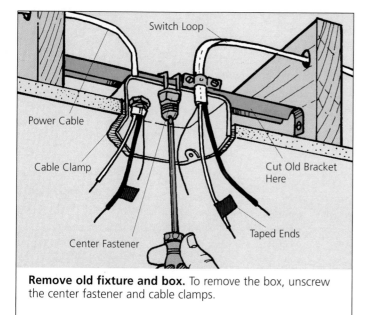

Remove old fixture and box. To remove the box, unscrew the center fastener and cable clamps.

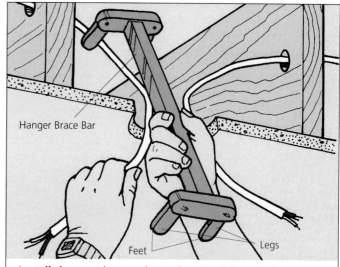

Install the new hanger brace bar. Feed the new brace bar into the cavity along the direction of the joists, then rotate it 90 degrees so that it spans crosswise in the cavity and the feet rest on the ceiling drywall.

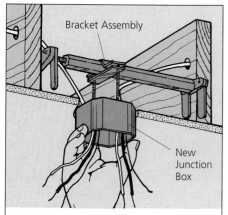

Attach the new box. Attach the new hanger assembly to the bracket and box (refer to the kit instructions for details).

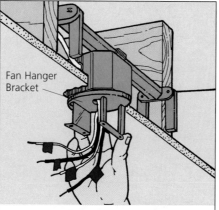

Attach the fan hanger bracket. Mount the fan hanger bracket on the junction box according to manufacturer's instructions. Pull the wires through the bracket.

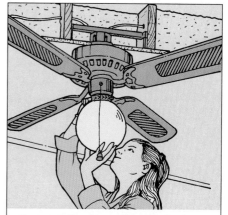

Connect the fan. After the fan is mounted, attach the light or cover plate.

9

Wiring Switches and Dimmers

Sometimes all you want to do is flick on a light. If so, the simple, tried and true on/off toggle switch will do the trick. But increasingly, modern lighting design calls for more than the flick of a switch. Greater efficiency and effect are both created when you step up to dimmers and more sophisticated control systems.

Efficiency comes into play because you rarely need full brilliance of a light source all the time, so you can reduce electrical costs and prolong bulb life through dimming. But efficiency is only a small part of the reason to use dimmers. Truly the stage setters for lighting, dimmers allow you to create precisely the mood you wish in any environment. With controls, you can then gear lighting to various activities. You can be as sophisticated as you wish. As an added bonus, the efficiency savings may offset the costs of dimmers.

Still the humble single-pole on/off switch has one outstanding advantage: It's the cheapest switch you can buy.

As a result, budget-conscious lighting design will usually include various kinds of switches. In this chapter, you'll learn how to select and install every kind of switch, from the simple single-pole on/off switch, to three-way switches that let you control light from two or more locations, as well as various types of dimmers. But first, let's take a look at ways to incorporate switches into your lighting design.

Joining the Gang

Designers detest the unsightly clustering of switches, dimmers, fan-speed controls, receptacles, and the like. Achieve a more satisfying effect by placing switches and dimmers together in the same electrical wallbox to create an unobtrusive dimming center. This is called ganging them.

When applicable, you can easily remove side sections of the dimmer switch front plates. This allows you to install the dimmers closer together

so you can get several in one box. But when dimmers are ganged with their side sections removed, you'll probably have to reduce the allowable electrical load. Called derating, this is necessary because dimmers are 98-percent efficient with 2 percent of the power dissipating as heat, and the dimmer side sections are designed to release heat, giving the dimmer longer life. When dimmers are ganged and side sections are removed, the load must be derated so less heat is produced, to ensure the dimmer's longer life. Most losses are small in comparison to the benefits of visually cleaned up, ganged dimmers.

In planning your runs, consider how you can gang the controls. Use advice from lighting salespersons and the manufacturer's literature to determine how to plan your wiring runs per dimmer and the capacity you will need. Most residential dimmers allow a load of 600 to 1,000 watts, although larger capacities are available.

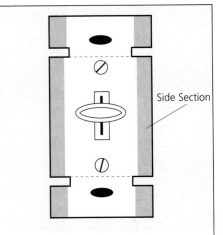

Side Section

Removing Side Section. The side sections of dimmer switches can be removed to allow you to gang them in a box.

Modern dimmer switches come in a range of styles and configurations. The one at left combines an up-and-down slider with a switch below so you can turn lights on and off at a preselected light level. The switch at right has buttons that let you select from five light levels.

For a coordinated look throughout the rest of the space, some manufacturers have incorporated similarly styled faceplate units for telephone jacks, groundfault circuit interrupter (GFCI) receptacles, cable TV jacks, and 15 AMP receptacles. If all this is intriguing but not as sophisticated as you need, consider the rewards and satisfactions of installing a control system.

Total-Room Control Systems

These systems include a master control that governs independent lighting zones/channels. In some cases, the zones can be assigned to different lighting types, such as incandescent, magnetic low-voltage, neon, fluorescent lighting, or nondimmed lighting. Scenes can fade into one another at programmed time intervals. They can come with built-in wireless remote control receivers. Auxiliary controls enable you to adjust parts of the system separately.

In a single console, you can create independent lighting scenes (preset lighting levels) for different moods or occasions. In modern open-plan homes, having as many as 16 different lighting scenes preprogrammed can gear the lighting specifically to the functions to be undertaken and the kind of natural lighting that needs to be balanced.

To understand how these work, consider where they were developed—at the theater. Remember those plays

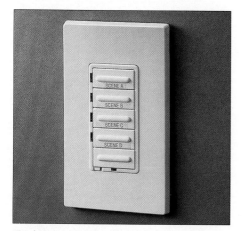

Total-room control systems feature switches such as this one which allow you to choose from four preset scenes.

where everything took place in one room. The scenes often were divided into "early morning," "high noon," "dusk," and the final act "just at midnight" or something equivalent. The scene setter was the lighting, the only major difference in the set. The name carried over into residential and even commercial lighting, which now refer to a predetermined combination of lighting effects as a "scene."

The name is apt because in creating scenes not all lighting is raised or lowered together. Rather, a new lighting arrangement is created. For instance, you might want to set one scene to raise the light level of wall grazing lights and lower the general lighting in the center of the room. Use this scene to create dramatic highlights that would work best with a roaring fire. Then on a gray, drab, rainy day, you may want to access another scene that raises the light level in the center of the room, pooling on warm-colored furniture, and let the walls fall off into soft background lighting. These are only a hint of the possibilities.

Ascertaining Needs

Control systems that cover a number of outlets and light fixtures must have a capacity greater than the sum of the parts, and the lights to be used on them must be similar types. Here are the steps to follow to set up a dimming system:

- Determine what you want to control: whether lighting will be tungsten-halogen, low-voltage, incandescent, or fluorescents.

- Determine total capacity required. Start by listing total watts of fittings or fixtures and totalling them, then adding any additional factors that would contribute to the overall electric load, such as transformer losses as well as loss of wattage caused by ganging controls. Manufacturer's specifications will give the figures you need.

- Determine the number of switch locations in a room to turn on/off the fixtures or fittings you want to control.

- Determine where you want the dimming control to be located and where you want switches to be located for operating the same lights.

- Double-check that the dimming system you have selected is designed to carry the wattage you have designated. Otherwise, use a larger capacity dimmer or more than one dimmer system. Most residential grade dimmers for incandescent use are rated for 600- or 1,000-watts.

Total-Home Control Systems

Systems can also be set up so that master controls are situated in strategic locations in your home, controlling all rooms. Advantages in terms of safety and security make these systems extremely desirable, especially in larger homes. Some of the key features include:

- Creating pathways of light activated at the touch of a button, such as bedroom to kitchen, garage to bedroom, family room to pool, etc.

- Turning all lights on at once with one button.

- Integrating lighting with security systems and controls, including time clocks, occupant sensors, audiovisual equipment, driveway sensors, and even a vacation mode that memorizes and then repeats light-use patterns while the homeowner is away.

- Master controls showing where lights are on in other parts of the home.

- Integrating with other residential electronic functions. (Note: dimming needs to be separated from lines that govern appliances and the like that cannot safely be run on lower electrical levels.)

The technology is increasing and becoming more affordable as new kinds of lighting control systems are redesigned from commercial installations for use in the home.

Working with Single-Pole Switches

It is not difficult to replace or add a single-pole switch. The process may vary slightly, depending on your wiring and whether the switch is grounded. A grounded switch has an extra terminal screw at the base that is green or shows the letters GR. This redundant grounding system is more reliable than systems that don't connect the ground to the switch. If wires are encased in metal conduit, the conduit is usually grounded, but not always.

When replacing a switch or adding a new one, buy switches with a ground-terminal screw, even though it may be necessary to modify your wiring, as explained in this section. Detach only those wires that are connected to the switch itself.

Reading Switches. Switches are stamped with code letters and numbers. Learn how to read these codes so you buy the right products. Here's what the codes on a typical switch mean:

UL means the switch is listed by Underwriters Laboratories, a testing organization.

AC ONLY means the switch will handle only alternating current—the kind used in house wiring in North America.

CO/ALR is a wire code indicating that the switch will handle copper, copper-clad, and aluminum wire.

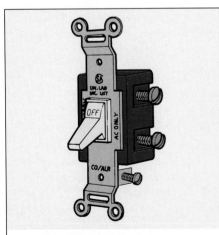

Reading the switch. Codes are stamped on switches so you know which one to buy for a project.

15A—120-V means the switch will handle 15 amperes and 120 volts of power. A new switch must have the same amp and volt rating as the switch it replaces.

Connecting Wires. Connect wires to terminals by looping the end around the terminal screw in the direction the screw tightens. This is usually clockwise.

The best way to form a loop in the wire for terminal screws is with needle-nose pliers. Strip about ½ to ¾ inch of insulation off the wire end of the wire and bend the bare wire around the jaws of the pliers, forming a perfect loop. Then hook the loop onto the terminals in the direction the screws turn down, and tighten the screws. As the terminals are tightened, the wire is forced under the screw-heads and clamped.

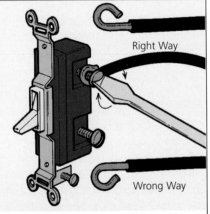

Connecting wires. Wire is looped around the terminal screws in the direction the screws tighten.

Removing Outlet Tabs. To install a receptacle with the lower outlet functioning as an "always on" outlet but the upper outlet controlled by a switch, you must break off the metal link between the terminal screws. Use a screwdriver to pry the link up, then break it off with pliers.

Connect the incoming hot (black) power wire and one switch wire to the lower outlet terminal. Connect the white wire and other switch wire to the upper outlet terminal.

Single-Pole to Light

The easiest switch/light wiring hookup is probably a single-pole switch controlling a light fixture. Follow these procedures:

1. Turn off the power at the main service entrance when you work.

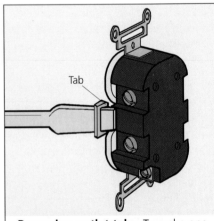

Removing outlet tabs. To make one half of a receptacle switch-operated, remove the side link.

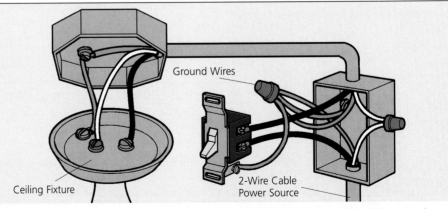

How to wire a single-pole switch to a light fixture. A single-pole switch controlling one light fixture with power coming from the switch is wired this way. White wire bypasses switch; ground connects to both metal boxes and to the green grounding terminal on the switch.

If the circuit is a new one, run the wire from the service panel to the switch and light, but do not connect it to the panel. Have a licensed electrician do this.

2. Cut the wire at the switch.

3. Strip off about ½ to ¾ inch of wire insulation on each end of the wire. Use wire strippers.

4. Connect the black wires to the terminals, hooking the wire loops around the terminals in the direction the screw tightens.

5. The white wire bypasses the switch completely.

6. Connect the grounding wires in the cable from the light and in the power cable to a pigtail (a short piece of wire of the same gauge) that is attached to the grounding terminal in the box and to the grounding terminal on the switch. Use a wire nut.

Note: When romex is used the ground is bare copper, so cover terminal screws with electrical tape.

Single-Pole Switch Controls Light, Constant Power to Outlet

In this single-pole connection the power is supplied by a two-wire cable with ground. A three-wire cable with ground goes to the light and a two-wire with cable ground to the outlet.

1 **Wiring the Switch.** With a length of black-insulated wire pigtail (same gauge wire), connect the black power wire to the switch and then to the black wire in the three-wire with ground cable. Wrap the wire nut with electrician's tape. Now connect the white wire from the power source to the white wire in the three-wire cable. Use a wire nut and tape it. Connect the red wire in the three-wire cable to the open switch terminal. Finally, connect the cable grounding wires (green or bare) to a pigtail that is attached to the box ground terminal and the switch ground terminal.

2 **Wiring the Outlet**. Connect the black wire to the brass terminal and

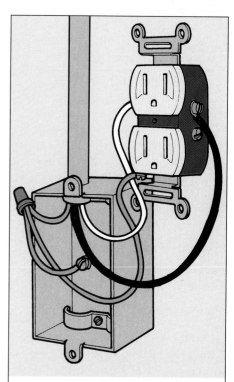

Wiring the switch. Connect the black power wire to black wire in three-wire cable; white wire to white wire, red wire to the brass switch terminal.

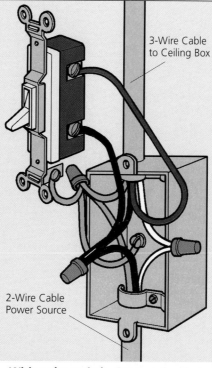

Wiring the outlet. The black wire goes to the brass terminal on the outlet; white wire goes to silver terminal. Ground goes to terminal and box.

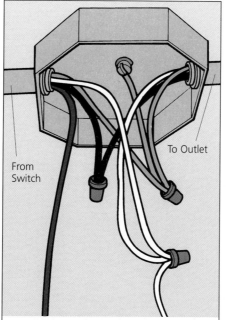

Wiring the ceiling box. Splice red wire to black wire of lamp or to brass terminal. Black wire goes through box to outlet; white to light/outlet.

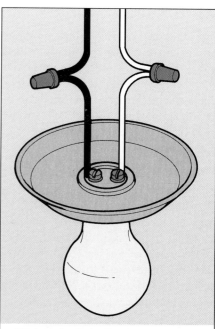

Wiring the light fixture. The red wire goes to the black light wire, if prewired; if not, to the brass light terminal. White to white. Wire nut, tape any splices.

the white wire to the silver terminal of the outlet, using the two-wire with ground cable. With a pigtail, splice the ground and connect it to the box and the outlet ground terminal.

3 **Wiring the Ceiling Box.** Connect the black wire from the switch to the black wire from the outlet. Add a wire nut and tape. Connect the grounding from the

switch box cable to pigtails from the receptacle ground terminal and the box ground terminal.

4 Wiring the Light Fixture.
Connect the red wire from the switch to the black light wire, if the light is prewired. If it is not, then connect the red wire to the brass-colored light terminal. The white wire is spliced to the light's white wire or connected to the light-colored terminal on the light.

Single-Pole Switch Controls Light, Outlet; Power Through Fixture

In this hookup, power runs through the light fixture to switch and then to an outlet. Both outlet and fixture are controlled by the switch. This circuit requires three-wire cable with ground and two-wire cable with ground, plus pigtail wire.

1 Wiring the Ceiling Box.
Power is supplied by a two-wire cable with ground into the box at the light.

Splice the black wire from the power source to the red wire of the three-wire cable. Splice the white wire to the white wire of the three-wire cable, and hook the black wire to the black wire of the light fixture. Also splice the white wire of the power source cable to the light. Use wire nuts and tape the nuts.

2 Wiring the Light Fixture.
The black wire coming from the switch is connected to the fixture. The white wire, connected to the power source and the white wire of the three-wire cable, is fastened to the silver terminal of the light fixture. Or the wires are spliced to the white and black wires of a prewired light.

3 Wiring the Switch.
Fasten the red wire to the top brass terminal of the switch. Make a pigtail of black-insulated wire and connect it to the bottom brass switch terminal. Connect the pigtail to the black wires in the fixture and receptacle cables. Connect the white wire to the white wire in the cable that goes to the outlet. Use wire nuts. The grounding wire (green) is pigtailed and fastened

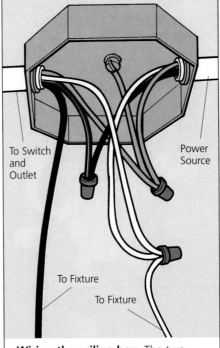

To Switch and Outlet

Power Source

To Fixture

To Fixture

Wiring the ceiling box. The two-wire power cable connects to the three-wire cable from the light to the switch. Splice black to red; pigtail the ground wire.

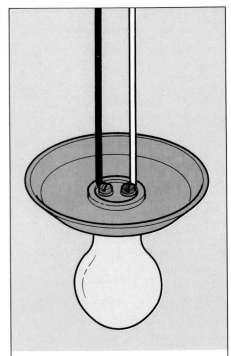

Wiring the light fixture. Connect the black wire to the brass light terminal and the white wire to the silver or light-colored light terminal.

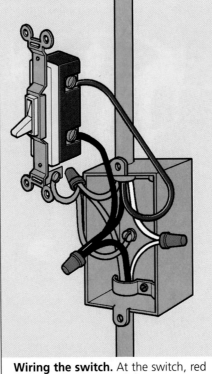

Wiring the switch. At the switch, red hooks to the top terminal and black to the bottom terminal. White bypasses the switch; ground is connected.

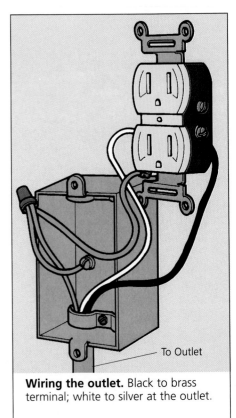

To Outlet

Wiring the outlet. Black to brass terminal; white to silver at the outlet.

to the box and the switch as shown.

4 Wiring the Outlet.
Fasten the black wire to the brass terminal

and the white wire to the silver terminal. Connect the ground with a pigtail to the box and the outlet.

Single-Pole Switch Controls Outlet Only

If you're operating a light or other device from an outlet and want to control it with a switch, here is how to wire it.

Use two-wire cable with ground throughout. **Turn off the power before starting to work.**

1 **At the Outlet.** Connect the incoming white wire from the power source to the silver terminal on the outlet. Connect the outgoing black wire to the bottom brass-colored terminal on the outlet. Then connect the incoming black wire to the outgoing white wire. Mark the white wire HOT by taping the insulation with a few wraps of black electrician's tape. The ground wire is pigtailed to the metal box, to the outlet grounding screw, and to the outgoing ground valve. Twist wire nuts around all splices and wrap the joints with electrician's tape.

2 **At the Switch.** Connect the white wire to the top brass-colored terminal. Then wrap this white wire with electrician's tape to indicate a hot wire. Connect the black wire to the other switch terminal. Fasten the ground wire to the junction box. If the switch has a ground terminal, pigtail the ground wire and connect it both at the box and the switch grounding terminal.

General Procedure. To make terminal connections, you will need approximately 6 inches of wire in the box to make the connections easily. Strip about ½ to ¾ inch of insulation from the ends of the wires without nicking the metal conductor. Use a pair of needle-nose pliers to bend each wire end into a hook that goes around the terminal screw with the opening to the right. Tighten each screw firmly to secure its wire. Fold the extra wire accordionwise as you place the switch or receptacle in its box. The wire is stiff, but use your fingers, not pliers, to avoid damaging it.

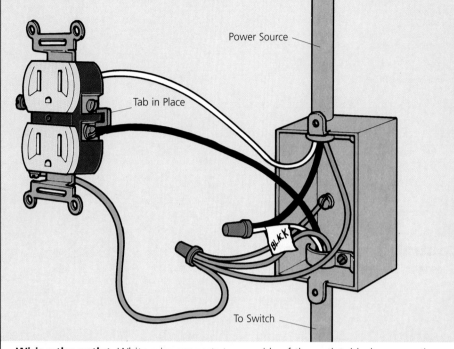

Wiring the outlet. White wire connects to one side of the outlet; black power wire from the switch goes to the other side of the outlet.

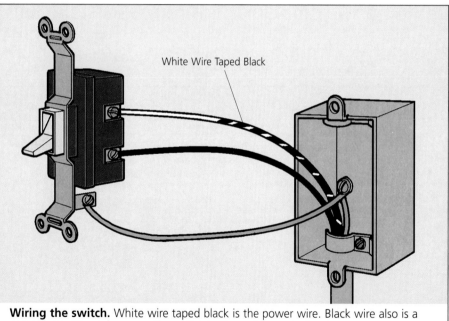

Wiring the switch. White wire taped black is the power wire. Black wire also is a power wire. Power bypasses the outlet to the switch control.

Single-Pole Switch Controlling Split Outlet with Power Through Outlet

Use this hookup when you want a single-pole switch to control half of an outlet with the other half of the outlet (bottom) hot at all times. This installation might be in a living or family room where you want to control table lamps along a circuit with a switch, but want other outlets hot at all times.

A two-wire with ground cable is used throughout this circuit with the power coming through the outlet. If this project involves a new circuit, make all the wiring/outlet/switch hookups and then let a professional electrician connect the circuit to the power supply.

1 Wiring the Outlet. Turn off the power before doing any work on the circuit.

The black wire, using a pigtail, is connected from the power source to the bottom brass terminal of the outlet. The white wire is connected to the upper silver terminal of the outlet.

Wrap the white wire running from the outlet to the switch with electrician's tape to indicate that it is now a hot wire. This wire is then spliced to the black wire pigtail and incoming black power wire. The ground is connected, with a pigtail, to the metal box and the grounding terminal of the outlet.

Use a screwdriver or pliers to remove the tab between the brass terminals of

the outlet. The switch will then control the upper half of the outlet and the bottom half will always be hot.

2 Wiring the Switch. The black power wire is connected to one brass terminal of the single-pole switch. The white wire, coded black with electrician's tape, is connected to the other brass terminal. The ground wire is screwed to the metal box. It may be pigtailed and connected to the switch ground terminal if the switch has a ground terminal.

Adding or Replacing Three-Way Switches

Three-way switches control the power to a light or other electrical device from two separate points. An example is a light in a hallway that can be operated from both the first floor and the second floor. Another example is a light in a garage that can be turned on/off from the garage and also from the kitchen or living room.

Three-way switches require a three-wire system: a power wire and two interconnecting wires called travellers. A fourth, grounding, wire is also required except with metal conduit. The proper cable is marked 12/3 WITH GROUND or 14/3 WITH GROUND.

Two three-way switches are also required. Each switch has three terminal screws on the side or back: two on one side, one on the other side. One terminal will be a distinctive color—often black—or will be marked COM, for common. This terminal is for the prime power wire, the black wire in a cable. The other two terminals are for so-called traveller wires that interconnect the switches. When a white wire is used as a traveller in a three-way switch hookup it must be marked with black tape because it too carries power.

Code Requirements

The National Electrical Code specifies that all wire must be spliced inside a

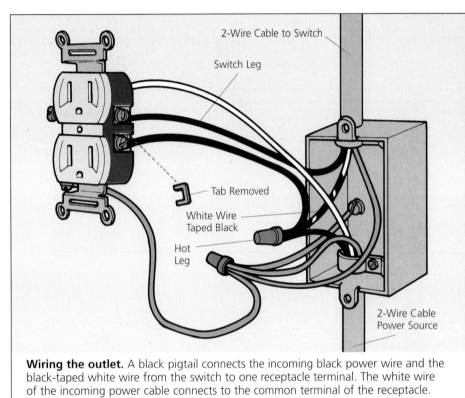

Wiring the outlet. A black pigtail connects the incoming black power wire and the black-taped white wire from the switch to one receptacle terminal. The white wire of the incoming power cable connects to the common terminal of the receptacle.

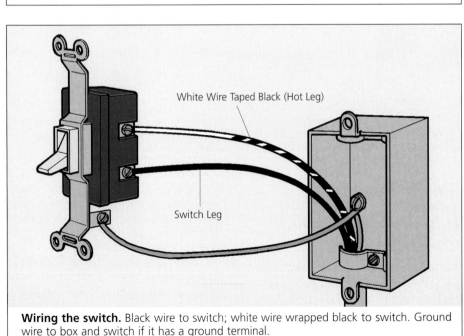

Wiring the switch. Black wire to switch; white wire wrapped black to switch. Ground wire to box and switch if it has a ground terminal.

switch, outlet, or junction box. If you splice wire outside the box and there is an electrical fire at this point, your fire insurance coverage could be void.

If you're simply replacing a switch—removing the old switch and installing a new switch—additional wire will not be necessary. In this situation, just connect the new switch to the same wires as the old switch.

You cannot add a three-way switch circuit using two-wire with ground cable.

To add a three-way switch circuit, you will need either (1) three-wire with ground nonmetallic or BX armored cable, or (2) three wires (black, red, white) to pull through metal conduit. The conduit itself can act as a grounding wire.

How Much Wire?

To figure how much wire you need, measure the distance between the new outlet and the power source. Add an extra foot for every connection you will make along the line. Then, to provide a margin for error, add 20 percent more. For example, if you measure 12 feet of cable between a new and existing receptacle, add another 2 feet for the two connections, making the total 14 feet. Then add 20 percent, about 3 feet to the total. To do this job you should buy 17 feet of cable.

As mentioned above, wire may not be spliced outside a box. Inside a box, the wire must be spliced together using a twisted wire splice covered by a wire nut and electrician's wire tape.

The wire may be attached to a fixture, switch, and outlet terminals. To make connections, pull the wire through boxes about 6 inches. Then cut the wire and strip the insulation from the end. See "Working with Nonmetallic Cable," page 95.

Wiring Three-Way Switches

On the following pages, you will find wiring diagrams for three-way switches. By following the paths of individual wires carefully, you can make the connections properly.

Whether you are installing a new circuit or are adding three-way switches to an existing circuit, be sure to identify which wire brings the power into each switch box. It must go to the common terminal of the switch. This is the key to wiring the switches correctly.

Solving the Puzzle

In wiring three-way switches you will use two-wire (black and white) and three-wire (black, white, red) cables with ground to make connections between two switches and one or more fixture, all in individual boxes. Electricians use the procedure described here to make the work go faster:

1. Run lengths of cable from box to box in the circuit. Add enough to make the connections, as explained above.

2. If the power source cable comes into a switch box, connect its black wire to the common (COM) terminal of the switch there. If the power cable comes into the fixture box, connect its black wire to the black wire running to one of the switches, and connect that to the COM terminal.

3. The power cable white wire must connect to the silver terminal of the fixture. If the power comes into the fixture box, connect it directly to the fixture. If it comes into a switch box, connect the power cable white wire to the white wire of the other cable there. Depending on the hookup, the power cable white wire may go to the fixture box, where you can connect it. If it goes to the other switch box, connect it to the white wire there that goes to the fixture.

4. Connect the COM terminal of the second switch to the black wire that goes to the fixture box, and there connect to the brass fixture terminal.

5. Two unconnected wires remain at each switch, red and black or red and white, depending on the layout. Connect these traveller wires to the two open terminals on each switch. If one wire is white, tape both ends black to mark it as a hot wire. If the travellers pass through the fixture box, connect them there: red to red, and black to black (or taped whites together).

6. Where there are two or more grounding wires, connect them with a pigtail to the ground terminal in the box. Where there is only one grounding wire, connect it to the box terminal.

One Fixture Controlled by Two Switches, Power Through a Switch Box

In this circuit, the power cable comes into the first switch box. The path goes through the second switch, and on to the fixture.

To install this circuit, you will need three-wire cable with ground between the two switches, and two-wire cable with ground between the second switch and the fixture. Local codes may require the use of conduit, especially for an outdoor light.

Turn off the power to this circuit at the service panel before starting work.

1 **Wiring No. 1 Switch.** Power enters the first switch box on a two-wire cable with ground. Hook the black or power wire to the common terminal on the switch. Connect the white wire to the white wire of the three-wire cable going to switch No. 2. Connect the red and black wires in the three-wire cable to the two lower terminals on switch No. 1. Connect the grounding wires in both cables to a pigtail connected to the box ground terminal and the switch ground terminal.

2 **Wiring Switch No. 2.** Connect the black and red wires in the three-wire cable from switch No. 1 to the two lower terminals of the switch. Connect the white wire to the white wire of the two-wire cable that goes

to the light. Connect the black wire in the light cable to the common terminal of switch No. 2. Connect the cable grounding wires to a pigtail attached to the box.

3 Wiring the Fixture. Connect the black wire in the two-wire cable from switch No. 2 to the black lead or brass terminal of the fixture. Connect the cable white wire to the white fixture lead or silver terminal. Connect the cable grounding wire to the box grounding terminal.

Fixture Controlled by Two Switches, Power Through Fixture Box

In this setup, the power comes into the light fixture on a two-wire cable with ground. The power is wired to pass through the fixture box to the two switches and then return to the fixture. A two-wire cable with ground is used between the fixture and one switch, and a three-wire cable with ground between the two switches. In this circuit the white wire in both cables becomes a hot wire. Therefore it must be marked with black tape.

Turn off the power at the service panel before starting work.

1 Wire No. 1 Switch. Connect the black wire from the cable between switches to the common terminal. Tape the white wire black and connect it to one lower terminal. Connect the red wire to the other terminal. Connect the grounding wire to the box terminal.

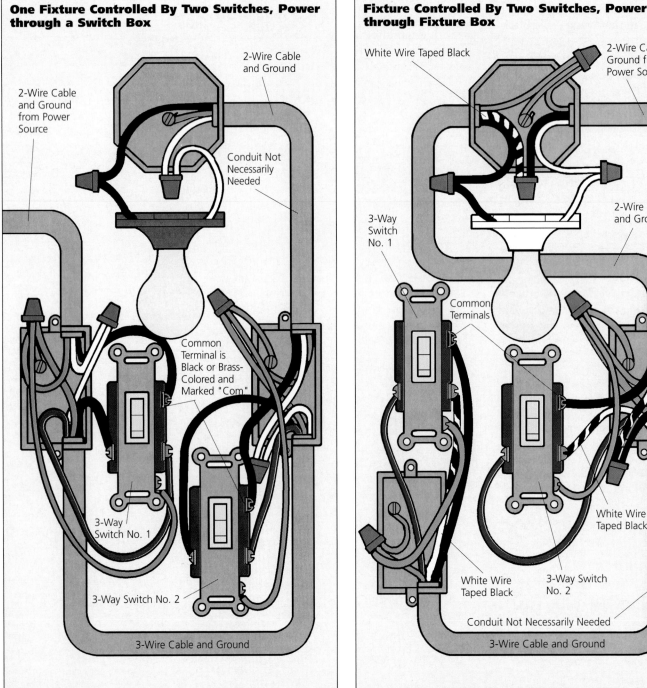

One Fixture Controlled By Two Switches, Power through a Switch Box

- 2-Wire Cable and Ground
- 2-Wire Cable and Ground from Power Source
- Conduit Not Necessarily Needed
- Common Terminal is Black or Brass-Colored and Marked "Com"
- 3-Way Switch No. 1
- 3-Way Switch No. 2
- 3-Wire Cable and Ground

Fixture Controlled By Two Switches, Power through Fixture Box

- White Wire Taped Black
- 2-Wire Cable and Ground from Power Source
- 3-Way Switch No. 1
- 2-Wire Cable and Ground
- Common Terminals
- White Wire Taped Black
- White Wire Taped Black
- 3-Way Switch No. 2
- Conduit Not Necessarily Needed
- 3-Wire Cable and Ground

2 Wire No. 2 Switch. Connect the red wire from the cable between switches to one lower terminal. Tape the white wire in this cable black and connect it to the other lower terminal. Tape the white wire in the fixture cable black and connect it to the black wire in the switch cable. Connect the black wire in the fixture cable to the common switch terminal. Connect the cable grounding wires to a pigtail to the box ground terminal.

3 Wire the Fixture. Connect the black wire in the cable from switch No. 2 to the brass terminal. Tape the white wire in the switch cable black and connect it to the black wire from the power source. Connect the white wire in the power cable to the white fixture wire or silver terminal. Connect the cable grounding wires to a pigtail to the box terminal.

Fixture Between Two Three-Way Switches, Power Through Switch

Here, a light fixture is between two three-way switches with power coming to the first switch on a two-wire cable with ground. The power passes on through the fixture box to the second switch, and returns to the fixture. Three-wire cable with ground is used between both switches and the fixture. The cable grounding wire (bare or green) is connected to the box of switch No. 2, and to pigtails in the fixture and switch No. 1 boxes. The white wire in the cable between the fixture and switch No. 2 becomes a hot wire in this circuit, so it must be marked with black tape as shown.

1 Wire No. 1 Switch. Connect the incoming black power wire to the common terminal of the switch. Connect the white wire to the white wire of the three-wire cable to the fixture box. Connect the red and black wires of that cable to the other two switch terminals. Pigtail ground wires to terminals in the box and on the switch.

2 Wire the Fixture. Connect the red wires of the two switch cables. Wrap black tape onto the white wire coming from switch No. 2 and connect it to the black wire coming into the fixture from switch No. 1. Connect the white wire from switch No. 1 to the white lead or silver terminal of the fixture. Connect the black wire from switch No. 2 to the black lead or brass terminal of the fixture.

3 Wire No. 2 Switch. Wrap black tape around the white wire. Connect the incoming black wire to the common terminal. Connect the white wire taped black to the terminal below the common terminal. Connect the red wire to the terminal on the opposite side. Make ground wire connections as for No. 1 switch.

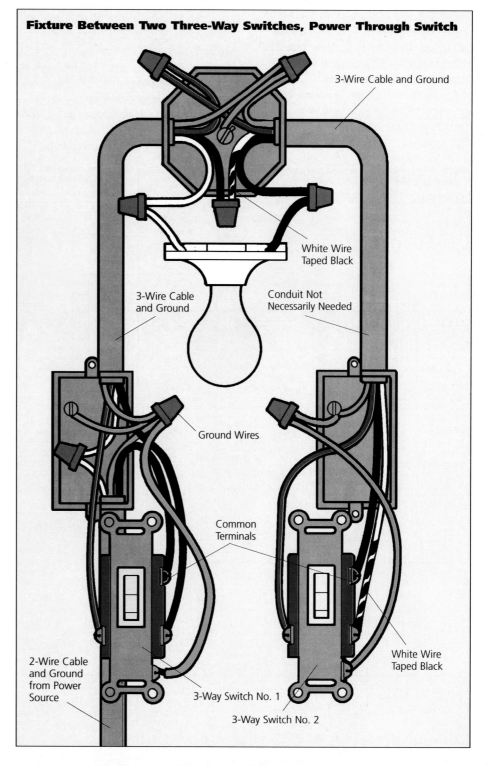

Fixture Between Two Three-Way Switches, Power Through Switch

3-Wire Cable and Ground

White Wire Taped Black

3-Wire Cable and Ground

Conduit Not Necessarily Needed

Ground Wires

Common Terminals

White Wire Taped Black

2-Wire Cable and Ground from Power Source

3-Way Switch No. 1

3-Way Switch No. 2

Fixture Between Three-Way Switches with Power Source at the Light

In this hookup you can use three-wire cable with ground very easily. The power comes through the light ceiling box. Then you connect it to the switches, which are powered on separate lines from opposite sides of the fixture.

Note that the white wire in the power source cable connects directly to the silver terminal of the fixture. The black power wire is connected to the common terminal on switch No. 2. Power is fed back and across to switch No. 1 by white wires coded black with tape to indicate that they are hot between the switches.

1 Wire No. 1 Switch. The black wire in the cable from the fixture box connects to the common terminal. The white wire is taped black. It and the red wire connect to the other two switch terminals. The grounding wire connects to the switch and to the box.

2 Wire the Fixture. The white wire of the power source cable connects to the white lead or silver terminal of the fixture. The black power wire connects to the black wire of the cable to switch No. 2. The red wires of the switch cables connect together, and the white wires of these cables, taped black, connect together. The black wire from switch No. 1 connects to the black lead or brass terminal of the fixture. The grounding wires all connect to a pigtail attached to the box.

3 Wire No. 2 Switch. The connections are the same as at switch No. 1. The black power wire goes to the common switch terminal. The white wire is taped black. It and the red wire go to the other two terminals. The grounding wire connects to the switch and to the box.

Two Lights Between Two Three-Way Switches with Power Through Switch

Power comes into switch No. 1 on a two-wire cable with ground. Three-wire and two-wire cables with ground are used between the four boxes.

Note that two white wires specified below must be taped black because they become power-carrying wires.

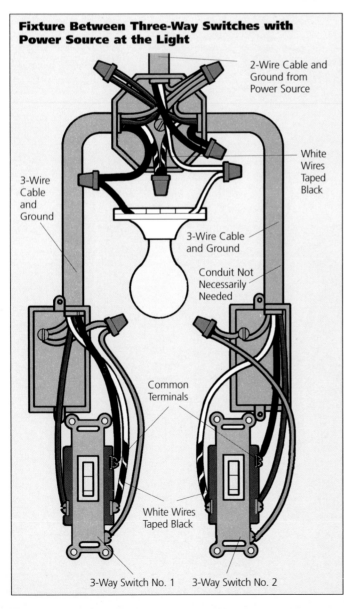

Fixture Between Three-Way Switches with Power Source at the Light

- 2-Wire Cable and Ground from Power Source
- White Wires Taped Black
- 3-Wire Cable and Ground
- 3-Wire Cable and Ground
- Conduit Not Necessarily Needed
- Common Terminals
- White Wires Taped Black
- 3-Way Switch No. 1
- 3-Way Switch No. 2

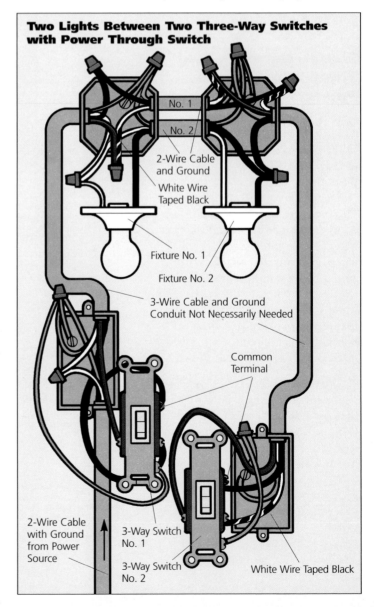

Two Lights Between Two Three-Way Switches with Power Through Switch

- No. 1
- No. 2
- 2-Wire Cable and Ground
- White Wire Taped Black
- Fixture No. 1
- Fixture No. 2
- 3-Wire Cable and Ground Conduit Not Necessarily Needed
- Common Terminal
- 2-Wire Cable with Ground from Power Source
- 3-Way Switch No. 1
- 3-Way Switch No. 2
- White Wire Taped Black

1 **Wire No. 1 Switch.** Connect the black wire in the incoming power cable to the common switch terminal. Connect the white wire to the white wire of the outgoing three-wire cable. Connect the outgoing red and black traveller wires to the other two switch terminals. Pigtail the grounding wires to the box, and to the switch.

2 **Wire the Fixtures.** In No. 1 fixture box, connect the black from switch No. 1 to the black in cable No. 1 to the next box. Connect the red traveller to the white—taped black—in cable No. 1. Connect the whites from switch No. 1 and cable No. 2 to the silver terminal of the fixture. Connect the black wire of cable No. 2 to the brass fixture terminal.

In No. 2 fixture box, tape the white wire in cable No. 1 black and connect it to the red traveller to switch No. 2. Connect the black in cable No. 1 to the white—taped black—going to switch No. 2. Connect the black wires from cable No. 2 and the switch cable to the brass fixture terminal. Connect the white wire in cable No. 2 to the silver fixture terminal.

In both fixture boxes, pigtail all grounding wires to the box terminals.

3 **Wire No. 2 Switch.** Connect the incoming black wire to the COM terminal of the switch. Tape the white wire black and connect it to one open terminal; connect the red wire to the last terminal. Connect the ground wire to the box and switch terminals.

Two Three-Way Switches Controlling Two Lights, Power Through Light

In this arrangement, power comes into one fixture box on a two-wire with ground cable. The two fixture boxes have a three-wire leg between them, as do the switch boxes, but the leg between switch box and fixture box requires only a two-wire cable. The (green) grounding wires are connected to the metal boxes throughout the run.

1 **Wire No. 1 Fixture.** Connect the power source black wire to

the black wire in the three-wire leg to the next box. Connect the white power cable wire to the white wire in the ongoing leg and to the silver fixture terminal. Connect the red wire in the ongoing cable to the brass fixture terminal.

2 **Wire No. 2 Fixture.** Connect the black wire from the first fixture box to the black wire in the cable to switch No. 1. Connect the white wire from the first box to the silver fixture terminal. Connect the red wire to the white wire—taped black—to the switch, and pigtail it to the brass fixture terminal.

3 **Wire No. 1 Switch.** Connect the black wire coming from the fixture box to the common terminal. Tape the white wire of that cable black and connect it to the black in the three-wire cable that goes to switch No. 2. Tape the white traveller in the cable to switch No. 2 black. Connect it to

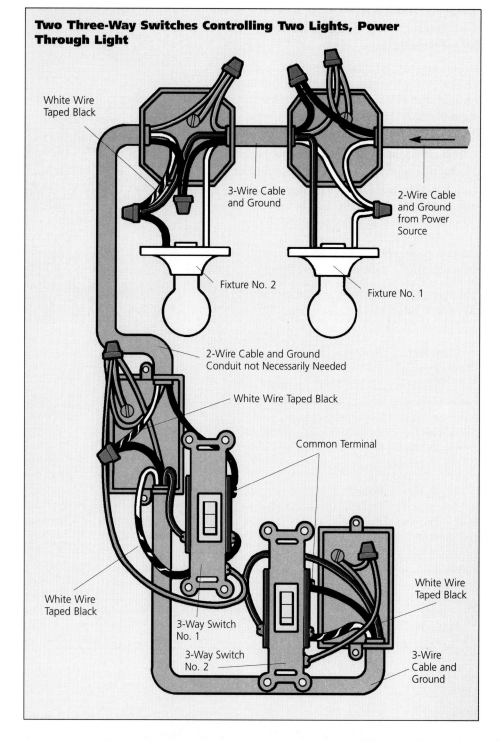

Two Three-Way Switches Controlling Two Lights, Power Through Light

White Wire Taped Black

3-Wire Cable and Ground

2-Wire Cable and Ground from Power Source

Fixture No. 2

Fixture No. 1

2-Wire Cable and Ground Conduit not Necessarily Needed

White Wire Taped Black

Common Terminal

White Wire Taped Black

3-Way Switch No. 1

3-Way Switch No. 2

White Wire Taped Black

White Wire Taped Black

3-Wire Cable and Ground

one open switch terminal and connect the red traveller to the other terminal. Pigtail the grounding wires to the switch and box terminals.

4 Wire No. 2 Switch. Connect the incoming black wire to the common switch terminal. Tape the white wire black and connect it to one open switch terminal. Connect the red to the other terminal. Pigtail the ground wire to the switch and box terminals.

End-of-Run Lights Controlled by Two Three-Way Switches

In this hookup, two lights are at the end of the circuit with power coming through the first switch, running to a second switch, and then on to the light fixtures.

Since only two-wire cable is needed for the fixture-fixture and fixture-switch wiring, you will save money if either or both of these legs in the run is long. Note that in this circuit the red and black wires in the three-wire cable between the switches are the traveller wires.

Throughout the circuit, the grounding wires connect to each other and to pigtails to the metal boxes.

1 Wire No. 1 Switch. Connect the incoming black power wire to the common terminal. Connect the power cable white wire to the outgoing white wire. Connect the outgoing red and black traveller wires to the open switch terminals. Pigtail the grounding wires to the switch and box terminals.

2 Wire No. 2 Switch. Connect the incoming red and black to the two lower switch terminals. Connect the incoming and outgoing whites together. Connect the outgoing black to the common terminal. Pigtail the grounding wires to the switch and box terminals.

3 Wire No. 1 Fixture. Connect the incoming and outgoing black wires together and to the brass terminal. Connect the two white wires together and to the silver terminal.

4 Wire No. 2 Fixture. Connect the incoming black wire to the brass fixture terminal and connect the white wire to the silver terminal. Connect the grounding wire to the box terminal and check that the grounding connections are correct and secure in the other three boxes.

End-Wired Switches with Power Through Fixture Box

Power comes from a two-wire cable with ground coming into the first fixture box. It is routed to the first switch, then by the traveller wires

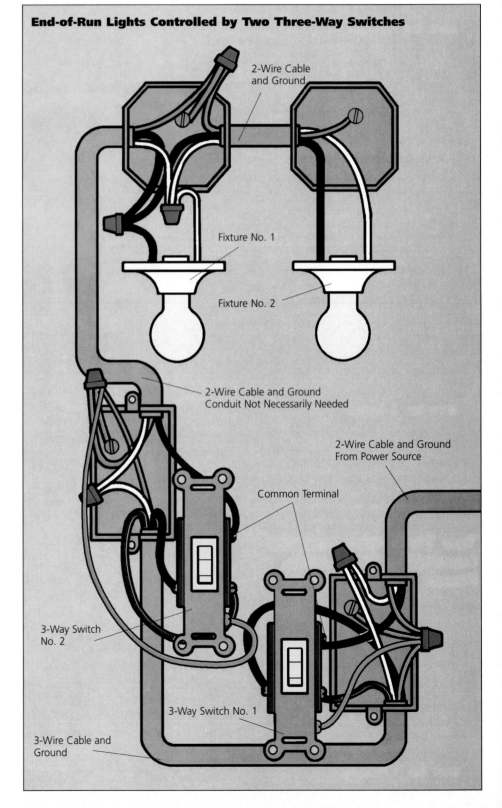

End-of-Run Lights Controlled by Two Three-Way Switches

2-Wire Cable and Ground

Fixture No. 1

Fixture No. 2

2-Wire Cable and Ground
Conduit Not Necessarily Needed

2-Wire Cable and Ground
From Power Source

Common Terminal

3-Way Switch No. 2

3-Way Switch No. 1

3-Wire Cable and Ground

to the second switch, and finally back to the lights. One traveller is red, the other a white wire marked with black tape. The grounding wires are pigtailed to the metal fixture boxes, and connected directly to the switch box terminals. As in the previous two-light hookups, the switches operate both lights, but the wiring arrangement ensures that if one bulb burns out, the other will still work.

1 **Wire No. 1 Fixture.** Connect the incoming power cable black

wire to the black wire going to switch No. 1. Connect the power cable white wire to the white in leg No. 2 to the other fixture and to the silver terminal of the fixture in this box. Connect the black wire in leg No. 2 between fixtures to the brass fixture terminal. Connect the black wire in leg No. 2 between fixtures to the brass fixture terminal. Connect the red wire from switch No. 1 to the black in leg No. 1 to the other fixture. Tape the white from switch No. 1 black and connect it to the black-taped white wire in leg No. 1.

2 **Wire No. 2 Fixture.** Connect the white in leg No. 2 to the silver fixture terminal. Connect the black in leg No. 2 to the black to switch No. 2 and to the brass fixture terminal. Connect the black in leg No. 1 to the red going to switch No. 2. Tape the whites in the leg No. 1 and switch No. 2 cables black and connect them together.

3 **Wire the Switches.** Both switches are wired the same way. Connect the incoming black wire to the common terminal. Tape the white wire black and connect it to one lower terminal. Connect the red wire to the other terminal. Pigtail grounding wires to switch and box terminals.

Choosing Dimmer Switches

For incandescent lighting, solid state dimmers most often used today work by switching the current on and off 120 times per second. Dimming occurs by controlling the amount of time current is flowing versus the amount of time current is not flowing. While the dimmer is off, current flow stops. The longer current is off, the more the lights are dimmed. Because the switching on and off is done so rapidly, the eye perceives a steady level of light even when lights are dimmed to less than one percent of full light.

Perceived Light

What the human eye sees is not the same as the actual dimming level. At the upper end of the dimming range, significant changes in the measured, actual light levels result in only minimal changes in the perceived light level. You can dim lights just slightly to extend lamp life and save energy, but there will be very little perceptible change in light level. For instance, dimming the light to 50 percent will be perceived as though the light were only dimmed to 70 percent. Therefore, there is no dramatic dilation or constriction of the eye due to light level change.

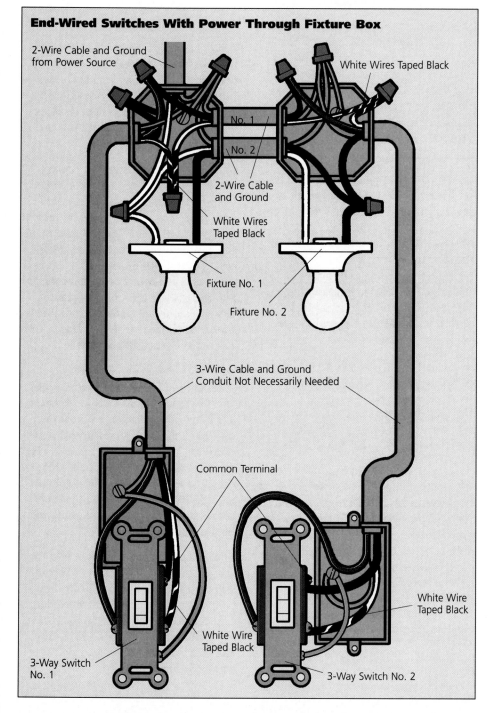

End-Wired Switches With Power Through Fixture Box

2-Wire Cable and Ground from Power Source

White Wires Taped Black

No. 1

No. 2

2-Wire Cable and Ground

White Wires Taped Black

Fixture No. 1

Fixture No. 2

3-Wire Cable and Ground Conduit Not Necessarily Needed

Common Terminal

White Wire Taped Black

White Wire Taped Black

3-Way Switch No. 1

3-Way Switch No. 2

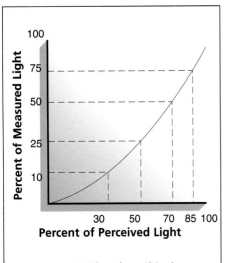

100
75
50
25
10

Percent of Measured Light

30 50 70 85 100
Percent of Perceived Light

Square Law Dimming. This chart shows that in upper lighting ranges, a significant reduction in measured light results in only minimal reduction in perceived light.

Square Law Dimming

To compensate for the difference in perceived and measurable light dimming levels, gradual movement of a linear dimmer slide results in a proportional change in the perceived lighting level. Dimming with direct correlation between the position of the slider and the light perceived by the eye is known as "Square Law Dimming." When the slider is half-way up a linear dimmer, the light is at the 50 percent perceived level in this system.

Advantages of Light Control

Being able to control the light:

- Increases productivity, especially when used around computer areas where users can adjust light levels for themselves. Depending upon age, people require different light levels for the same tasks.

- Adds flexibility, so you can suit lighting to a variety of activities in the same space. For instance, eliminates going "snowblind" when turning on a bathroom light in the middle of the night and can be used as a night light in a child's room.

- Gives greater control when specialized controls are used to set specific scenes of light.

- Improves aesthetics by creating beautiful atmospheres that vary with needs and preferences. The proper light level can be adjusted for outside lighting conditions or task-at-hand to save electricity and for comfort.

- Saves money by enabling you to lower light levels to reduce electricity consumption and increase bulb life or, in the case of table lamp dimmers, by providing control without costly three-way bulbs.

Styles of Dimmers

Dimmers can look sleek and contemporary, with ergonomically easy-to-use rocker pads to depress, or they can have toggles that resemble other switches in your home. Keep switch styles uniform and select a dimmer switch that goes with other switches. Consider the convenience and features of different styles.

Toggle Dimmers. Old-fashioned styles look like regular toggle switches, but light is increased as the toggle is gradually moved. They may also incorporate an on/off switch that clicks to off as the lowest light level is reached. There are other versions as well that incorporate true preset dimming; a small slider to dim or brighten lights is preset, while the toggle turns the light on or off at the dimming level set with the slider.

Rotary Dimmers. Controlled by turning a round knob, which adjusts the light level. Switch rotary dimmers on or off either by turning all the way in one direction or by pushing the knob in, depending on the model.

Slide Dimmers. Operated by moving a sliding knob up or down. The most convenient models have a separate on/off rocker switch that give you the ability to preset light levels. Adjust the slide to the light level you prefer and use the rocker switch to turn it on or off. Contemporary models are easy to use and sleek.

Paddle or Rocker Switches. Often incorporated with slider dimmers and other more contemporary designs for dimming.

Touch-Pad Units with Mini-Slides

These unit are easy to operate once the level is set, and suit ergonomic needs of those who can't easily use conventional switches. More sophisticated units allow you to tap switches once for on/off function, tap twice to adjust dimmer function to full, then press a dimmer rocker to adjust light levels including a 10 second fade-to-off feature for exiting a room. Light Emitting Diodes (LEDs) indicate the light level at which the unit is working and include a night light indicator.

Other Considerations

Personalized features with dimmers include many choices. Fan/light combinations that separately control these two functions are one selection. Some styles lend themselves to being ganged together at one location for a sleek look.

Remote dimmer sets enable you to dim a fixture and still have control from two locations, as with an ordinary three-way switch. In some remote sets, the master enables you to dim the light and the remote is a simple on-off switch. In more sophisticated units, you can dim from the master and the remote unit. Some remote sets can be incorporated into a system similar to those that open garage doors or control your television set.

You may want to use dimmers on all your lighting in a given space, or just dim the lighting that calls for greatest flexibility. For example, a simple on/off switch may suffice for a bedroom overhead light that is rarely used, while dimmers for task and ambient light in the same room might make a substantial difference. In that case, dimmers that match the switches are going to be most attractive.

For efficiency and safety, it is important to follow manufacturer's recommendations. You can burn out the lamps, burn out the dimmer, void Underwriters Laboratory's specifications and manufacturer's warranties and in a worst case scenario, cause an electrical fire.

Dimming Fluorescent Lights

You cannot use incandescent lighting dimmers for fluorescents, and that includes compact fluorescents that screw into conventional incandescent fixtures. However, fluorescent lighting can be dimmed using a system involving a special fluorescent dimmer and ballast. The dimmer works in conjunction with the ballast to regulate the light. Usually, fluorescent dimmer manufacturers make the whole system or specify exactly what kinds of fluorescent lighting is suited to the dimmers.

Cove lighting with a fluorescent base, undercabinet lighting in a kitchen/ dining room area or even lighting in a luxurious bathroom all lend themselves to dimmer control to go from brisk and utilitarian to relaxed and inviting.

Low-Voltage Lighting

With the aid of transformers, low-voltage lighting lends itself to dimming as well. In fact, there are few kinds of lighting that do not have a corresponding dimmer system specifically applicable to them.

Installing Dimmer Switches

A dimmer switch allows you to select different intensities of light to create a mood or to conserve electricity. You must not use them to control receptacles into which you may plug appliances or power tools. This could result in damage to the dimmer switch and possibly to the appliance or tool.

A high-low dimmer switch has a toggle that lets you select one of three positions: OFF, LOW, and HIGH.

A rotary slide, paddle or rocker dimmer switch lets you set the control for light output thatis fully on, fully off, or any intensity in between.

A line dimmer switch has a rotary dial that sets the light output. This switch comes in a cord set for use with table or freestanding lamps. You will have to rewire the lamp (see pages 109, "Rewiring Freestanding Lamps") so the lamp can be dimmed properly.

Fluorescent lamps may be controlled by a special fluorescent dimmer switch and ballast combination.

Like toggle switches, dimmers are available as single-pole and three-way switches. A single-pole dimmer has two wires, or leads (usually black). A three-way dimmer has three leads, usually one red and two black. Determine whether the switch you want to replace with a dimmer is a single-pole or a three-way type.

Single-Pole Incandescent Dimmers

Turn off the power and remove the faceplate and switch from the electrical box. Test for power using a voltage tester to be sure the power is off. Disconnect the circuit wires from the old switch and attach them to the leads on the new dimmer switch. The dimmer's wires are interchangeable, so they each can be attached to either of the free wires in the box. If there was a ground wire attached to the old switch, attach it to the ground screw in the electrical box.

Three-Way Incandescent Dimmers

To function properly a three-way dimmer must be paired with a conventional three-way toggle switch, so in a three-way circuit replace only one of the two conventional switches. Turn off the circuit breaker and pull the old switch from the box. The switch has a black screw that indicates the common terminal. To test for absence of power, touch one of the voltage tester's leads to this screw and wire and the other to a ground. Once you're sure the power is off, disconnect the wire from the common terminal and mark it. This wire may be red or, more likely, black. Disconnect the other wires, called travelers, from the old switch.

Middle-of-Run Switch. If the switch is in the middle of a circuit run, the travelers may both be black wires or they may be a red wire and a black wire.

End-of-Run Switch. If the switch is at the end of the run, the travelers may be a red wire and a white wire marked with black tape or a black wire and a white wire marked with black tape. Connect the marked common wire from the circuit to the red wire on the dimmer switch. In either switch

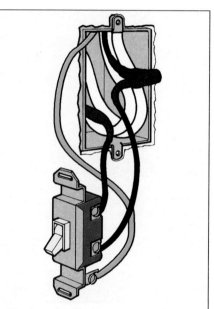

Single-pole dimmer. Remove the old switch and replace it with a dimmer switch. Splice the wires with wire nuts and tape.

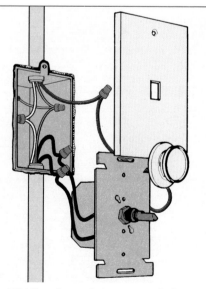

Middle of run three-way switch. Conect the common wire from the power source to the red wire on the dimmers switch. Connect the traveler wires to the black wires on the switch.

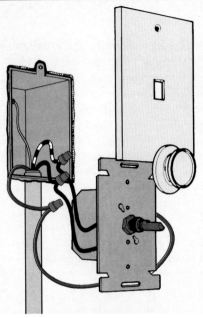

End-of-run three-way switch.
Connect one traveler wire from the fixture to one black wire from the dimmer and the other traveler wire to the other dimmer black wire. Connect the common wire from the fixture to the red wire on the dimmer.

connect the two traveler wires from the circuit to the remaining two black wires on the dimmer switch. Either of the travelers may be attached to either of the dimmer's black wires. If there is a ground wire running in the circuit cable that was attached to the old switch, attach it to the ground screw in the electrical box. Push the wires and dimmer switch into the electrical box and fasten the dimmer housing to the holes in the box. Install the faceplate and the control knob.

Fluorescent Dimmer Switches and Ballasts

Fluorescent fixtures with external or instant-start starters require extensive work to adapt them for dimmer switches. Here you'll find directions for installing a dimmer to control a 40-watt rapid-start fluorescent light.

1 Remove the Ballast. Turn off the power to the circuit and remove the fluorescent lamp and metal lid that covers the ballast and wiring. Remove the terminal screws.

Remove the wire nuts and untwist the wires. Don't disconnect the equipment grounding conductor.

Unscrew the ballast lock nuts. Lift out the ballast and terminals.

2 Unhook Lamp Terminals. Notice the wiring setup. Two sets of wires extend from the ballast, one from each end. The wires at one end have the same color insulation. At the other end they are white, black, and a third, different color.

Disconnect all of these wires from the lamp terminals. Align the new dimmer ballast wires with those in the old ballast, so the new hookup will be identical with the old. If there is a short white wire protruding from one of the lamp terminals, connect it to the white wire from the dimmer ballast. This terminal is prewired.

3 Connect Dimmer Ballast. Wire the new dimmer ballast to the lamp terminals by pressing the clamps,

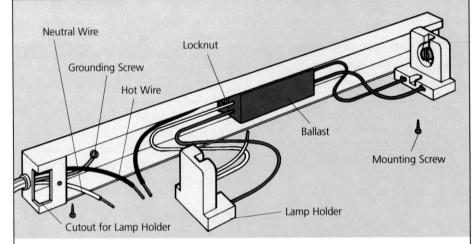

Remove the ballast. Turn off the power on the circuit. Remove the fluorescent tube and cover plate. Unscrew the ballast locknuts and remove the ballast. Then slip the lamp holders out of their retaining brackets. Dimmer are easy to install on rapid-start units.

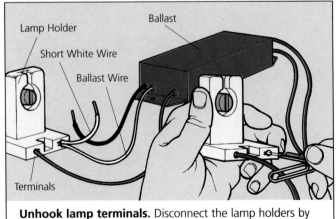

Unhook lamp terminals. Disconnect the lamp holders by inserting a stiff wire, such as the end of a paper clip, into the opening beside the ballast wire to release the circuit wire. Note color-coded wires so you can reassemble the unit with the new dimmer-type ballast.

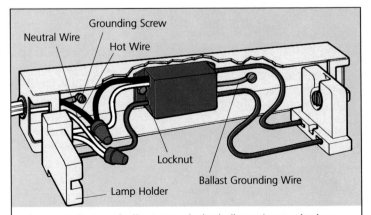

Connect dimmer ballast. Attach the ballast wires to the lamp holders; slip the holders into position, and then fasten down the ballast. Splice the house and ballast wires using wire nuts and electrician's tape. You must now install a dimmer switch.

pushing the wires into the respective slots, and releasing the clamps.

Attach the dimmer switch ballast to the fixture with the lock nuts. Reinsert the two lamp terminals and fasten them in. Then connect the ballast wiring to the house wiring by splicing the hot wires together, and the neutral wires together. Reinstall the fixture cover and fluorescent lamp.

Installing a Fluorescent Dimmer Switch

A dimmer switch for a fluorescent light can control as many as eight fluorescent bulbs simultaneously. However, the ballast of every fluorescent fixture you want to control must be replaced with the special dimmer ballast. A dimmer switch also is larger than most conventional or special switches. It will fit into a standard box. You may need to replace an old-style box with a larger one to accommodate the new switch and wires.

Dimmer switch markings are similar to those on conventional switches. A dimmer switch also has data that tells you the total maximum bulb wattage that may be used with the switch. Buy a switch that can handle your fixtures.

Mechanically, a fluorescent dimmer switch is installed the same way as an incandescent one. Turn off the power to the circuit. Remove the faceplate and then the switch. Remove the wires from the terminals.

1 **Connect the New Switch.** Splice the leads on the switch to the incoming hot wire in the box and to the outgoing wire to the fixture. One of these will be black, the other will be white taped black. Use wire nuts and tape them in place. Then mount the switch in the box.

2 **Set the Dimmer.** Turn on the power. Push the dimmer control knob onto the dimmer switch shaft. Then turn the control knob so the light is turned down to its low lighting capacity. Now turn the knurled adjustment nut, located at the base of the shaft on which the control knob fits, counterclockwise with pliers until the lamp flickers. Then turn the nut clockwise until the lamp stops flickering. The adjustment is made.

3 **Install the Cover Plate.** When the control knob is set to your satisfaction— high to low light—remove the control knob and mount the face-

plate on the switch housing. It screws on just like a conventional faceplate. Then reinstall the control knob. Test the light from high to low. When the knob is on the high setting, the light should be fully on. When it's on low, the light should be at its lowest level. If not, you will have to remove the faceplate and adjust the nut.

Interference Trouble

The addition of a dimmer switch may cause interference with television, radio, and stereo systems. Although dimmer switches usually have a filter to block out signals created by the switch, some signals can penetrate the filter.

One way to lessen interference is to plug television, radio, and stereo equipment into a circuit other than the one serving the dimmer switch. If this does not work, purchase a power-line filter from a TV supply store and attach it, as directed, between the equipment and the receptacle into which you plug the equipment. A power-line filter traps interfering signals created by dimmer switches.

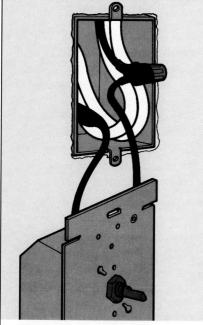

Connect new switch. Join the switch leads to the incoming power and fixture hot wires. Power and fixture white wires join directly.

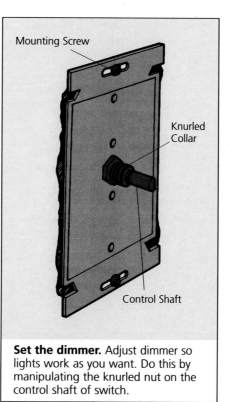

Mounting Screw

Knurled Collar

Control Shaft

Set the dimmer. Adjust dimmer so lights work as you want. Do this by manipulating the knurled nut on the control shaft of switch.

Install cover plate. The cover plate goes over the switch housing. Push the control knob on the projecting shaft and test the full range of the light.

10
Exterior Lighting

Techniques for lighting outdoors are in many ways similar to indoor lighting techniques. Outdoors and in, designs include wall grazing, spotlighting, floodlighting, creating pathways, and layering lighting with exciting varieties of bright and mood-setting light.

Be sure to use lighting components such as wiring, bulbs, and fixtures designed for outdoor use where weather and temperature extremes are more rigorous than indoors. Note that some bulbs are not designed for use with the base up. Do not use them in fixtures with the sockets at the top.

A major difference in planning an outdoor lighting scheme is that it often means pointing at a moving target. While entrances, walkways, and the house don't move, the trees, shrubs, flowers, and even grass sway and change during the seasons. One section blooms and another goes to seed. A key ornamental is trained or pruned into an attractive shape. And, most important of all, major elements in the outdoor lighting scheme *grow*. Within a few years, a spotlight placed too close to a shrub can be enveloped by it. You need to keep up with the landscape changes through shifts in lighting emphasis.

Besides growth, a good outdoor lighting plan takes into account these factors:

■ What is the visual focus or focuses you want to create? Perhaps you want to focus on a fabulous specimen tree, a swimming pool, a winding pathway, deck, or entranceway.

■ What is the mood or intent of the lighting? Bright for taking out the garbage, but dim for the hot tub?

■ What light level best suits household members? Are they old enough to need brighter lighting for safety?

■ Will any landscaping plans affect the lighting, and how will the natural maturation process affect the scheme? Should you anticipate wanting more lighting in a specific location or an extension of lighting to be used in years to come?

In addition to these considerations, a good outdoor lighting plan provides pleasing light when viewed from inside your home and approaching it. It allows for the safe navigation of the landscape, properly illuminating changes in grade, rough paving surfaces, and other obstacles. It gives a nighttime garden a sense of depth and color. It provides a selective focus of light through highlighting, and it uses bright areas to lead your eyes pleasantly around the landscape. It models special parts of your landscape through contrasts and shadow, revealing the sculptural forms to their best advantage. And outdoor lighting sets the mood, creating a new nighttime environment integrated into the architecture of your home.

The artistic challenge of designing exterior lighting is deciding how to distribute the light. From which direction should the light come? How intense should it be? An outdoor lighting design orchestrates the light's movement and determines how the eye is drawn to favorite objects, such

as a trellis archway or birdbath, or is persuaded to follow a path through a garden. These choices create the visual treats that are the magic of exterior lighting.

There also are visual pitfalls to be avoided. For instance, outdoor lighting should not glare into your home or your neighbor's. Many light sources are best concealed, drawing attention to what they light rather than to themselves. You often can hide fixtures behind shrubs, embedded in borders, or lodged below ground.

People are more comfortable if they see one definitive light source, even though all the lighting could not possibly come from that fixture. Select a fixture that is a decorative asset for your home, such as a carriage post lantern fixture, for instance.

Don't over light. Eyes accommodate to nighttime and are able to see well with surprisingly little illumination. There's no reason to brightly light. It is not daylight, and you cannot recreate daytime, so do not try. However, do provide adequate transitional lighting from inside to outside, allowing eyes to adjust. That's one reason to have a front porch light.

Lighting for Effect

Drive around neighborhoods and you will see the lighting you admire. Make a mental note of what you like and see if you can apply the same principles in your own lighting scheme. Here are some of the techniques that are effective:

Downlighting or Area Lighting

For highlighting flower beds, paths, or steps, a downlight is positioned close to the ground. To cast broad illumination over wide areas, lights are mounted high up in trees or on the house. This floodlighting enables you to entertain in your backyard or outdoor area after dark. Lighting an area away from your house, such as a glade within a group of trees, visually extends your property and makes it seem most spacious. Area lighting also can surround your home with a bright moat for security and safety.

Uplighting. Theatrical but interesting, uplighting capitalizes on the beauty of trees and statuary or grazes interesting walls. Uplights can even be buried to spotlight large trees or small walls or bushes. Rain, snow, and autumn leaves are displayed in full glory with uplighting.

Accent or Spot Lighting. Accent lighting highlights the focal points of a garden, such as statuary, flowers, small shrubs, or decorative structures. These areas of interest, more strongly lit than anything else, give the scheme its necessary sparkle. A controlled intense beam is focused specifically on the object.

Spread or Diffused Lighting. Some areas, such as patios, decks, driveways, and pathways, are best lit with even, diffused light. Other areas that are best lit with circular patterns of light such as flower beds, ground cover, or shrubbery, benefit from spread lights that cover a wide area of low-level illumination. Mushroom and bollard lighting fixtures, deck lights, and even wall fixtures can provide these effects.

Moonlighting. This lovely effect sends light filtering through branches and casting interesting complex shadow patterns, much as real moonlight does. The iridescent color of translucent leaves, backlit, also adds to the magic. To create the effect, install soft light sources very high up.

Low downlighting. Position downlighting close to the ground for emphasizing flower beds, steps, and paths.

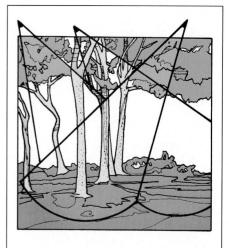

High downlighting. To floodlight a broad area mount downlighting high in trees.

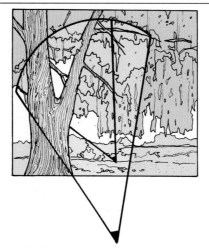

Uplighting. Use uplighting for dramatic effect such as to highlight interesting trees, statuary, or textured walls.

Accent or spotlighting. An intense beam of light is focussed on a special object you want to emphasize.

Spread or diffused light. Areas such as patios, decks, driveways, and walkways are best lit with a even, diffused light.

Moonlighting. Much like the light of the moon, fixtures set high filter light through branches and leaves.

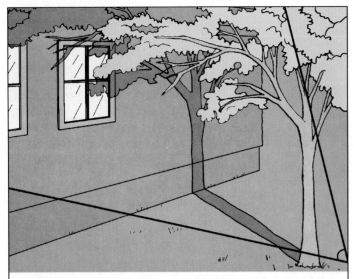

Shadowing. Use the shadowing effect to provide a sense of depth and project intriguing shadows on vertical surfaces behind the object.

Silhouetting. The reverse of shadowing, silhouetting lights objects from behind, obscuring detail and emphasizing shape.

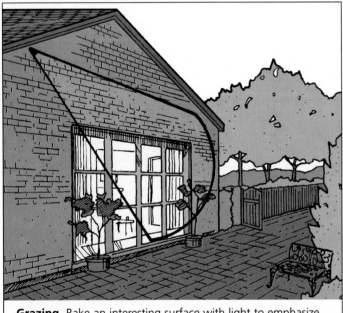

Grazing. Rake an interesting surface with light to emphasize its texture.

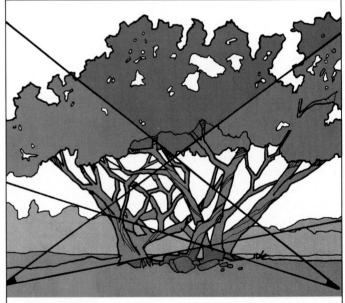

Cross Lighting. By using more than one light source you will create an effect that is softer, deeper, and more pleasing.

Shadowing. Shadowing provides a sense of depth. As the flip side of your lighting scheme, it plays a balancing role. Dramatic shadows often are as stunning as the lighting in other areas of a landscape.

To project intriguing shadows on a wall or other vertical surface behind an object, light the object such as a tree or sculpture from diagonally in front and below it.

Silhouetting. Take advantage of an interestingly shaped object by doing the reverse of shadowing. Light the vertical background behind an object so that it is silhouetted in front of the light, much as it would be silhouetted against the sky if it were on a ridge.

Grazing. Textures take on added excitement at night because it is easy to create strong contrasts. Wonderful tree bark, masonry walls, stucco, or wood shingles are all worthy of special grazing lighting. Place the light source close to the surface to rake across it, creating shadows to emphasize the relief and protrusions.

Cross Lighting. Softer shadows, added depth and dimension, and a more pleasing, rounded effect are achieved when more than one single light source is used. This method reveals the three-dimensional form of a tree or object, illuminating both sides. Cross two or more floodlight beams high above the subject, or light from below. Make sure, however, that the light beams do not extend to areas (such as windows) where they produce glare.

Contour Lighting

Define borders of paths, reflecting pools, and flower beds with lighting that is designed to specifically highlight those areas. Specialized downlighting with low, hooded fixtures (such as mushroom lights or tier lights) create this effect. Adjustable units allow you to direct the light at exactly the landscape feature you want to highlight.

Mirror Lighting. You may not have a formal garden with a huge reflecting pool, but even a small body of water can create a wonderful calming design element when lights are reflected upon it. Select lighting that will be reflected by the pool from favorite views, such as off the deck or beyond the family room windows. Ponds can be transformed at night with mirror lighting. Consider this effect for water gardens as well.

You can use a balance of uplighting and silhouetting from the real moon to show off a variety of trees and shrubs, here reflected in a pool.

Concealed lighting dramatizes bare tree limbs, defining the homeowner's property.

An ornamental lamp sets the tone and visually justifies other light sources that make the most of ornamental shrubs.

Use of the same fixture style outside and inside decoratively unifies this patio and living room.

Plan outdoor lighting with views from your windows in mind for the most enjoyment. Here, a magnificent tree is spotlighted and blends inside and out.

Low-voltage tier lights outlining plantings cast light directly on the most decorative garden assets.

Low-voltage lights delineate stone walls, a pool with a waterfall, and a two-level patio.

Balance underwater pool lighting with lighting of surrounding trees for greatest aesthetic appeal.

Underwater Lighting

Pools and fountains create dramatic focal points when lit from beneath, although they usually lose the natural look. A word of caution: if your pool is overhung and subject to fallen leaves and the like, underwater lighting silhouettes all this unwanted debris to make it show more. Mirror lighting might be a better choice in this case.

For any underwater applications, check for code regulations and obviously, use systems designed specifically for underwater use. Electricity and water do not mix unless properly handled.

Lighting for Safety and Security

Aesthetics aside, lighting plays an important role in outdoor safety and security. Stairway lights should shine down toward the riser so the treads will not be in shadow. Police recommend that, in addition to eliminating overhanging shrubs near your home, you use exterior lighting to illuminate the front entry, vulnerable areas close to the house, and the garage.

Timers and controls that are located inside your home are part of an overall security and safety system. Areas for special attention include the following:

Entryways. Usually lit by wall-mounted fixtures or overhead lights,

A combination of low-voltage exterior lights that graze the walls, highlight shrubs, and provide ambient lighting, all transform this home into a dramatic presence at night.

Floodlights positioned behind shrubs that illuminate all possible entrances deter burglars.

Entryways. Light the front entry to your home with wall-mounted or overhead fixtures or both.

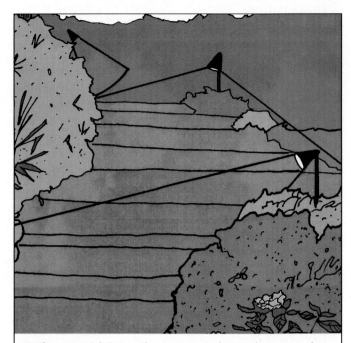

Pathways. Lighting pathways to your home does more than say "welcome." Proper pathway lighting is essential to safety.

entryways require adequate illumination for front steps, house numbers, and the keyhole. If one bracket only is used, place it on the keyhole side of the door. Flanking wall lanterns should be centered 66 inches above standing level at the door, with each lantern having a range of 20 to 60 watts, or if placed far apart, 75 to 100 watts.

Under a porch or other overhang, recessed or close-to-ceiling fixtures with 60 to 100 watts are best. Wall mounted fixtures centered over a house or garage door should be 75 to 100 watts.

There are compact fluorescent and other energy-saving variations, such as halogen, for virtually all exterior entrance lights. Another convenience to look for are controls for timing and motion sensing. Some of these screw in to sockets; others are separate units or are integral with the fixture.

Pathways. Lighting leading from the curb to the front door can illuminate landscaping features along the way or become part of the overall decorative impact of your home. Entrance walkways illuminated with a post lantern are traditional ways of saying welcome. Locate the post at a critical point, such as at steps or

where a path or driveway begins or separates. Plantings below or around the post itself add to its decorative effect. Energy-efficient fluorescent bulbs are suitable in this location.

For safety, provide at least 5 lumens of light at all pathways, ramps, and stairways. Stairway lights should shine down toward the risers so that the treads will not be in shadow.

Low-profile lights or bollards which stand 30 to 36 inches off the ground can help delineate a pathway route.

Generally, it is best to use matching fixtures along the same path. You also will want to coordinate all entrance lamps beside the door, lamp post, and up the pathway for a cohesive look. In most cases, the lamp post lantern should set the style.

Garages and Driveways

Plan to delineate driveways with equally spaced low-profile lights, leading to a lighted garage door. Low-profile lights or bollards standing

Garages and Driveways. Position lights to illuminate the garage door and use low-profile lights to delineate the driveway.

30 to 36 inches off the ground will be easy to see from the car and will stay above snow in many climates.

Garage exterior lights should be positioned to illuminate the door and area directly below the door, without blinding the driver. Mount lights under a soffit or on the wall above the door. Or mount lights centered between double garage doors. Many homeowners prefer to leave exterior garage lights on for security throughout the night, installing photocells or automatic timers or motion detectors. Pull into the driveway and on clicks the light.

Steps and Pathways. Don't overlook back stairs, deck stairs, and pathways behind the home. Illuminate these as carefully as the front of a home for safety and security.

Types of Landscape Fixtures

Some outdoor lighting fixtures are showy, while others are meant to be hidden. Here is a rundown of the multitude of general lighting options available:

Wall Brackets, Ceiling Close-ups, and More. Wall brackets, ceiling close-ups, chain-hung lanterns, and outdoor combination fan/lights are meant to be seen. These fixtures cast ambient and direct light. They are usually mounted at entry doors, over garages, or on porches.

Lamp Post Lights. The signature entrance to your home. They cast ambient light. Some local codes allow them to be gaslight. The fixture itself and the post on which it will sit generally are purchased separately. Since the fitter for the post light is universal in the industry, you can mix most posts and post lights from different manufacturers.

Cylinder, Box, or Bullet Flood Mounts. These help focus and direct light beams. Some of the fixtures are designed to cut off glare and protect the lamp and socket from debris and moisture. They are used for general illumination.

A high mushroom tier light leads the way for a walkway.

Spread and Diffused Fixtures. Low to the ground, spread and diffused fixtures are designed to cast illumination in a broader pattern for flower beds, perimeter plantings, driveways, steps, and paths. They often are mushroom shaped.

Spot or Accent Fixtures. Versatile and adjustable, spot or accent fixtures are used for uplighting, crosslighting, accenting, and grazing. When mounted high up, they provide focused downlighting and moonlighting.

Bollard and Post Fixtures. Standing fixtures for pathways, steps, garden walks, deck, and pool areas. They also are used for driveways.

In-Ground or Well Fixtures. These fixtures can be buried flush with the ground to conceal the light source. They are useful for uplighting trees and shrubs, and grazing textured walls.

Swimming Pool and Fountain Fixtures. Installed at the ends and in sides of swimming pools and bottoms of fountains. Wet niche fixtures can be removed to change the lamp, while dry niche fixtures require access to the back of the pool shell.

Recessed in-ground lighting like this planter lighting with a grille uplights without being seen.

Other Considerations

Timers, transformers and photocells, motion sensors, and dimmers (be sure that fixtures and bulbs are suitable for dimming) can produce as sophisticated an exterior lighting system as you want. They can be controlled from inside or outside the house.

Both low-voltage and line-voltage outdoor systems can be further customized through use of colored bulbs, filters, and sleeves. These can intensify floral colors, but must be used sparingly so that the effect is not garish.

Selecting a Power System

Before you focus on the specific kinds of lighting available, consider the power supply and system you want to use. Most systems are accommodated with either 120-volt electricity and corresponding line voltage fixtures, 12-volt systems and corresponding fixtures, or a combination of both. The 12-volt system can be branched off the 120-volt system.

Whichever you select, you will need to plan logical runs of power throughout your property. It's also a good idea to plan ahead for any future lighting and make sure that extra wire and power can be delivered where you might want it in the future.

Consider the light you want and where you want it in planning power delivery. For instance, energy-saving fluorescent lighting, which requires 120-volt power, may be your preference for showing off a tree canopy. Because they have more voltage, the high-intensity discharge (HID) family of lights can provide longer distance light throw and higher intensity. Mercury vapor bulbs offer strong illumination, but project a cool color suitable only for greenery. HID lights are most often limited to commercial applications and for security because of the distortion of color that affects the beauty of a flowering garden. Also, they do not go on immediately but must warm up. HID also includes high pressure sodium as well as mercury vapor.

Other 120-volt bulb type options include incandescent "A" and "R" bulbs in both spot and floodlight styles. The R bulbs produce about twice the light output of A bulbs, and incandescent PAR bulbs produce about four times the projected light of an A bulb. The PAR bulbs are generally the best of commonly used residential incandescent bulbs for floodlighting and long light throws.

120-Volt System

This generally lights larger areas more brightly and provides longer beam throws. Security lighting usually requires the powerful beam throw of a 120-volt system. The National Electrical Code requires permanent rigid installation for 120-volt lighting.

Low-Voltage Systems

Most low-voltage systems are designed to work with cable extending no farther than 200 feet from the transformer. So you may need to break your cable runs down or use more than one transformer. The size of the area you want to light and the amount of brightness you want will determine

whether a low-voltage, line-voltage, or combination of both is best.

Low voltage systems require a transformer to convert 120-volt household current to 12 volts. However, the system has a number of advantages, including lower electrical costs than 120-volt systems. The 12-volt system is an ideal choice for do-it-yourselfers with smaller properties that don't require long wiring runs. Here are other advantages:

- Simple do-it-yourself installation for most systems. A screwdriver and small shovel are all that's needed in many cases, instead of the trenching required for 120-volt line installation. Some low-voltage systems can be installed in less than an hour.

- Lower overall costs for installing this system, since no special disruption and possible replanting is needed. Lines need to be protected from lawn mowers, but often, just covering with bark or wood chips is sufficient. No need to worry about favorite plants and their roots. Cable can be buried without conduit and junction boxes or it can be left above ground.

- More energy-efficient and often more light output per watt than line-volt systems. A typical 6-light

set uses less electricity than a single 75 watt bulb.

- Little or no risk of shock or other electrical hazard. Even if you touch bare wires or cut a buried cable with a garden tool, you will not get a shock. This makes 12-volt systems safe around children and pets.

- Fixtures are easily relocated when desired.

Low-voltage often is the preferred choice for decks, stairs, pathways, and near pools. (But don't confuse it with underwater lighting.)

How and where you plan to run your power and where fixtures can be attached to it are determined by the kind of light you want. No matter what voltage system you use, you will need to bring electricity from inside your home out. The only exception is solar-powered lights.

Solar Accent Lighting

A solar panel collects and stores sunlight in rechargeable batteries for use after dusk. Many turn on automatically at night.

The advantages of these systems include easy installation (no plugs or wires), portability, self-containment, efficiency, and flexibility of placement.

Decorative colors in low-voltage lights can make your garden festive at night, but make sure the colors don't unpleasantly distort natural colors.

They can be used long distances from a conventional power source or where laying cable would be difficult.

On the other hand, they have a relatively high initial cost compared to low-voltage systems. They are dependent upon good strong sources of direct sunlight, so that they work better in areas such as the Southwest. Also, there is a limited amount of time the light works each day.

While solar paneled lights continue to have appeal for their great convenience and energy efficiency, low-voltage systems or a conventional fixture with a compact fluorescent bulb may be better choices.

Wiring for 120 Volts Outdoors

Before you start an outside electrical project, contact the municipal building inspector to determine the requirements that have been established for your community concerning outdoor wiring. In some communities, only a professional electrician can make the final hookups. In other areas, the work must be inspected before it can be put into operation. You will have to find out whether the municipal electrical code permits the use of Type UF cable, or if it specifies Type TW wire and conduit.

Generally, local codes require that 120-volt outdoor wiring be protected by conduit whenever it is installed aboveground. If the wiring is to be buried, most codes allow Type UF cable. However, some require that Type TW wire and conduit be used.

Always, without fail, turn off the power at the main electrical service panel before working on a circuit.

Planning Outdoor Wiring

Whether you plan to light the walkways or paths for safety, or spotlight a lawn feature, it's a good idea to draw a plan of the wiring scheme you want. This will save you plenty of time and help you estimate the materials needed.

Paths for Cable. As you plan, try to place all fixtures and receptacles so that they are easily accessible, both for installation and for future maintenance. Keep the total distance between fixtures to a minimum.

If you have to dig to bury cable, contact the local utilities first. They will need at least three days' notice to plot underground wiring and plumbing for you. Do not dig until you contact the utilities. Driving a spade blade through an electrical cable can be dangerous.

Equipment. Outdoor electrical equipment, such as fixture boxes and receptacles, is especially manufactured to meet codes and resist the elements. You also should use weatherproof light bulbs in outdoor fixtures. These resist shattering when the temperature drops.

Do not use electrical products specified for indoor use outdoors.

Connectors and Fittings. An LB fitting is a right-angle connector that is used with a conduit to bring cable through the wall of a house. The fitting routes cable toward a trench that has been dug from the house to the area where the electricity is needed.

LB fittings are threaded on both ends. Conduit passing through the house wall to the outside is screwed to one end. Conduit leading down the side of the house to the trench is screwed to the other end. Thus, cable is enclosed in the metal to provide an efficient seal from the time it leaves the house to the time it enters the ground. LB connectors are outfitted with thick gaskets and metal cover plates.

Box extenders are used when tapping an existing outdoor receptacle or fixture junction box for power. The extender may have a nipple and a 90-degree elbow so that the wires may be brought from the fixture, through the conduit, to the point where power is wanted.

Outdoor Conduit. Three types are available, but check the codes before you buy.

Rigid aluminum and rigid steel conduit provide equal protection to the wires that pass through them. Rigid aluminum is easier to work with, but if it is going to be buried in concrete, first coat it with bituminous paint to keep it from corroding.

Both types of metal conduit come with a variety of fittings, including elbows, offsets, bushing, couplings, and con-

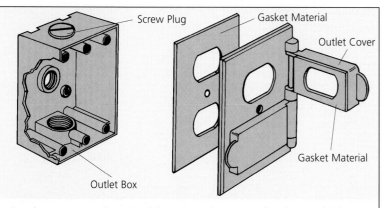

Outdoor receptacles. Outside receptacles are made of extra-thick metal with screw fittings and gaskets between faceplates and openings to the outlets. In stores, you may find these products in the lawn and garden department.

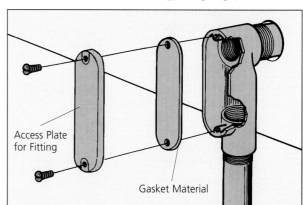

Outdoor fittings. Fittings for conduit and wire used outdoors include these basic products. An LB fitting is L-shaped and has a back opening for conduit. The fittings have weatherproofing gaskets.

nectors. If offsets and elbows do not provide the necessary turns in rigid metal or EMT conduit, you will need a bending tool called a hickey.

Nonmetallic conduit is made from either polyvinyl chloride (PVC) or high-density polyethylene, both of which are suitable for burial. If PVC is going to be exposed to direct sunlight, it must be labeled as suitable for use in sunlight. But before you purchase nonmetallic conduit, be sure you check local codes. Don't assume that it's approved. An inspector might require you to replace the nonmetallic materials with another product; this can be very costly and time-consuming.

Extending Power Outside the House

There are two main ways to extend electricity from the house to the outside. You can run the power cable through the basement—or basement crawl space—or through the attic.

Through the Basement. Follow these procedures for a basement exit:

1. Locate the exit point for the cable. It may be near a water pipe that extends through the wall or at a corner. The spot where you go through the wall should be at least 3 inches from a joist, sill plate, or floor to allow clearance for a junction box.

2. Outside, measure from the common reference point to the spot selected

for the exit. If the spot is on the foundation, make sure the spot does not fall on a joint between concrete blocks or where two pieces of siding join. The spot has to provide a firm base for the LB fitting. At this point outside, drill a small hole through the wall to verify that the path is clear. If the hole is in a block wall, don't drill through the top block. Blocks below the top have a hollow center; top blocks often are filled with concrete.

3. Cut the opening for the nipple that will extend through the masonry. You can do this with a star drill and baby sledge hammer or you can use an electric hammer drill and masonry bit which you can rent. Wear safety glasses and gloves while working.

4. Back inside, open one of the knockouts from the back of a box and mount the box so the hole matches the hole through the wall. The box is mounted with masonry shields (anchors) and screws.

5. Outside, dig the cable trench.

6. Onto an LB fitting screw a nipple long enough to extend from inside the box through the hole to the outside. Outside, attach conduit to the LB fitting and run the conduit down the side of the house to the trench. Then seal the joint around the fitting with quality caulking compound. Inside, secure the nipple to the box with a con-

nector. The opening is now ready for the cable.

Through the Attic. To bring power through the attic and an eave, you will need an outdoor outlet box, nipple, 90-degree corner elbow, and a length of conduit to extend down the side of the house to the trench.

1. Hold the assembly against the overhang of the roof so the box and nipple are against the soffit and the conduit is against the wall. Try to run the conduit near a downspout to make it inconspicuous.

2. Mark the soffit where the cable will pass through the soffit into the box. Use a 1⅛-inch bit to drill a hole through the soffit for the cable. Then remove a knockout to correspond with the hole, and fasten the box to the soffit with screws.

3. Run the cable from the attic power source and out the hole in the soffit. Clamp the cable to the box. With conduit straps, strap the nipple and conduit into place and complete the installation by running conduit down the side of the house. The path is now ready for the cable installation. Be sure to check the codes for the type of cable and/or conduit you can use.

The Connection. You will have to pull the cable through the pathway you have made for it. Then the cable can be connected to the power source inside the house. The best plan is to

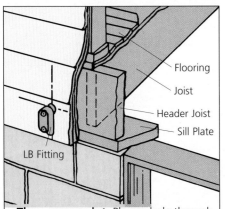

The access point. Place a hole through the wall for cable at least 3 in. from joists, sill plate, and flooring. The LB fitting goes on the outside wall.

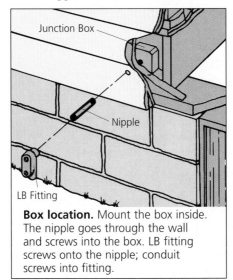

Box location. Mount the box inside. The nipple goes through the wall and screws into the box. LB fitting screws onto the nipple; conduit screws into fitting.

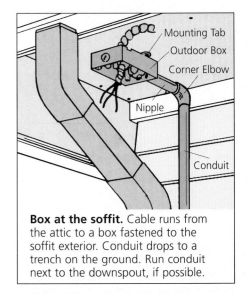

Box at the soffit. Cable runs from the attic to a box fastened to the soffit exterior. Conduit drops to a trench on the ground. Run conduit next to the downspout, if possible.

complete the entire project first—hooking up the outside lights—before connecting to power. If you are creating a new circuit, see "Adding a Circuit Breaker," page 129. If you are connecting to an existing outlet, make sure the circuit has enough amperage to handle outdoor demands for power. See "Wattage Ratings," page 127.

Installing Power Cable Outside

Running the cable from the house out to the yard, pool, garden, or wherever you want it involves digging a shallow trench and building an anchor for each receptacle. Here's how:

Digging a Trench. First, call the utility company for a plot of pipes and wiring that may be running underground on your property. In some areas you are required by law to do this. Check your local code on depth requirements. Generally, cable not in conduit (but with proper installation, see "Selecting Cable," page 89) must be buried at least 24 inches deep, with expansion loops. Put intermediate metallic conduit at least 6 inches deep, rigid nonmetallic conduit at least 18 inches deep.

Trenches under Slabs. If the wires have to go under a walkway or driveway, you can use this technique: Dig the trench up to the obstruction. Then continue the trench on the other side of it. Cut a piece of conduit 10 inches longer than the span. Hammer a point on one end of the conduit. Now hammer the conduit under the obstruction. When it appears on the other side, cut off the point with a hacksaw. You now can connect another piece of conduit to it or run the cable through the conduit under the obstruction.

Installing a Lamppost

A lamppost must be buried at least 24 inches deep for stability and protec-tion from frost heave. Some posts are adjustable. They come with an opening for NMWU cable. If you are using conduit, extend the opening in the lamppost.

1. Mark guidelines, 18 inches long and ⅞ inch apart, on the post.

To cut out the outlined strip (see illustration "Install a Lamppost" page 166), use a hacksaw that has a blade-type grip. Once the sides are cut, bend out the strip and saw it off, using a file to smooth sharp edges. If the post has a middle-of-the-run hookup, cut another slot in the direction that the cable continues.

2. If you're using conduit throughout, measure and cut a piece that extends from the already-positioned conduit at the house to the top of the locknut of an adjustable post or to the top of a nonadjustable post.

3. Dig the trench and attach the conduit capping it with a plastic bushing to protect the cable.

4. Once all the receptacles, lights, and other features are in place, fish the wires through the conduit. Hook up all wiring as you would for conventional systems.

5. Dig the postholes 24 inches deep and about 8 inches wide. Position the conduit, if needed, as described above. Position the post over the conduit, or thread NMWU cable through the cable opening.

6. It's a good idea to set the post in concrete, although you can lay down alternating layers of dirt and large gravel around the post. Tamp and compact the fill after every addition.

If you are creating a new circuit for the lamppost, run the cable to the main electrical service panel. Make the power hookup after you complete the rest of the lamppost project. If you tap into an existing power source inside (or outside) the house, make sure that the circuit can handle the extra load.

The Concrete Mixture. At home center stores and building material outlets, you can buy already-mixed concrete in 80-pound bags. You simply add water to the mixture and stir. One bag of concrete mix will yield about two-thirds of a cubic foot of concrete. For a lamppost, you may need two bags of material.

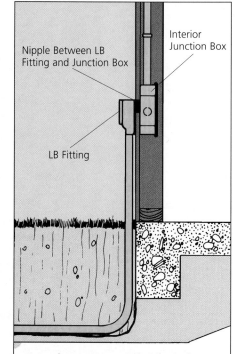

From house to trench. Here's the hookup for outdoor wiring as it leaves the house on its way through a trench to a receptacle or appliance in the yard area.

Interior Junction Box

Nipple Between LB Fitting and Junction Box

LB Fitting

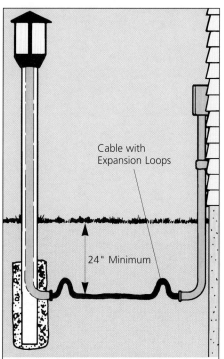

Cable with Expansion Loops

24" Minimum

Bury cable at least 24 in. Bury the cable at least 24 in. underground—or according to local code requirements. Loop the cable as shown to allow for expansion.

After the mixture is dumped into the hole with the post in position, round off the top of the concrete in a crowned configuration with a trowel. The crown will help drain water away from the lamppost. Then brace the post with a length of 2x4 to steady it until the concrete sets—a couple of days is best.

About Wires and Conduit. The wires you pull through conduit must be insulated, but they may be single strands since the conduit takes the place of cable insulation.

The neutral wire must be coded white. The other wires may be black or one red and one black.

Adding a Single Exterior Outlet

An exterior outlet may be necessary to your outdoor lighting scheme because low-voltage transformers are designed to plug into a 120-volt transformer.

Going Through Siding. If at all possible, locate the exterior outlet directly opposite an interior outlet. This way, you can use the same power source for both outlets.

1. Shut off the power to the circuit that operates the interior outlet. Remove the faceplate and the outlet. Then with a long ¾-inch drill bit, drill a hole through an opening in the back of the box through the sheathing and siding.

2. Outside, locate the drilled hole. Then with a keyhole or saber saw, cut away the sheathing and siding to fit the exterior box that you will install in the exterior wall. Set the saw so that the blade won't enter the interior box.

3. Remove the back of the knockout on the cast metal box and screw this box into the house with the knockout hole aligned with the hole in the wall. Insert a 10-inch length of cable in the hole.

4. Connect the cable inside to the terminals of the receptacle and the cable outside to the new GFCI receptacle. Then install a waterproof

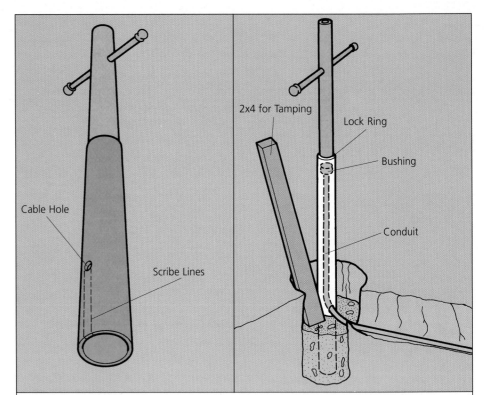

Install a Lamppost. To slot a post for conduit (left), mark 18-in.-long lines, ⅞ in. apart, on the post. Extend beyond the opening for UF cable. Cut along the lines with a hacksaw. To anchor the post (right), dig a hole 24 in. deep and 8 in. wide. Bend the conduit to come up in the middle of the hole, almost to an adjustable post's lock ring or a fixed post's full height.

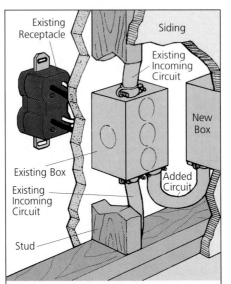

Tap into existing outlet. Turn off the power and remove the existing outlet from the interior box. Drill a hole through the back of the box to the exterior. You will tap this outlet.

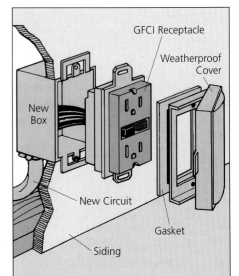

Install outside box. Cut a hole in the siding and sheathing from outside and insert the exterior box. Run cable through the knockout to the inside box and make the power hookup.

gasket and faceplate over the outside outlet.

Through Masonry Walls. Outline the shape of the box on the concrete block with masking tape. Put on safety

glasses and gloves. Then drill a series of holes within that border with a masonry bit in a power drill. Clean out the area with a cold chisel and baby sledge.

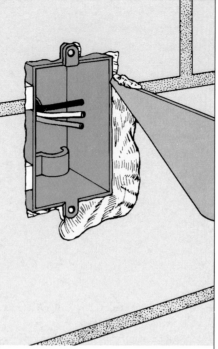

Drill and chisel hole. Drill a series of holes in concrete block for the exterior box. Remove the back knockout, insert the box, and drill a hole to the interior for power cable.

Mortar box into block. Mortar the exterior box in place. Connect the outlet to power in the interior junction box, which may be surface-mounted to the block with masonry shields.

Drill a hole through the wall, matching a knockout in the back of the box. The cable will run through this hole to a junction box on the interior wall.

Adjust the ears of the exterior box so the box will extend about 1/16 inch from the block. Then cement the box in place. Connect the outlet and install a weatherproof cover as shown.

Low-Voltage Outdoor Lighting

Low-voltage lighting transformers or power packs convert 120-volt household current to 12 volts. The pack supplies the electricity to low-voltage cable, which transmits the electricity. Low-voltage fixtures are attached to the cable. A typical low-voltage lamp delivers between 15 and 30 footcandles, the level of illumination which is about 18 to 25 percent as bright as a 75-watt lamp. This lower light level seems much brighter in the surrounding exterior darkness.

Transformers range from lower wattage units that can power a single

entrance light to large models that can safely operate 25 or more fixtures.

Selecting Transformers

To determine the transformer you need, simply add up the wattage of all fixtures/lamps you plan to use (this wattage is referred to as total nominal wattage or TNW). Then select a transformer that most closely matches the total nominal wattage of your lights (see the chart,

"Transformer Selection" below). For example, to power six 11-watt lamps, you need a transformer that has an output of at least 66TNW. It also may be listed as a volt-amperes (VA) rating, which indicates the maximum rate of current flow with which the transformer should be used.

As a general rule, the total low wattage of the lamps should not be less than half of the transformer's TNW, nor should it exceed the transformer's maximum capacity. Using fewer lamps and less total wattage causes more electricity to go to each lamp, shortening the lamp/bulb life. Overloading the transformer will cause the ground fault circuit breaker to trip or the dimming of all lights below appropriate levels.

(Note: In maintaining low-voltage, it's important to replace burned-out bulbs to rebalance the electrical pull on the transformer.)

Special Features

Transformer units can offer versatile controls. Convertible power packs are geared for add-ons so that functions can be combined. For instance, combining an optional photo cell with a timer transformer results in as many as nine ways to operate lights. The control options to consider include the following:

■ Manual control may be all that's needed for areas that are only lit for specific occasions. Gazebos, decks, pool areas, and patios are favorite

Transformer selection						
Total nominal wattage of transformer	150W 16-gauge cable		200W 14-gauge cable		250W 12-gauge cable	
	max. watts	max. length	max. watts	max. length	max. watts	max. length
25 watts	25	100	25	125	25	150
44 watts	44	100	44	125	44	150
88 watts	88	100	88	125	88	150
121 watts	121	100	121	125	121	150
196 watts	150	100	196	125	196	150
300 watts	150	100	200	150	250	200

locations for manual controls.

- Automatic timers are useful when lights are used for set periods each evening, such as on at 6 p.m. and off at 11 p.m.

- Photo control is the option when you want light to stay on all night for security. The control eliminates the need to turn off lights during the day. The light is triggered by dusk and dawn, adjusting seasonally from winter's short days to summer's longer ones.

- Photo control/timer combination is the option when you want lights on at dusk, but want to have them automatically turn off at a set time, such as when you normally go to bed. This combination conserves energy. This system also can be programmed to simulate a "still at home" lighting pattern when homeowners are on vacation.

- Dimmer controls give you brighter light for barbecuing, candle glow for moon gazing, or something in between. All are available with dimming systems. Select this option where your outdoor living space, a patio or deck, calls for more than one light level. You can have dimmer packs that manually turn lights off and on, or select one that operates with an automatic timer for the lights.

- Motion sensor controls are a great choice for security lighting and are highly convenient for garage entrances. Your lights will automatically be triggered as you step out of the car. Motion and heat sensors take over when lights are turned off, reacting to heat in motion (a person) up to 40 feet away, providing protected coverage area of more than 600 square feet. These mount on walls, beneath eaves, and even on fences, connected to a power pack by a 25-foot cord. A word of caution: make sure the motion sensor can be adjusted so that wandering wildlife such as deer in the far reaches of your yard will not trigger a midnight "lights on" alert.

Selecting Low-Voltage Cable

Low voltage cable is a weather-resistant, self-sealing, insulated stranded copper wire that is available in 18-, 16-, 14-, and 12-gauge sizes.

For most installations, 16-gauge cable is perfect. However, for runs longer than 100 feet, or more than 150 total lamp watts, you may experience insufficient light output. The effect is especially noticeable with lights farthest away from the transformer. Voltage drop is easy to understand if you remember how the flow of electricity compares to the flow of water through a pipe.

As water travels from the pump house, it begins to lose pressure. Like water, electricity must flow from a "pump house" to its final destination. With a low voltage lighting system, however, the "pump house" is the transformer and the "pipe" used to transfer the current is the cable.

As the electricity travels farther away from the transformer to remote parts of the yard, it loses electrical energy due to resistance from the cable. This lost energy is given off as heat.

Voltage drop can be minimized by using a heavier gauge wire, switching to a more powerful transformer, or both. As a rule of thumb, 16-gauge cable is recommended for runs up to 100 feet, 14-gauge for up to 150 feet, and 12-gauge for up to 200 feet. See the "Cable Selection Chart," below.

A third way to reduce voltage drop is by dividing the cable into shorter lengths. While most low voltage lights are installed "in series" (i.e., one light after another), this type of installation will only allow 16-gauge cable runs of approximately 100 feet. In contrast, by dividing 16-gauge cable into two or more legs, it's possible to use as much as 150 feet of cable.

One wire in the cable will have ridges on the insulation to denote polarity. Whichever layout you use, be careful to connect the same wire ends to the proper transformer terminals by noting the ridge on one side of the cable. Here are four alternatives to running the lights in series:

- Split the load: run up to the recommended maximum distance in two or more directions from the transformer.

- The tee method: allows more even distribution of power to the center of a run or to a run some distance off, i.e., across a driveway. Heavier gauge cable (10- or 12-gauge) or a double run of cable should be used to make the tee. All connections should be soldered.

- Split tee: allows relative uniform distribution of power to both legs, i.e., to both sides of the yard. Otherwise, the layout is the same as the other tee method.

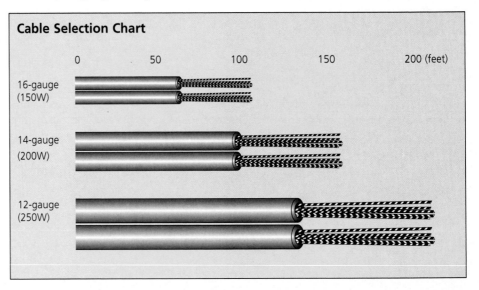

Cable Selection Chart

	0	50	100	150	200 (feet)
16-gauge (150W)					
14-gauge (200W)					
12-gauge (250W)					

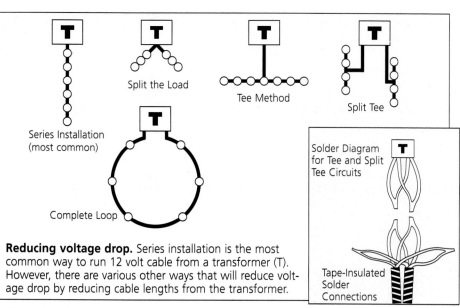

Series Installation
(most common)

Split the Load

Tee Method

Split Tee

Complete Loop

Solder Diagram
for Tee and Split
Tee Circuits

Tape-Insulated
Solder
Connections

Reducing voltage drop. Series installation is the most common way to run 12 volt cable from a transformer (T). However, there are various other ways that will reduce voltage drop by reducing cable lengths from the transformer.

Special fixtures can direct light precisely where you want it, here both down and away towards the plants.

■ Complete loop around yard: allows for relatively uniform light output.

On runs over 150 feet or when 10 or more lamps are connected to one line, consider using heavier cable (12- or 14-gauge) which will reduce voltage drop and produce greater efficiency from the lamps.

Selecting Low Voltage Lamps

The final component in the low voltage lighting system is the bulb. More impact-resistant than a conventional 120-volt bulb, these tiny lamps are mechanically stronger and offer greater economy.

Several types of bulbs are available. Two of the most common types are the bayonet base lamp, which features a copper base that twists into the fixture socket, and the wedge base lamp, which plugs into the socket. Since the wedge base lamp is all-glass, it is not subject to corrosion and therefore requires less maintenance than bayonet base lamps.

The floodlight lamp consists of a "burner" enclosed in a plastic or glass casing with a parabolic reflector to beam light in one direction (such as on a wall or a fence).

One of the newer designs is the halogen bulb, which offers even greater economy. This energy-efficient floodlight lamp is whiter and brighter than conventional incandescent floodlamps, providing more light per watt of power.

Using Higher-Wattage Lamps. Should a higher-wattage bulb be used to achieve a brighter lighting effect, be certain you don't overload the transformer or cable.

If you live in an area where voltage surges or high voltage are common, your lamps may burn out more frequently.

To extend bulb life, some manufacturers offer an inexpensive "lamp-saver" kit that can be installed in minutes. The lamp-saver kit consists of a small resistor that is screwed into place on the terminals of a floodlight bulb or installed between one of the bulb socket leads of a wedge or bayonet based bulb. Lamp-savers are easy to install, and extend bulb life by as much as 50 percent by reducing voltage at the bulb.

Selecting Low-Voltage Fixtures

A variety of fixtures to achieve different effects can be combined to customize your system. Most popular include low-profile tier lights and floodlights, bollard lights, mushroom lights, tier lights, well lights, globe lights, and floodlights. These fixtures adapt and adjust relatively easily, so that you can use the same fixtures as the garden grows, to highlight exactly what you want.

Low-Profile Tier Fixtures. Short fixtures with covers that direct light downward. They are relatively unobtrusive light sources.

Low-Profile Zoom-Focus Floodlights. Unobtrusive, easy-to-conceal light available with a zoom-focus that changes the light pattern from a floodlight to a spotlight with the turn of a wrist.

Bollard Lights. So named because they resemble the vertical posts at wharf-side used for securing nautical ropes. Bollards are meant to be seen. A cylindrical diffused light is projected a full 360 degrees, or can be shielded to compress the light at smaller angles. Use these when you want to create a pathway of light.

Mushroom Lights. Project light downward, shielded by a mushroom-shaped shade atop the fixture. This is especially good for showing off low foliage, borders, and decorative ground covers, as well as pathways without visual glare.

Tier Lights. Higher than low-profile models. These fixtures have an exposed light source that is diffused to eliminate glare. Additions of tiers and a broader top tier cuts down on the amount of horizontal light while still providing lighting directed toward ground covers and shrubs.

Prismatic Tier Lights. Similar to tier and mushroom lights. These adjustable units have a highly efficient prismatic design of the diffuser that projects light downward in controlled patterns with even light distribution. More light goes on paths, walkways, and steps than is deflected upward and lost.

Well Lights. Fixtures hidden from view. These fixtures create a magical setting by lighting up shrubs, walls, and any vertical plane. They are also useful for security lighting around a home.

Globe Lights. Meant to be seen and cast light in all directions. They are decorative additions that should be in keeping with the home's design.

Floodlights. Feature a sealed beam automotive-type lamp, especially designed to cloak the light source. High-intensity halogen lamps used in some floodlights are whiter and brighter than incandescent floodlight lamps. Round or rectangular, many are easily adjusted to be positioned exactly where the light is wanted.

Variable Focus Floodlights. Have a prismatic lens with a special reflector inside that produces more footcandles of light and cuts light absorption and glare. A zoom-focus allows you to adjust light from a tight focus to a flood focus or anything in between. Light patterns can be changed by rotating the lens 90 degrees from horizontal to vertical.

Putting It Together

Once you have decided what lighting you want and generally where you want it, you can make a plan. Use the grid sheets at the back of the book to lay out your landscape and lighting plan. Remember to account for growth of trees and shrubs.

Installing Low-Voltage Outdoor Lights

Low-voltage outdoor lights are great for do-it-yourselfers because a complete system often can be installed in less than an hour.

1 Install the Transformer. Once you have decided where the lighting fixtures will be located and what type of wiring layout will be used, install your transformer.

Mount the transformer next to a grounded indoor or outdoor electrical outlet. It can be hung on a wall, fence or post. For outdoor installations, hang the transformer at least one foot above the ground.

Use the terminal screw to attach the low-voltage cable to the bottom of the transformer. Plug in the transformer, turn it on, and stretch the cable to full length.

2 Bury the Cable. To cross a lawn or open area, make a cut in the surface at a 45-degree angle. Pry up the sod, drop in the cable, and press the sod back into place.

To run the cable under walks or driveways, dig a hole on the opposite sides of the pavement several inches deeper than the pavement is thick. Attach a short length of pipe to a garden hose with a pipe-to-hose coupling. Use water pressure through the pipe to sluice away a tunnel under the pavement and connect the two holes.

Attach the cable to the free end of the pipe through the tunnel, pulling cable with it. New construction should have a ¾-inch conduit laid under the pavement for access prior to construction.

Use shaded tier lights to direct light downward to safely light a pathway or brighten up pretty floral plantings.

Use a conventional low-voltage floodlight for wall grazing, silhouetting, uplighting and general floodlighting.

Install the transformer. For outdoor installation, mount the transformer near a grounded outlet, at least 1 ft. off the ground.

Bury the Cable. There is no requirement to bury 12-volt cable deep in the ground. You can bury it in a shallow ditch to get it out of sight and out of the way.

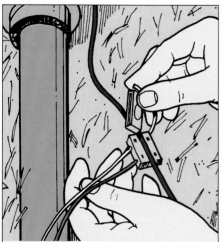

Connect the Lights. Some 12-volt outdoor lighting systems come with a fast-lock connector that makes connecting the lights as simple as snapping the connectors in place.

Complete the Installation. In soft ground, you can simply push the lights into place. Otherwise, use a garden spade to dig a small hole.

3 Connect the Lights. Connecting the low-voltage cable to the light fixtures is a simple task that can be completed in seconds. Some manufacturers have a fast-lock connector that does not require splicing, soldering, or tools to make the electrical connection.

The fast-lock connector has a pair of teeth that pierce the cable to make the connection. Since the power pack already is on, to test the connection, simply press the cable against the teeth. The light should turn on.

Complete the connection by firmly sliding the connector lock over the low voltage cable into the slots on the fast-lock connector until it snaps into place. For other types of lighting fixtures, follow manufacturers' instructions.

4 Complete the Installation. If the ground is soft, you can push the lights into place. If the fixtures can't easily be pushed into the earth, use a garden spade to dig a small hole. Insert the fixture (ground stake first) into the hole and refill the hole with either dirt or gravel. Under no circumstances should you use a hammer to drive the fixtures into the ground.

Before burying any cable, removing sod, or digging any holes, verify that your lights work and you are pleased with the lighting results. Now is the time to experiment with different lighting arrangements. Remember, low voltage lights are portable and the cable is self-sealing, so you can change connections as often as you wish, without fear of shorting the cable or creating an electrical hazard.

Low-Voltage Lighting for Decks

There are low-voltage lighting systems specifically for decks. Lights can be affixed almost anywhere. You will get even greater pleasure from a deck when its use is extended into evenings through adequate lighting.

Safety First. The most critical areas for deck lighting are those that govern safety. At a minimum, steps and stairways leading from the deck to the yard need to be lit top and bottom. Do not overlook lighting the flat area leading away from the lowest step.

On the deck, corners of planters and benches or any other shaded hazards need to be properly delineated. Lighting directly beside house doorways leading to the deck helps bridge the transition from bright indoor light to deck night lighting. This area is especially important since often there is a slight change of level to a lower deck that is hard to perceive if not properly lit.

Function is Foremost

The great American cookout works best if the chef can see when the meat is done. You can incorporate into lighting plans special lights near the cooking area. Other special areas to consider include outdoor showers, cleanup areas from lawn chores or gardening, transitions of decks to pools (keep lights 60 inches away from water), and hot tubs.

Turn decks into rooms usable even at night with low voltage lighting. Be sure to adequately light stairs.

Expanding the Deck

Fill light creates the effect that a large deck is an outdoor room extension to your home. Spotlights dressing the house walls act as a backdrop for the deck as well as adding fill light. In designing deck lighting, consider the extension of lighting that goes to the rest of the landscape and coordinate both effects. For instance, unify a deck with a line of mushroom lamps that extend into the yard pathway.

Floodlights. Floodlights originating from the deck can be used to uplight trees, trellises, or hanging gardens. Use floods also to downlight interesting foliage or ground cover adjacent to the deck.

Deck Lights. These are unobtrusive and can be mounted almost anywhere: on walls, fences, even deck surfaces, as well as beneath benches, steps, and railings.

Decorative Lights. These can include tier lights, mushroom lights, shaded tiers, and globe lights. They are effective decorative lighting when mounted on posts, railing corners, or walls of the house.

Switches and Dimmers

Both of these controls are easy custom touches for deck lighting. Switches to turn lights on and off from various locations on the deck are convenient and serve as safety precautions, especially near stairs. A dimmer for some if not all deck lights enables you to change the mood to suit your outside activities.

Installing Deck Lights

1 **Lay the Cable.** Make a layout of your deck and the position of the lights and cable. Establish the positioning of the transformer and power pack. If possible, lay the cable before attaching decking planks to the joists. Feed the cable through the joists or beneath them, leaving enough slack to make it easy to connect the lights later on.

2 **Install the Lights.** When you are ready to install the lights, drill a small hole in the deck surface and use a wire coat hanger or pliers to pull the cable above deck level. Turn on the power pack and connect the lights. If they work properly, mount the lights following manufacturer's instructions.

Cable also can be mounted to the underside of railings or benches. To install lights on steps, run cable beneath or along the bottom of the steps.

Lay the Cable. If you have the opportunity, it's easiest to attach wires to a deck frame before decking boards are installed.

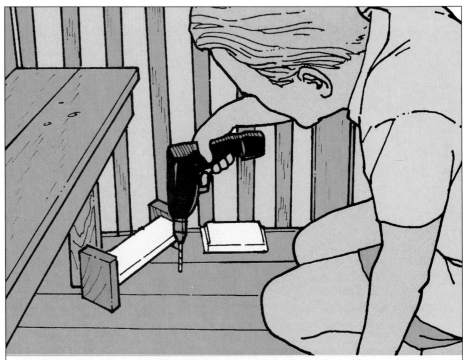

Install the Lights. Drill small holes in the deck below where lighting fixtures will be installed. Pull the wire through.

Photo Credits

Back Cover:
(top) Bill Rothschild Photography, Wesley Hills, NY
(L.) Thomas Lighting, Accent Division, Louisville, KY
(R.) Intermatic Inc., Spring Grove, IL

p1   #717P8, Top Brass, Baltimore, MD

p6   Bill Rothschild Photography
Wesley Hills, NY

p7   Thomas Lighting, Accent Division
recess lighting, Louisville, KY

p13   Bill Rothschild Photography
Wesley Hills, NY

p15   Thomas Lighting, Consumer Division
#SL9256-1, Louisville, KY

p17   Thomas Lighting, Consumer Division
#SL7258-1, Louisville, KY

p20   Icarus Cable System, Expo Design
Locust Valley, NY

p21(L.)   Panasonic Lighting, Secaucus, NJ
p21(R.)   Lights of America Inc., Walnut, CA
p24   Panasonic Lighting, Secaucus, NJ
p25   Panasonic Lighting, Secaucus, NJ

p26   Fibertwist, Fiberstars Inc.
Freemont, CA

p27   #717P8, Top Brass, Baltimore, MD

p28   Jill Floor Fixture, P. King/S. Miranda
Flos USA, Huntington Station, NY

p29(top)   Pao Floor Fixture, Matteo Thun
Flos USA, Huntington Station, NY

p29(bot)   Stylos Floor Fixture, A. Castiglioni
Flos USA, Huntington Station, NY

p30(L.)   #299V7, Top Brass, Baltimore, MD

p30(R.)   Silver Moon, Fine Art Lamps
Hialeah, FL

p31(L.)   Jac, Luxo Corp., Port Chester, NY

p31(R.)   Pao Table Lamp, Matteo Thun
Flos USA, Huntington Station, NY

p32   #563B1, Top Brass, Baltimore, MD

p33(L.)   Ted Harden Photography
New York, NY

p33(R.)   Bill Rothschild Photography
Wesley Hills, NY

p34   Shelf Lighting, Lucifer Lighting Co.
San Antonio, TX

p35   J.B. Grant Photography
West New York, NY

p36   Intermatic Inc., Spring Grove, IL
p37   Intermatic Inc., Spring Grove, IL

p38(L.)   Gary Novasel, Patdo Light Studio
Port Chester, NY

p38(R.)   Thomas Lighting, Consumer Division
#SL8429, Louisville, KY

p39   Thomas Lighting, Consumer Division
#SL8447-1, Louisville, KY

p40   Thomas Lighting, Consumer Division
#M2523-1, Louisville, KY

p41(L.)   Thomas Lighting, Consumer Division
#SL8496, Louisville, KY

p41(R.)   Aurora Suspension Fixture
P. King/S. Miranda
Flos USA, Huntington Station, NY

p43(L.)   Trio-ADA, Lightolier, Wilmington, MA

p43(R.)   Ambience Collection, Justice Design
Group, Culver City, CA

p44   Thomas Lighting, Consumer Division
#GY6223-1, Louisville, KY

p45   Thomas Lighting, Consumer Division
#SL7128-8, Louisville, KY

p46   Sof-Tech, Lightolier, Wilmington, MA

p47   (clockwise from top right)
Altima Lightpoint, Lucifer Lighting
Co., San Antonio, TX

SightLine, Edison Price, New York, NY

Truss System, Lucifer Lighting Co.
San Antonio, TX

Metal-Men Cable System
Expo Design, Locust Valley, NY

Sof-Tech, Lightolier, Wilmington, MA

Lyteflood, Lightolier, Wilmington, MA

p50   Zumtobel Staff Lighting Inc.
Highland, NY (all fixtures)

p53   Thomas Lighting, Consumer Division
#SL7042-53, Louisville, KY

p54   Bill Rothschild Photography
Wesley Hills, NY

p55   Judy Collins, Mendham, NJ (designer)
Melabee M. Milller (photo)

p56   Thomas Lighting, Consumer Division
#SL8450-1, Louisville, KY

p58(L.)   J.B. Grant Photography
West New York, NY

p58(R.)   Bill Rothschild Photography
Wesley Hills, NY

p59   Thomas Lighting, Consumer Division
#SL8443-1, Louisville, KY

p60(L.)   Stair Rail Light, Lucifer Lighting Co.
San Antonio, TX

p60(R.)   J.B. Grant Photography
West New York, NY

p62   Bill Rothschild Photography
Wesley Hills, NY

p63   Marilee Schempp, Design I
Summit, NJ (designer)
Melabee M. Milller (photo)

p64   Bill Rothschild Photography
Wesley Hills, NY

p65(top)   J.B. Grant Photography
West New York, NY

p65(bot)   Bill Rothschild Photography
Wesley Hills, NY

p66(top)   J.B. Grant Photography
West New York, NY

p66(L.)   Thomas Lighting, Consumer Division
#M2522-75, Louisville, KY

p66(R.)   Thomas Lighting, Consumer Division
#M2235-1, Louisville, KY

p67(L.)   J.B. Grant Photography
West New York, NY

p67(R.)   Bill Rothschild Photography
Wesley Hills, NY

p67(bot)   Bill Rothschild Photography
Wesley Hills, NY

p69   Gary Novasel, Patdo Light Studio
Port Chester, NY

p70(L.)   Robert Valleau, NY, NY (designer)
Melabee M. Milller (photo)

p70(R.)   Judy Collins, Mendham, NJ (designer)
Melabee M. Milller (photo)

p71(top & R.)   Bill Rothschild Photography
Wesley Hills, NY

p71(L.)   Sharon Draznin, Short Hills, NY
(designer), Melabee M. Milller (photo)

p72(L.)   Kathy Maraglio, Fair Oaks, CA
(designer), David Livingston (photo)
NKBA

p72(R.)   Gail Whiting, Bedminster, NJ (designer)
Melabee M. Milller (photo)

p73   J.B. Grant Photography
West New York, NY

p73(R.)   Beth Mellina, Westfield, NJ (designer)
Melabee M. Miller (photo)

p74   J.B. Grant Photography
West New York, NY

p75   Kathleen Donohue/Neil Kelly
Portland, OR (designer)
David Livingston (photo), NKBA

p76-77   J.B. Grant Photography
West New York, NY

p77(bot)   Cove Lighting, Lucifer Lighting Co.
San Antonio, CA

p78(top)   J.B. Grant Photography
West New York, NY

p78(bot)   A. Simon/M.A. Imbriaco, Springfield, NJ
(designer), Melabee M. Miller (photo)

p79   J.B. Grant Photography
West New York, NY

p80   Miss Sissi Table Fixture, P. Starck
Flos USA, Huntington Station, NY

p81   Intermatic Inc., Spring Grove, IL

p82(L.)   Peggy Deras
San Bruno, CA (designer)
David Livingston (photo) NKBA

p82(R.)   William Earnshaw, Wyckoff, NJ
(designer), NKBA

p84   Karen Shapiro, Randolph, NJ (designer), Melabee M. Miller (photo)

p85-86   Ambience Collection, Justice Design
Group, Culver City, CA

p136-37   Decora Series, Leviton Maufacturing
Co., Little Neck, NY

p157   Design and photo by
David Story Design, Seattle, WA

p158   (clockwise from top left)
Design and photo by
David Story Design, Seattle, WA

Geco Wall Sconce, L. Pagani
Flos USA, Huntington Station, NY

Intermatic Inc., Spring Grove, IL

Thomas Lighting, Accent Division
Louisville, KY

p159-171   Intermatic Inc., Spring Grove, IL

Glossary

Accent Lighting Lighting that highlights an area or object emphasizing that aspect of a room's character.

Amperes (Amperage, Amps) A unit of measurement that describes the rate of electrical flow.

Ballast In a fluorescent fixture, a component that provides the necessary high starting voltage and limits current to the proper operating value.

Cable Two or more wires grouped together inside a protective sheathing of plastic or metal.

Candela A measurement of luminous intensity roughly equivalent to 12.57 lumens.

Candlepower The luminous intensity of a beam of light (total luminous flux) in a particular direction from an international candle measurement standard (the candela).

Color Rendition Index (CRI) Measures the way a light source renders color. The higher the index number, the closer colors are to how an object appears in sunlight.

Compact Fluorescent Bulb Fluorescents that screw into medium or Edison bases just like incandescent bulbs.

Correlated Color Temperature (CCT) Compares the warmth or coolness of light as it is produced, or the source as it appears to the viewer.

Dichroic Reflector A reflector that projects light forward while deflecting heat backwards toward the socket so that the light beam itself is cool.

Dimmer Switch A switch that can vary the intensity of the light it controls.

Downlighting A lighting technique where objects or areas are illuminated from above.

Efficacy The efficiency of a lamp (bulb or tube) measured in ratio of lumens per watt (LPW).

Efficiency Relates to the light output from a fixture (luminaire) as a percentage of light output from the bulb or bulbs it uses.

End-of-the-run Box with its outlet or switch at the final position in a circuit; only one cable enters the box.

Faceplate The plate installed over a switch or receptacle. The plate covers the wall opening and thus protects the wiring.

Fish Tape Flexible metal strip used to draw wires and cables through walls, raceway, and conduits.

Fluorescent Lamp A glass tube coated on the interior with phosphor, a chemical compound that emits light when activated by ultraviolet energy. Air in the tube is replaced with argon gas and a small amount of mercury.

Footcandle A unit that is used to measure brightness. A footcandle is equal to one lumen per square foot of surface.

Footlambert The brightness of a surface which emits or reflects 1 lumen per square foot of its surface.

Ganging Joining two or more switch or receptacle boxes for greater capacity.

General Lighting Lighting that provides overall brightness for an area.

Halogen Bulb A bulb filled with halogen gas that causes the particles of tungsten to be redeposited onto the tungsten filament. This process extends the lamp's life and also makes the light whiter and brighter.

Harp On a lamp, the metal frame that holds the shade.

Illuminance The density of light on a surface when it is uniformly illuminated.

Incandescent Bulb/Lamp A bulb/lamp that converts electric power into light by passing electric current through a filament of tungsten wire.

Incandescent ER Ellipsoidal Reflector Bulb A bulb that focuses its beam of light approximately 2 inches in front of it.

Incandescent PAR (Parabolic Aluminized Reflector) Bulb A bulb with vaporized aluminum on the glass backing. The aluminum forms a reflective coating that forces light forward. The back and front lenses are made of hard, heat-resistant glass, and stippling of the front lens determines the angle of the beam.

Incandescent Reflector Bulb "R" A bulb that directs light out in front by bouncing it off its cone-shaped, silver-coated inside walls.

IR PAR Halogen Lamp A bulb that has an infrared-reflective coating. The coating redirects infrared energy onto the filament.

Junction Box Metal box inside which all standard wire splices and wiring connections must be made.

Knockout A perforated piece of metal in a box that is removed with a punch and hammer to permit insertion of wire.

Lamp Life The average rated life of a bulb or lamp. Usually the lamp life is printed on the package.

Low-Voltage Lighting System Lighting that functions on 12-volt or 24-volt current, as opposed to 120 volts.

Lumen The amount of light cast upon 1 square foot of the inner surface of a hollow sphere of 1-foot radius with an international candle in its center.

Lumens Per Watt (LPW) The ratio of the amount of light provided to the energy (watts) used to produce the light—measurement of the bulb's efficacy.

Luminaire The lighting industry uses this term to encompass a "lighting fixture" or "fitting." Luminaires are grouped by mounting type and locations.

Lux One lux is equal to the illuminance provided by an ordinary wax candle.

Middle-of-the-run Box with its outlets or switch lying between the power source and another box. Cable(s) enters and leaves this box.

Moonlighting A lighting effect that sends light filtering through branches and casts interesting complex shadow patterns, much as real moonlight does.

National Electrical Code Body of regulations spelling out safe, functional electrical procedures. Local codes can add to but not delete from NEC regulations.

Pigtail A short piece of wire used to complete a circuit inside a box.

Polarized Plug Plug with an equipment prong longer that the two blades, one of which is wider than the other.

Polarized Receptacle Outlet with prong openings that accommodate polarized plugs.

Raceway Surface wiring that adds outlets, switches, and fixtures without extensive structural work.

Seasonal Affective Disorder (SAD) A depression that occurs in individuals due to lack of sunlight during the winter months.

Service Panel The point at which electricity provided by a local utility enters a building's wiring system.

Single Pole Type of switch with only two terminals.

Task Lighting Lighting that concentrates in specific areas for tasks such as preparing food, applying makeup, reading, or doing crafts.

Three-Way Bulb A bulb that has two filaments; when used with a corresponding three-way socket, either or both filaments can be lit to provide three light levels.

Three-Way Switch One of two switches controlling a single outlet or fixture; it has three terminals.

Torchiere A lamp designed to direct light upwards. Most of the light is thrown against the ceiling and reflected back.

UL, Underwriters Laboratories Independent organization that tests electrical products for safe operation and conformance with published standards under various conditions. Products that pass may display the UL logo.

Voltage The electric potential difference that drives the current through a circuit, or the force of electrical pressure.

Wall Grazing An effect that treats the wall itself and its texture as artwork.

Wall Washing An effect where the entire wall is lit up to bring out the beauty of wallcoverings, scenic murals or painted effects, grouped artwork, or books.

Watt, Wattage A unit of active electric power; the rate at which electric energy is used.

Wavelength In lighting, the distance between two similar points of a given wave, as measured in nanometers (1 nm equals 1 billionth of a meter).

Wire Connector Plastic cover for a wire splice; the inside is threaded metal.

Zip Cord Electrical cord designed with a thin section between the insulating coverings of the wires. The cord easily splits when pulled down the middle.

Index